The
EDUCATION
of an Accidental
LAWYER

Told in True Stories

DEDICATION

This book is dedicated to my wife Stephanie. She read every word of the drafts, and offered a number of incisive suggestions for improvement. Her comments were particularly valuable because she lived through many of the experiences described here.

Stephanie could easily write her own book about her independent accomplishments and awards in the larger world, but I doubt that she will. She does not like to talk about herself and I know that she would be embarrassed if I wrote at length about these things or about her great gifts to our immediate family and to me.

Perhaps Stephanie won't mind if I describe what she means to me with some words borrowed from Mark Twain. In his recreation of "The Diaries of Adam and Eve," Twain's imagined Adam sums up his feelings about Eve this way:

"Wheresoever she was, there was Eden."

That says it all.

CONTENTS

COVER IMAGES Top to bottom, Stephanie Abbott and Tom Leary wedding 1954; Tom Leary and Otis Smith at GM function 1980; Igor Artemyev and Tom Leary at Moscow press conference 2004; Barrett, Dan, Mary Caroline, Tom, and Margot with parents Margaret and Daniel at Skytop 1940.

ADDITIONAL IMAGES can be found after page 301.

INTRODUCTION

Late in the year 2002, I was asked to give an after-dinner talk at a "Masters Course" sponsored by the Antitrust Law Section of the American Bar Association. Since an after-dinner audience is in a relaxed, if not exuberant mood, a speaker has to entertain as well as inform.

Most of those who attend these annual "Masters" programs are in private practice, and I wanted to stress the key role of private lawyers in the enforcement of the antitrust laws. I was serving as a member of the Federal Trade Commission in 2002, but I had been in the private sector for most of my professional life and always believed that the system depended on the efforts of the private Bar.

I decided that the best way to convey some of the things that I had learned from my experience was simply to tell stories. The talk, later published as "True Stories that Illustrate the Art and Science of Cost-Effective Counseling",[1] seemed to be well received by the intended audience. Now, in semi-retirement with time to spare, I decided that my fellow lawyers and lawyers in training might like to hear more stories. There are a lot of them to tell. In fact, just about everything I have learned in over 50 years of practice as an antitrust lawyer is based on an event that can be described in a story. (Some pretty good yarns, of marginal importance or undue length, did not make the cut but are included in a final Appendix labeled "Outtakes." Reading is optional.)

Rest easy. I do not propose to bore a reader with details of my personal life. This is not an autobiography, and personal matters are discussed only as needed to "set the stage" for the story to follow. Many close personal friends, who have been important in my private life, are not mentioned at all. It also is not an exercise in self-glorification. I am not the central figure in a lot of these, only a bit player, or a passive observer.

By pure dumb luck, however, I have witnessed events of some lasting significance. I was often no more important than the character Woody Allen played in *Zelig*, who somehow popped up repeatedly in gatherings of the famous, but I was there and I remember.

I have met a lot of famous people, but I cannot claim any celebrity on that account. Most assuredly would have no reason to remember me. What I think is important is not the meeting, but what I may have learned from it (in most cases, anyhow). I may throw in a few celebrity contacts just for the hell of it. For example, I did meet someone who is more likely to be remembered 500 years from now than anyone in the world who was alive in the last century. I'll talk about him later.

Some of my personal philosophical or political views will be disclosed in the stories that follow because they sometimes had an effect on the way that I approached the practice of law, and the way that I decided cases when I was in a position to do so. These personal views have been shaped in large measure by my experiences as a lawyer and occasionally by cold logic. Like everyone else, however, I am also profoundly affected by value judgments formed in early life. That is why a lot of early experiences are included in this memoir. I also realize that other people have different views of the world based on their own value judgments, and I don't expect to change their minds. So, I'll try not to preach. Moreover, as will become apparent, I am frequently not at all sure that I am right, anyhow.

Finally, a comment on a theme that appears over and over again in these stories. Before I embarked on this project, I really was not so aware that so many of my life choices seem to have been shaped by chance. I am not one of those people who consistently had the same specific goals for the future, or who carefully weighed the pros and cons of life-changing decisions. Most of my major decisions were triggered by unexpected events. I picked my profession, and my career choices within that profession, almost by accident.

Hence, the title of this memoir.

Now, for some stories:

EARLY LIFE

This will be as brief as I can make it. The details of a "happy" childhood are of little interest to anyone other than me – and, perhaps my siblings, if they are in a generous mood. I will highlight only a few things that seemed to foreshadow the approach I later brought to my professional life.

Restraint and Respect for Different Opinions

My lineage is wholly Irish-American. I am third generation on my father's side and fifth generation, at most, on my mother's side. But, the home atmosphere did not conform to the stereotype of a boisterous and quarrelsome Irish clan. I grew up in an atmosphere of emotional reserve, where discussion of unpleasant subjects was avoided and disagreements were muted. In fact, vehement opinions on any subject were discouraged.

One remark by my father stands out in memory after some 65 years. Like many adolescents, I was beginning to voice some maverick opinions. Once, I upset the mandatory decorum of the dinner table with a strong denunciation of someone's views on a public issue. My father interrupted me in full flood, and simply said: "Tom, why don't you just let someone else be wrong?"

Implicit in this criticism is not only impatience with crusades of any kind, but also some skepticism about whether it is possible for me or anyone else to be too sure we are right. The reason I remember the remark so well is not because it turned my life around immediately; it didn't. But, as the years went by, my fundamental approach to the legal profession and to the world seems to have been shaped by it. Additional specific examples will be described later on, but it's no exaggeration to say that some of my significant shortcomings, as well as my strengths, are foreshadowed in those ten words.

My father taught me another, clearly-allied lesson, expressly and by example. He was always courteous and respectful to the people he encountered, regardless of their station in life. I rarely had the opportunity to observe him in his office environment, but those who had once worked with him would mention his unfailing kindness and consideration, years after he was gone. I personally could see these qualities when he spoke to people who served him, at home or in a public place. He once said to me: "If you ever have a position of authority, never ever speak harshly to subordinates because they can't fight back." I suspect he treated any adversaries the same way – I don't think he had an enemy in the world.

Again, my efforts to follow his example may have had mixed effects on my life as a lawyer. Lawyering, after all, can be a combative calling, and anger - real or feigned - is sometimes effective. It's just not one of my tools.

Finally, it should be obvious from these tales of an unusually nomadic professional life that was strongly influenced by another example of his parental advice. He once said to me: "It's a mistake to set longterm goals." He went on to explain that longterm prospects can be affected by too many things that will be entirely outside my control, and that fixation on one objective may cause me to miss out on unexpected opportunities that may offer greater satisfaction. "If you apply your basic intelligence and do your best in whatever your present occupation may be," he said, "I promise you that you will have a rewarding career, even though it could be in a field that you may not imagine today."

He was right.

Priorities in Life

My father was a self-made man. The son of a policeman, who died when he was five, he went to work at the age of 15, to help support the fragmented family. He never had the benefit of a college education. By intelligence and hard work, he rose to become an executive vice president of the largest bank in the State of New Jersey and chairman of an affiliated auto finance company.

Unlike many self-made men, however, he never was particularly interested in the accumulation of wealth. He earned enough to provide all five children with an excellent education and to support an expansive lifestyle. He respected achievement but not money for its own sake. He believed that significant inherited wealth could cripple ambition and a sense of self-worth. He had some friends with inherited money who "never did a day's work in their lives," but they were spoken of with tolerant amusement rather than respect.

My mother, by contrast, grew up in a privileged environment. For most of her life she did not have to cook meals, clean the house, or take care of infants. But she had as diverse interests and quick intelligence as anyone I have ever known. She graduated from college, with a major in mathematics, and earned a Masters in English at Columbia, at a time when few women had advanced degrees. She had a vast reservoir of poetry in her memory bank, and she encouraged us to enjoy it; she read to us for hours when we were little; and she took us to museums and events of cultural significance. (My father's expeditions were sometimes more interesting for a young boy. I still remember the overwhelming bulk of the Hindenberg, close to the ground at Lakehurst, New Jersey, shortly before it was destroyed in the famous explosion.)

My mother's best friends were people who shared her intellectual curiosity and she had no interest whatever in the preoccupations of her many affluent acquaintances. "Rich people can be very boring," she once said to me. "All they want to talk about is their golf game, their social life and the servant problem." The most worthwhile possessions, she said, are "mental furniture," acquired by an accumulation of interesting experiences. I still feel that way, and am fortunate to have a spouse who agrees.

In summary, when I was growing up, money never was a subject of much interest. There always seemed to be enough of it, but I knew a lot of kids from families that had a lot more, and therefore I did not feel defined by it. This attitude has also continued throughout my life.

When I decided to become a lawyer, I assumed that I could earn enough to have a comfortable life, but never expected to get rich. The "business side" of law firm life - which has become increasingly important in recent years - has never interested me. I never cared whether someone else attracted more clients, logged more hours, or earned more money than I did. I never wanted to "compete" with my law partners. This should be understood as a comment on my own preferences, not as a criticism of anyone else. Changes in the legal profession were foreshadowed by the Supreme Court's 1975 decision in *Goldfarb*,[2] which essentially taught that lawyering was a competitive business like any other. And, clients that have been pressured by intense and growing world wide competition have in turn expected their lawyers and other suppliers to compete hard for their business. It's just hard for me to "sell myself."

Worse, I do not have a strong competitive streak. In the days when I competed in team or individual sports, I would obviously rather win than lose, but enjoyment of the game itself was always more important. In grade school and high school, at Newark Academy, a private boys' school, a gold medal was awarded annually to the kid with the highest grades in each class. I went to the school for nine years, and have six of them. However, the perennial number two, and occasional leader, cared a lot more than I did. Each month, he asked about the grades on my report card, but I was never interested in his. I have always cared more about satisfying my own standards than winning the prize.

Peace of Mind

My paternal grandmother was an Irish immigrant, born in rural Cavan County in 1867. She came to this country in the mid 1880's, and married another immigrant - a policeman who, as mentioned, was accidentally killed in 1899. As a widow, with two young children in a more callous age, she had a difficult time.

Later on, she had a much more comfortable life. She lived with us in a very large house while I was growing up, and survived to see the arrival of a number of great-grandchildren - a rarity in those days. But she knew sorrow, as well. When she finally died in 1964, she had outlived all her children and most of her surviving close friends.

Withal, she had the most even and serene disposition of anyone I have ever known. Outsiders noticed it and, in her extreme old age, she was sometimes asked to explain the secret. Her answer was always the same: "I never worry about things that I cannot do anything about."

These may be the most sensible words I have ever heard, but it's not advice that is easy to follow. A lot of people have been programmed to think that worry is a form of common prayer, and that there is a collective obligation to join in common expressions of concern. It can be particularly difficult to maintain this sensible detachment if you are in a personal service profession like a doctor or a lawyer. Clients can really get upset.

But, as we shall see, some of my legal mentors have said much the same thing to me, and I have come to believe that clients are best served if counsel can maintain a certain detachment. In law as in life, it is sometimes best to just accept the inevitable, let go of past grievances and adapt to changed circumstances.

Other Family Influences

I cannot conclude this discussion of the things I learned in early life without mention of my brothers and sisters.

We five children were in many ways treated as members of two separate families: the "three boys" who were a little more than a year apart, and the "little girls" who were several years younger. This division was probably typical of the times, but it really was unfair to the girls who resented it and it had mixed effects on me.

I owe a lot to my two older brothers, Dan and Barrett. For example, they taught me to read before I ever went to school, and this head start contributed to a confidence about schoolwork that I never lost. Their insistence that I participate in their sometimes rough sports, even when I was a lot smaller, helped to give me a physical confidence that was particularly important for boys and men when I was growing up.

The paternalistic, almost condescending treatment of my sisters, Mary Caroline and Margot, reflected a reality of the time. Men and women really inhabited separate worlds. In the setting where I was raised, we were not educated in the same schools and consequently did not really get to know each other very well. I was brought up to believe that women were frail and had to be treated with special consideration. Physical violence was, of course, unthinkable, but even a harsh tone of voice was too threatening. In other words, women should be treated as gently as people in a subordinate position - which they actually were at the time.

My two sisters seem to have survived this paternalistic upbringing. They are witty and intelligent women, who can hold their own anywhere today. But it's hard for me to shake it. I may have acquired an undeserved reputation as a closet feminist later in life, when I went out of my way to support women as they entered the professional ranks. I guess the support was welcomed. In retrospect, however, I believe it was largely prompted by old-fashioned paternalism. If I sometimes slip into that mode today, I apologize.

One member of my extended family was anything but frail. My Great Aunt and Godmother Elizabeth Barrett Rothschild (1859-1943) had an amazing life. I want to say some things about her here because she is such a vivid example of an unconventional woman in an era when those qualities were not encouraged.

"Aunt Lizzie" married a Jewish man, at a time when it was a daring thing for both of them to do. In 1912, Martin Rothschild went down with the Titanic, but Aunt Lizzie survived. (She may have owed her life to the male gallantry of her time, but she never looked for it again.) She was in the famous lifeboat No. 6, in company with the "Unsinkable Molly Brown". This was the boat on which the women rebelled against the pusillanimous direction of the crewman in charge, and ensured their own rescue.

I remember Aunt Lizzie as a formidable lady of strong opinions, and considerable wealth, who pretty much did whatever she pleased. She really deserves a chapter, if not a book of her own, and I expect to write down some of my most vivid memories as a tribute to her next year when the Centennial Anniversary of the Titanic disaster will be commemorated across the country.

In a small cemetery in Watkins Glen, New York, where she grew up, there is a rather imposing marble mausoleum that she built to honor her husband, Martin Rothschild. Inside, there is a stained glass window for him and burial places for several generations of family members, including her brother Monsignor Thomas Barrett, whose name I bear.

There is one story about Aunt Lizzie that has a really close connection to our present home. In the early years of the last century she used to travel across the country by rail and stay at the Hotel del Coronado, a short distance up the same road from where we live now. Sometimes she brought along a young niece by marriage named Dorothy Rothschild, the product of a broken home. "Poor little Dorothy," as Aunt Lizzie called her, probably chafed in the company of her overbearing relative. When she became a successful writer in the 1920s, under her married name Dorothy Parker, she was famous for her irreverent wit and radical political views.

I want to tell one more wholly irrelevant story that is connected to Aunt Lizzie, and then promise to move on. For a long time, she lived with an older half-sister who had the same name. I don't remember much about "Aunt Lib" because she died when I was seven, and it was hard to communicate with her because she was stone deaf and as feeble as Aunt Lizzie was feisty.

One thing, however, has stuck with me. Aunt Lib always claimed that, when she was a little girl she met a veteran of the Revolutionary War at some patriotic celebration. There is no way to verify the story, of course, but it is entirely possible since Aunt Lib was born in 1848, some 65 years after the War ended. And, I have treasured the thought that I once talked to someone who talked to a veteran of that War.

Maybe, my grandchildren will care, even if no one else does.

Brushes with the Law

There was no strong tradition of lawyering in my family. My mother's brother, Charles Barrett, was a trial lawyer and later a trial-court judge in New Jersey. But, he was the only member of my extended family in the legal field and had a limited influence on my early life, although I will say that his courtroom stories were a lot more interesting than some of my father's largely incomprehensible discussions with his colleagues in the financial world.

Sometimes, elder members of my immediate family would tell me that I should be a lawyer some day - probably for no better reason than the fact that I talked all the time. I chattered so much, in fact, that my maternal grandmother (not the serene grandmother already mentioned) would occasionally pay me a dollar just to be quiet for awhile. That was big money for a little kid in those days, and the bribe probably worked for ten minutes, or so.

I don't remember that I had any strong feelings about a legal career, one way or the other. However, I once did meet a very famous lawyer, indeed. The incident really has no bearing on my future approach to the law, but it makes a pretty good story.

Charles Evans Hughes was the Chief Justice of the United States in the Summer of 1940. At that time, my family used to vacation in Skytop, Pennsylvania, a quiet and unpretentious (albeit expensive) "family" resort of the kind that my family favored. Chief Justice Hughes also used to stay at the same resort, perhaps for similar reasons.

Hughes, who was then roughly the same age that I am now, had far more gravitas than I do. He wore a full white beard in the tradition of the previous century, was always formally dressed, and moved in a formal way. He was obviously someone important but, at the age of nine, I had no idea what a "Chief Justice" was.

Hughes did, however, have a fascinating automobile. It was a great, big, ponderous thing - probably some exotic foreign brand - that was stored in one of the guest garages behind the hotel. I sometimes saw his driver back there, busy with washing and polishing, and we had friendly conversations while I admired the car. It occurred to me that if I introduced myself to Mr. Hughes, I might be invited to take a ride in his wondrous machine. I asked my parents to arrange an introduction, but they pointed out that they did not know Mr. Hughes and were not inclined to intrude on his privacy. This was not a satisfactory answer.

At this same period of time, World War II had begun; France had fallen; the Battle of England was underway; and Winston Churchill, Prime Minister, was much in the news. I really did not know what a "Prime Minister" was either, but assumed it meant he was important, like a "Chief Justice".

You can see where this is going. One day I saw Mr. Hughes across the hotel lobby, and broke away from our family gathering to meet him. Walked right up and said, "Hello, Mr. Prime Minister." I have no idea what Mr. Hughes thought, but he courteously put out his hand, and said something like: "Well, hello to you, and what is your name?" Before I could tell him my name, and launch into a discussion of his automobile, I was interrupted and hustled away by my apologetic and mortified mother.

So, I never did get to ride in that car, but I have always been pleased to say that I once shook hands with Charles Evans Hughes.

Justice William Brennan was someone I met, and really did get to know well in my teenage years. Before he was appointed to the Court by President

Eisenhower in the early 1950's, he circulated amiably in the Northern Jersey Irish crowd.

During the summer of 1948, the Brennan family and my family had rented houses at another quiet resort on Cape Cod; and the families socialized a lot. Brennan was then a practicing lawyer in Newark, New Jersey, and my father was an older, and more established man. But he was impressed by Brennan, and liked him. Everyone did. That summer, my father said to me: "That young man will someday be either the Governor of this State or a Supreme Court Justice." Really!

Justice Brennan was particularly nice to me that Summer; he had teenage boys, too, and I think he recognized it was an awkward age. And, he always remembered me. In later years, when I would see him at Harvard Law School or Bar functions, he would always inquire about the progress of my legal career and the health of various members of my family. He was a cheerful and engaging man, without a trace of self-importance.

I did not agree with some of the opinions that Justice Brennan wrote during his long service on the Court. But I have always admired his well-known ability to maintain collegial relations with his fellow Justices. For example, when Justice Rehnquist was up for confirmation as Chief, he drew a lot of fire from the political Left. Brennan, the acknowledged leader of the so-called "Liberal" bloc, effectively undercut the opposition when he publicly declared that Rehnquist would make a "splendid" Chief Justice.

A collegial attitude, of course, is not entirely altruistic. It can be a useful strategy. Minority members can choose to dissent frequently, and hope for ultimate - perhaps posthumous - vindication when attitudes change. Alternately however, they can choose to dissent infrequently, engage in dialogue with the other members, and perhaps temper the views expressed by the majority. Brennan was widely considered to be one of the most influential members of the Court because he largely adhered to the more accommodating strategy.

In 1999, when I was confirmed as a Republican member of the Federal Trade Commission, which then had a Democratic majority, I chose to follow Justice Brennan's example, albeit in a far less imposing role, with generally less contentious matters to decide. On the relatively rare occasion when I felt compelled to dissent, I rarely stated my reasons publicly. Instead, I would circulate private statements to my colleagues. And, I always preferred to see our differences resolved by mutual compromises in a unanimous decision.

This was a conscious strategy, but it should be obvious that it came naturally to me because of the childhood influences that I have already described. For better or worse, this is the way that I am. And, although I cannot be sure, I suspect that William Brennan acted the way that he did because it also came naturally.

COLLEGE YEARS

My oldest brother was a senior at Georgetown and my next oldest brother was a sophomore there, when I decided that I wanted to go to Princeton. It may have looked like a "radical" step because I had always wanted to follow them everywhere. (At Newark Academy, the faculty referred to us as "Big Leary, Middle Leary, and Little Leary" and my brothers paved the way for me.)

But it really wasn't so daring. Princeton was not much over an hour away by a car or on the train, and I could easily go home for a weekend it I wanted to. My roommate Michael Hogan (later a successful plastic surgeon) had been my best friend since I was 12, and a number of family friends were loyal - indeed, fanatic - alumni.

I did not view my Princeton years as specific preparation for an ultimate legal career, or any other particular occupation. This attitude was encouraged. Dr. Dodds, the University President, in his opening address to the freshman class, said something like: "There are 24 hours in the day, and you will normally work for eight and sleep for eight. What we hope to do here is teach you some things that will enrich the other eight. So, don't be afraid to try out different things."

And, so I did.

The Man of the Millennium

Before a discussion of the Princeton experiences that did have an influence on my later working life, I have to digress, and tell a story about an event that did nothing more than contribute to later bragging rights.

I have sometimes asked people of my generation to name any individual alive in the 20th Century who is most likely to be remembered for centuries to come. Some will name conspicuous larger-than-life personalities like the leaders of the warring nations in World War II. But, the one name that is mentioned more often than any political leader is Albert Einstein - the man who irrevocably changed our view of fundamental reality. He is my choice as well, and I met him while I was a freshman at Princeton.

It happened because of the confluence of two seemingly unrelated facts: the then-lingering vestige of Princeton's religious heritage and the absence of girls on the campus. For at least the first two years at the University (and perhaps more - I don't remember), Princeton required students to attend a religious service of their choice in town on at least two weekends a month. Attendance was taken. I knew some girls in the vicinity of my home in New Jersey, and even more in New York, but there was a serious shortage in Princeton itself.

It has often been said that "where there's a will, there's a way" - and, when it comes to girls, the will of a teenage boy is very, very strong. So, I found a way. Remember, I would get credit for attending a religious service of my "choice". So, I chose to attend the Jewish services on Friday evening, and then dash for the train to Newark or New York. Plenty of time for a late date on Friday, and two full days of jollification thereafter.

The Jewish services in town were rather like those conducted by Unitarians, with an emphasis on ethical and moral questions rather than theology and ritual. The services frequently featured outside speakers, and one evening the speaker was Albert Einstein, then affiliated with the Institute for Advanced Study in Princeton and noted for his pacifist views. The gathering was small because Princeton imposed a disgraceful quota on Jewish students at that time, and the great man was able to shake hands and exchange a few polite words with everyone present.

So, that's how I got to meet the Man of the Millennium.

A Detour into Journalism

If someone had asked me about my future ambitions midway through my years at Princeton, I probably would have expressed a serious interest in journalism. *The Daily Princeton* newspaper was published five days a week, and I devoted far more time to the newspaper that I did to any other activity. I liked to write stories on a short deadline, to edit the stories of others, and occasionally - on a rotating basis - "put the paper to bed" at the print shop in the early hours of the morning. The paper was printed in a way that is now obsolete, with lines of lead type and headlines that were inserted by hand in a frame, letter by letter. You had to count words, and even letters, when you made the inevitable last-minute changes. You had to deal diplomatically with the experienced linotype operator, who was reliably grumpy and not reliably sober. I loved every minute of it.

As I advanced on the staff I was given the opportunity to make my own choices of subjects to write about. I co-authored a series of articles to guide underclassmen through the Club selection process, which was later put in booklet form and circulated to students for many years. I led a team that traveled to New Haven, to produce an issue on Yale for the benefit of Princeton students who expected to travel to New Haven for an upcoming football weekend. William Buckley, then Chairman of the Yale Daily and later a noted conservative journalist and raconteur, graciously made facilities available for our efforts.

Later, I impersonated an undergraduate with more money than brains, and wrote a lengthy expose of a well organized enterprise that would find capable graduate students to ghost-write a Senior Thesis or a term paper for a fee. Then, with some credentials as what would now be called an "investigative reporter," I was offered an even more challenging assignment, which ultimately demonstrated that I really did not have what it takes.

One day my fellow editors suggested that I solve an intriguing mystery, namely, the location of the famous statue of *The Christian Student*, created about 100 years ago by the well known sculptor Daniel Chester French, who also created the statue of Lincoln in his Memorial. The Princeton statue epitomized the image of what was then known as "muscular" Christianity, in the person of a young man with a firm jaw, a football under one arm, and a Bible under the other.

The undergraduates of the day, quite understandably, despised it. It was repeatedly splattered with paint and even more noisome embellishments; and it was sometimes toppled, dragged about, and left in the nearest gutter. The University finally gave up, and secreted the much abused Christian Student in an unknown location. To solve the mystery seemed like a worthy quest.

The University Administration, of course, was not about to disclose the secret. I interviewed a number of retired faculty members without success. Longtime janitors seemed a likely source, and, with them, I explored some musty basements. Nothing. Then I had what I thought was a bright idea. The not-inconsiderable cost of the statue had been contributed by a very wealthy and prominent family. One surviving member of the family, who would surely remember the gift and its ultimate deposition, still lived in the Princeton area. She was a very sweet and very ancient lady, who lived in seclusion.

We had several lengthy telephone conversations. I told her I was keenly interested in this great work of art that her family had generously given to the University, and that it deserved to be on public display - perhaps in the University Museum where it would be well protected. I assured her that we on the student newspaper were ready to demand action. It was all a lie, of course, and she was wary at first.

Finally, however, I seemed to be making headway. She invited me to come over for tea, and meet with one of her family advisors to discuss the matter further. The goal was in sight!

But, at the last minute, I simply couldn't go through with it. I felt as rotten then as I ever had in my young life. I called the good lady back, apologized for taking up her time, and explained that I was convinced after further inquiries that the project simply would not work. The "further inquiries" part was another lie, of course, but sometimes a gentle lie is less hurtful than the truth.

And I concluded then, and forever after, that I did not have a strong enough stomach for the journalistic profession. Some journalists, of course, are principled and even noble. But, overall, the profession seems to depend on sensation for survival at the expense of human dignity. (Consider how hard a shell you must have when you stick a microphone in front of an innocent citizen who has just lost her entire family in a fire, and ask "how she feels".) Of course, as a lawyer, I cannot assume a superior air about the frailties of other occupations. In my own profession, there are also some things that I simply cannot do.

The shift in my thoughts about a post-Princeton occupation actually did not have an immediate impact, because there was something else going on in the world that I expected to have a much more immediate effect on my future.

The Korean War

The Korean War started in June 1950 just after the completion of my sophomore year, and just before my 19th birthday, I immediately concluded that a life that had been sheltered and largely free from stress could become very serious, very soon.

This War is largely a "forgotten war" today, perhaps because it essentially ended in a draw. But over 40,000 U.S. servicemen died in Korea, almost as many as were killed in the much longer war in Vietnam - and it consumed a far higher share of the nation's resources. Korea cost well over 10% of the Gross National Product, equivalent to a yearly bill of about 2 trillion today. Even more important, it was widely believed that this war was just the opening salvo in a much longer battle against the Communist world. North

Korea was a Soviet client state, supplied with Soviet weapons, and then Red China entered the War in force about six months after it began.

As it turned out, Korea did not trigger World War III, and with almost 60 years of hindsight, it is easy to say that those grim expectations were unfounded. But it did not look that way at the time. Young men of my generation had been a little too young for World War II, but we believed that this time it would be our responsibility, and our privilege, to carry the heaviest burden in the defense of Western civilization.

If I may digress for a moment, I can never understand why we in the so-called "Silent Generation" have been characterized as self-satisfied and self-seeking. We were silent, by comparison with youth later on; we did not scream in the streets. We had no cause to be angry at parents who had nurtured us in comfort through the greatest depression in the nation's history or those who had so recently won a great war. Sycophantic academics did not encourage us to think that our generation could do a better job than our elders did; in fact, we weren't sure that we could do as well.

But, we were willing to try. About 70% of my Princeton class served in the military, without complaint. I think we were every bit as idealistic as the self-congratulatory Baby Boomers who came along later.

So, my last two years at Princeton had a surreal, quarter-to-midnight quality. I studied less, and partied more, because the music was about to stop. I decided to join the Navy right after graduation. As a backup, in the event something went wrong, I applied to Columbia and Harvard Law Schools, and was accepted at both. But I really didn't want to go.

ANCHORS AWEIGH

Military service today is voluntary; service during the Vietnam war was largely based on random selection in a draft; service during the Korean War years was mandatory for all males who were physically and mentally fit. The mandatory obligation could, however, be deferred until completion of college or graduate school. Some of my Princeton classmates who graduated in 1952 chose to go directly to a graduate school and serve later.

Along with many others, I wanted to serve as soon as possible after graduation. (As it turned out I reported for duty four days after.) The decision was partly promoted by uncertainty over what I wanted to do with my life. I thought I might want to go to law school someday, but I wasn't sure. And, I was horrified by the thought of three more years as a student, and really needed a break. Ever since I have had a great deal of sympathy for young people who want to take a break from the long slog of preparation that modern society demands. And I consider myself lucky that my country required me to take a break at some point, anyhow.

But, this wasn't all of it. I was genuinely eager to play a part, however small, in the battle to contain what I believed was then the greatest source of evil in the world - an international conspiracy with advocates who openly declared their intention to destroy Western civilization.

With the benefit of hindsight, many present-day commentators are critical of the anti-Communist sentiment that existed in this country in the 1950's. But they do not take adequate account of the way the world looked at the time. Communist forces had killed thousands of Americans, and were known to have killed millions of their own countrymen in order to impose a system that their acolytes wanted to import into the United States. I think it is understandable that most people in this country did not want Communists, or unrepentant former Communists, to poison the minds of their children in schools or in media messages. For a present analogy, consider the likely reaction today to teachers or script-writers who have affiliations with the Ku Klux Klan, White Supremacists, or the Taliban.

In this atmosphere, the Navy was a welcome choice for me. My oldest brother Dan, then a graduate of Business School, was serving as a supply officer in the Navy. My middle brother Barrett was trying to get in the Marines. (He ultimately wound up in the Army because the Marines looked askance at his history of asthma in childhood.) I decided to apply for the Naval Officer Candidate School in Newport, Rhode Island, where I could earn a commission in four months. By a stroke of good fortune, I had the opportunity to learn and to do some fascinating things in the Navy, which have had a significant impact on my later life.

The Initial Screen

In the Spring of 1952, I traveled to New York on a designated day when applications were taken for the Newport OCS Program. At the appointed place and time there were probably about 100 applicants there - mostly college seniors like I was. We were directed to a large room with individual desks, and given about an hour to take a written exam that looked something like a short version of a Scholastic Aptitude Test.

This didn't concern me at all because I had always done well on so-called "Intelligence" tests. The name is misleading, of course, because the format does not test for more important qualities like judgment or the ability to see the world through the eyes of another. My ability to do well on tests was probably a birthright, but I had to learn more important things from observation and experience. In any event, I took the test and then spent several hours undergoing individual interviews and the usual indignities of a physical, followed by some informative talks. At the end of the day those of us who had passed the initial screen - over half - reconvened in the big room. A man in authority then said that we would receive further orders by mail, and dismissed everyone except for two people whom he asked to stay behind. I was one of them.

The two of us, understandably puzzled, were ushered into a small room and introduced to a couple of officers we had not seen before. We were then congratulated and told we had done so well on the written test that we could qualify for an assignment in Naval Intelligence. But, before the necessary clearance process started, there was one vital question: "Do either of you have any relatives who live in a country behind the Iron Curtain?" If so, there was no point in proceeding further because the Soviets were likely to discover the identity of Intelligence Officers and they or their puppets might retaliate against innocent people. As it happened, the other fellow did have relatives in Poland, and was excused with apologies and assurances that the Navy would welcome him in another capacity. That left me.

There are, of course, a number of sub-specialties in the Intelligence field. I was told of one that I might find particularly challenging. Beginning in World War II and continuing into the Korean War, people designated as Air Combat Intelligence Officers were assigned to various aviation units. Their job was to gather information on enemy targets, ground defenses and the capabilities of various hostile aircraft - and then to summarize it in oral briefings for active Navy fliers and former fliers who commanded them. People who were teachers or lawyers in civilian life were considered to be particularly well suited for an assignment like this, but it was not an essential qualification.

Was I interested? You bet I was. And, without any advance planning, I took one more step toward my ultimate life's work.

Officers' Candidate School ("OCS")

It took a while for the FBI to conduct the necessary background checks, but finally I got my orders to report to OCS in Newport, Rhode Island. The night before I left, I had an odd conversation with my father, which is included here for no reason other than to show the whimsical side of a fun- damentally serious man. The spoken words in quotes are reproduced to the best of my memory; the italicized words represent my simultaneous thought processes.

Father: "Tom, will you come into the library for a minute."

TL: "Sure."

What's this all about? A summons to the library usually means something serious.

Father: "I know you've finished college, but you've really had a sheltered life up to now."

TL: "____"

This sounds like a prelude to something embarrassing.

Father: "I think it's time that we talked about women."

TL: "____"

Oh, God! I knew it! This is beyond mortifying. Maybe a bolt of lightning will strike the house, and this will stop.

Father: "In your Navy travels, you may someday find yourself in a railroad station. And a young woman will come up to you."

TL: "____"

Please, earth, swallow me now!

Father: "She'll be carrying a baby."

TL: "____"

Mild relief. Where is this going?

Father: "And she'll say: 'Would you please mind my baby while I go to the ladies' room?'"

TL: "_____"

Big relief!

Father: "Don't do it. She'll never come back … Any questions?"

TL: "I think I've got that; thanks."

With great enthusiasm.

For years, I couldn't figure out what this was all about. But now, I think the most likely explanation is that my anxious mother had urged my father to give me a farewell lecture on women and babies. He was probably as reluctant to have the conversation as I was, but afterward could honestly report that he had done it.

I got on a train the next day to Providence, R.I., in a buoyant frame of mind.

I expected OCS to be four months of hellish boot camp, but it was nothing like that. The physical side was actually rather light. Exercises were infrequent and mild, to most everyone's vast relief. (Men in my generation enjoyed sports, but pure exercise was something to avoid.) We marched in formation to and from classes, but we really weren't expected to be very good at it. (That was for the Marines and the Army - not for Sailors.)

But the mental part was intense. For example, we were taught how to navigate the very complex and old fashioned way, by sighting on the sun or the stars. We were taught how the then standard mechanical computers solved the problem of firing the ships guns at moving targets, by very sophisticated use of solid geometry. I loved it because the solutions were so elegant. Beautiful, really.

And, I didn't mind the daily pressure. In an odd way, it was a relief to have some higher authority script virtually every waking moment of the day. On most days, I had about 15 minutes to spare, just before we marched off to dinner, and I still remember the simple joy of sitting on the edge of my bunk, with an empty mind.

I wouldn't have wanted to live this kind of life forever, but the experience did teach me that I was happier with some structure. Today, in semi-retirement, I can appreciate the occasional day with nothing at all that I have to do. But a steady diet of it would be oppressive.

As graduation day approached, most in my OCS class were anxiously concerned about their next assignment. It was really a random lottery. The possibilities ranged from duty in Guantanamo Bay, Cuba (the best for those of hedonistic temperament) to a minesweeper in Korean waters (the worst for almost anyone). I didn't have to worry, because I knew what my next assignment would be. I would wear the uniform of an ordinary line officer, but I really wasn't one. I had an Air Intelligence designation (1355 AI, as I remember), which was really a staff position.

And, as it turned out, I have been in staff positions ever since. That's what lawyers do.

Graduation in late October 1952 was a glorious day. I got to wear my officer's uniform for the first time, and was pleased that my parents came up to Providence for the ceremony. A Vice Admiral Delaney, Commander of the Eastern Sea Frontier, was the speaker at the event, and I have never forgotten his closing words:

> "May all your cruises be on calm seas,
> And may all your missions be peaceful ones."

This may, at first, seem like an unusual message for a group of newly-minted officers who will shortly join the fleet in the midst of a bitter war. It does, however, reflect a profound truth. Most of the people with whom I served in the Navy did not crave violence and risk; they just accepted that these things might be part of the job. They thought of themselves as guardians of our country on its far frontiers, and they were willing to do what they had to do. I was proud then to serve with people like that, and I honor them still.

The top-ranked dozen in a class of over 800 were invited up on stage to get their commissions directly from the Admiral. I ranked number 12, and just made it. However, none of us was actually the smartest guy in the room. The smartest guy was a Chief Petty Officer - a crusty old salt in our training phase - who stood by one of the doorways as we filed out, with a big smile and a sharp salute for each new Ensign that went by. We each returned the salute, and handed over the dollar bill that new officers traditionally give for the first one.

Naval Intelligence School in D.C.

After graduation from OCS, and a brief leave, I spent six weeks at the Naval Air Station in Jacksonville, Florida, where I was introduced to the flying wing of the Navy, and to the very pleasant life of an officer ashore. We learned a lot about the characteristics of various kinds of aircraft, and the technical disciplines required to maintain and fly them off carriers. But, the pressure was off, and it was a welcome break from the intensity of OCS. Then, along with a number of OCS classmates who also were designated Air Intelligence Officers, I traveled to Washington, D.C. for a three-month course at the Naval Intelligence School, then located at the Observatory near the present home of the Vice President. This was a challenging, and sometimes unsettling experience.

We were told about the ways that intelligence is gathered around the world, and made aware of the current predictions about Soviet intentions - then in flux because Josef Stalin died while I was there. We were told about the strengths and weaknesses of the Russian and Chinese military forces. We were split into groups and given problems involving hypothetical targets and hypothetical defenses, information that we then were supposed to reduce to a manageable form and present in mock briefing sessions - which were then, of course, critiqued by our instructors.

The parallels between these hypothetical exercises and the conduct of litigation are, of course, obvious. And, something said at the beginning of our training summed up the process in a way that I have never forgotten and have often quoted in talks to other lawyers.

"The job of an Intelligence Officer," an instructor said, "is to serve as the enemy's representative on the commander's staff." Needless to say, this bold statement came as a shock when I first heard it. What the instructor meant, of course, is that an Intelligence Officer is supposed to learn a much as possible about the enemy, and to evaluate its capabilities and likely intentions for the benefit of the commanding officer.

And, that is exactly what a good lawyer is supposed to do. We are supposed to know as much as we can about our client's adversaries, or potential adversaries, to evaluate the strengths and weaknesses of their position, and predict their likely arguments and strategies. If a client interrupts a counseling session and says "whose side are you on, anyway," it probably means that you are doing a good job. (But, it might be prudent to explain why.)

There is one specific intelligence issue that is worthy of mention in a legal memoir, even though it has not arisen directly in my own practice. The description of intelligence-gathering methods included an extensive discussion of various methods of prisoner interrogation - employed in the U.S. and in other countries around the world. It was important for us to know about these things because one of our jobs would be to provide those about to fly over hostile territory with information about what they are likely to encounter if they are shot down and captured. And U.S. methods are also relevant because our nation's experience with what is effective and what is not may provide further insight into what an enemy might do. (The word "effective" here refers to the likelihood that information elicited will be accurate and useful; a determined interrogator can always get people to talk.)

The appropriate rules for POW interrogation raise an issue that erupts from time to time, particularly during the tenure of Presidents who are generally unpopular among the media outlets that publish the stories. Lawyers are particularly likely to become involved in discussions of what is "legal" and what is not. I do not know how much of our training in Intelligence School is still classified, or indeed is still accurate. But, after 58 years, a few general observations are probably safe and valid.

It is well known that the overall treatment of POWs in World War II occupied a wide range in a spectrum. Japanese treatment of prisoners was generally barbarous; and very few Russian or German prisoners survived capture on the Eastern Front. At the other extreme, the experience of German prisoners in the U.S. was so generally benign that significant numbers of them decided to emigrate to this country after the War. In the heat of battle, however, troops of any nation may simply ignore isolated attempts to surrender and no one, military or civilian, could "surrender" to people who are bombing or shelling them from afar.

I also am not aware that any of the belligerents in that War adhered strictly to the structures of the Geneva Convention and respected a prisoner's supposed right to disclose only "name, rank and serial number". The experience in the Korean War was the same, and I would be amazed if anyone has observed these rules in subsequent conflicts. (Terrorists are, of course, not covered by the Convention, anyhow.) We lawyers sometimes get so fixated on legal distinctions that we ignore common sense. It is simply not realistic to suppose that the figurative flutter of a white handkerchief will forthwith transform what had been a lethal confrontation into a polite dialogue governed by rules of conversational decorum appropriate for a royal levee.

It also may be useful to consider the larger context. The business of Intelligence, by definition, involves an effort by one nation to gather information that other sovereign nations want to hold secret. Methods involve not only interrogation but also trespass, theft and bribery - all of which raise legal issues if you want to be fussy about it.

I once heard a blunt comment by Judge Stanley Sporkin, onetime General Counsel of the Central Intelligence Agency that makes this point better than I can. At an ABA meeting in the mid-1980's, Judge Sporkin gave a talk on some corporate governance issue. (He had, of course, made his name as a vigorous enforcer of the Securities Laws.) During the question period that followed, some young fellow in the back of the room asked a wholly unexpected question about how he, as General Counsel, prevented the CIA from engaging in unlawful conduct.

Sporkin looked startled for a moment and then said something like the following:

> "Young man, the CIA is an intelligence agency. And, like all
> intelligence agencies, it sometimes does things that are illegal in
> every country in the world. That's the only way I can answer your
> question."

I mention this remark, and my own experience related here and later on, only to make a point that I believe has general application. It is very difficult to craft simple legal rules that can be applied consistently in a complex world. The outcomes may be whimsical or inane; evasion may be rampant; and general respect for the law can be undermined.

Perhaps the most egregious example is the rigid application of the "exclusionary" rule when it leads to the suppression of convincing evidence that points to the guilt of a violent predator. Surely, there are better ways to discipline overly aggressive policemen (like monetary penalties for overly aggressive searches) than to let loose someone who predictably presents an ongoing threat to public safety. I would also include in that category the failed experiment with National Prohibition and the harsh penalties for possession of some illegal drugs, or the prohibition of "profiling" in an age of terror. An example closer to my own experience would be some now-discredited _Per Se_ antitrust doctrines that penalized efficiency.

Before I take leave of my time at the Naval Intelligence School, I want to relate an experience that was mostly just a pleasant memory but also something that did have an effect on my later life.

Dwight Eisenhower was the first President I was able to vote for, and my first political hero. (It was really hard to warm up to Tom Dewey or Robert Taft.) My parents felt the same way. As it happened, the finance company that my father headed had an office located in a building that once stood on Pennsylvania Avenue near the location of the Canadian Embassy today. He and my mother jointly hosted a big party in this office suite so that their friends in town could watch the 1952 Inaugural Parade in comfort. I was invited, of course, along with my four roommates in a Georgetown house that we had rented for the three-month duration of our Intelligence training. (For $200 a month, fully furnished!)

One of my father's business friends was a wealthy gentleman with a younger wife, who was apparently well-connected in the Washington social scene. She told me that she had two extra tickets for an Inaugural Ball that night, and would like to invite me to attend the dance as her guest along with a young lady she knew who would be my date for the evening. I accepted, of course, and we agreed on an hour when she would pick me up in Georgetown.

At the appointed hour, a long black limo drew up to my house, with some guests already aboard. I really felt out of my league - in Ensign's uniform with a lonely gold stripe - when I was introduced to "General _____" in the limo. But, everyone was very pleasant, and my date was lively and pretty.

I believe there were only two Balls in town that night, and I'm not sure about the location of the one that I attended. But, unlike similar events today, there was plenty of space on the dance floor and a number of comfortable lounges on the side where we could retire for drinks and quiet conversation between dances. It seemed like every other man wearing a uniform in our particular retiring room had stars on his sleeve or shoulder, and every man in civilian clothes was some kind of ambassador with bright-colored sashes and glittering decorations. "The Grand Cross of Saint Olaf, madam," one said with a deep bow when my date admired a particularly spectacular example. (It may have been some other saint.)

I began to think the whole thing was hilarious, actually; might as well relax and enjoy it. But, then, something happened.

We were out on the dance floor, when suddenly the music stopped. After a pause, the band started to play "Hail to the Chief" and President and Mrs. Eisenhower entered the Ballroom. They walked down on a balcony overlooking the dancers and - once again, by dumb luck - we had been dancing just below. We had the best view in the place.

It's hard to describe the strange surge of emotion that I experienced in that moment. I felt so proud to be there in uniform in the presence of that great man that I thought my heart would explode. The undiluted patriotic fervor of the very young that, so often, can change lives.

* * * * *

Not long after that experience, all the students at the Intelligence School got their assignments for further duty with the fleet. I was initially assigned to a carrier, then serving in the Mediterranean, with a mission no more arduous than goodwill calls in the beautiful ports of our allied countries. By early 1953, the risk of a big war in Europe seemed diminished - although Stalin's death was a wildcard.

At one time, I might have considered it pretty good duty. I was then disappointed, however, because I wanted to get in the War. I went to the Commanding Officer at the School and asked whether I could be reassigned to the Pacific Fleet. In fact, I knew some guys who would be pleased to switch assignments with me. It is perhaps not surprising that the exchange was implemented promptly.

My new assignment was for a brief stop at one more training facility, located at the Alameda Naval Station across the Bay from San Francisco. We got a quick update there on the current situation in Korea, along with more work on hypothetical problems. After this stay of about a month, I was ordered to report to Fighter Squadron 123, then located at the Naval Air Station in Miramar, just north of San Diego.

If it had not been for my experience at the Inaugural Ball, I might not have asked for a change of orders. And, were it not for that change - which I requested after full reflection for about ten minutes - I would never have met my wife, Stephanie Abbott, would never have had the experiences that solidified my decision to go to Law School, and would not be writing this memoir at the place where I am living today.

I don't mean to imply that there is anything uniquely mystical or mysterious about all this. Most everyone has comparable life experiences. I also don't believe that whatever guiding intelligence has ordered the cosmos is concerned with my career development, any more than the outcome of athletic contests. But, it is just one more reason to be humble and grateful for things that have turned out well, and to be aware of the extent to which my life (and my attitudes) have been shaped by random chance.

Adventures in Fighter Squadron 123

The month at NAS Alameda passed quickly and uneventfully. I really was eager for the next assignment as the Air Intelligence Officer ("AIO") for Fighter Squadron 123 ("VF-123") then in pre-deployment training at NAS Miramar. I felt fortunate because a couple of my close friends, and roommates in Georgetown had assignments in the same area. We drove from San Francisco to San Diego together in a dilapidated Ford convertible I had bought for $500.

VF-123 was my home for over two years, about equally divided between Far East cruises on the carriers *Essex* and *Philippine Sea* and retraining at Miramar. The Squadron had relatively extended time ashore because the aircraft and equipment were becoming progressively more sophisticated, and it took time to break in the steady flow of replacement pilots. A number of experiences in VF-123 affected my view of the world for the rest of my life.

But, because this is the memoir of a "lawyer", I will concentrate on those that had a bearing on my future professional life and pass lightly over the rest.

The most important thing then, and forever after, is the fact that I met my wife Stephanie in June 1953 at a dance in the Officers' Club at the North Island Naval Air Station. It would take another book to describe the things she has accomplished in her own life, but she is too modest ever to write it herself and would be mortified if I attempted to do so. All I can say is that this beautiful, intelligent girl, not quite 19, had a powerful impact and things got very serious very fast. And, one way or another, she has been "ever on my mind" for almost 60 years.

A quick glance at some other things that had a powerful and lasting effect.

Perhaps most important was the fact that I had to earn the respect of people with very different life-experiences and ambitions. The handful of Intelligence Officers on the base were very much like me, and had generally similar educational backgrounds. The pilots in our squadron were a very different breed.

This is not to say that they were less intelligent. Anyone who flies a high-performance military airplane has to have a quick mind, as well as quick physical reflexes. But, they are not necessarily "intellectual" or verbally adept. The best ones are not at all reckless but, just as some professional athletes have a high tolerance for pain, military pilots had to have a high tolerance for risk.

Even as the Korean War was winding down, the fatality rate was about five percent a year, which is far higher than the rate which recently prevailed in Iraq when the fighting was intense. The principal reason was that the World War II carriers in the fleet had not been designed to handle a next generation of heavier aircraft with higher landing speeds.

The closest call that I ever had was when a plane bounced on a landing and crashed into the ship's superstructure just below an open platform where I was standing with a few other guys to watch the landings. I still can see that big prop which seemed to be heading directly at us. (The reason it fell short was that the ship was moving at the same time.) But, we all hit the deck so fast that there was no time to feel scared. So, I don't really know how I would handle the risks that the aviators handled routinely.

Let me give just one example, of many. One of the pilots in my Squadron had a midair collision, and ejected safely. But, for almost the entire fall, his chute was tangled, and he dropped like a stone. It popped open at the last minute. "The opening shock and the shock of ground contact were almost simultaneous," he said. The next day he was flying again.

These men were, in many ways, the most admirable people I have ever known. They were not "military" martinets and they maintained an easy and mutually respectful relationship with the enlisted men who maintained the complex machines that they flew and who worked with precision on the flight deck - which can be a very dangerous place. Beyond that, the fliers generally were world-class hell raisers at liberty ashore, a quality that I particularly appreciated at the time.

My close association with people unlike any I had ever encountered before is something that I still like to revisit in nostalgic memory. I love to see a pair of F-18 fighters sweeping by with a roar that splits the sky. When I sit on the upstairs terrace of the house we live in today, overlooking the Pacific Ocean, there sometimes is a magnificent warship heading out to sea. I fantasize that maybe the Navy could still benefit from the service of someone on the brink of his ninth decade, with skills almost sixty years out of date, and take me aboard for a month or two.

I also had the opportunity to experience close up some events that are still of some historic significance. A few examples.

The shooting war in Korea was suspended in July, 1953, when the parties agreed to a six-months truce. But, there was still a good chance that fighting would resume once the truce expired. (In fact, a Korean peace treaty has never been signed.) So, preparations continued on a wartime basis.

VF-123 and the other squadrons in the larger carrier Air Group embarked on the *Essex* in December, 1953, for an eight-month deployment in the Far East. I was one of three Intelligence Officers who were airlifted over in advance, to gather current information on the situation on the ground in Korea. The information was needed because the Navy provided what is known as "close air support" for frontline troops. Close air support consists of attacks on enemy targets very near the battle line, so continuous inter-service communication is necessary. The codes and recognition signs were continually changing and up-to-date information was critical. So, I wound up in a somewhat unusual place for a Navy man, on the ground in Seoul, Korea.

Seoul had been overrun four times during the War, and was a mass of rubble as far as the eye could see. Most of the buildings still standing had gaping holes for windows. People were still living in the rubble, and Korea was already a very cold place in December. An Army briefing officer told us that more than 100,000 people were expected to freeze to death in the city that winter!

It was my first sight of what was then third-world poverty. The people seemed sunk in misery, staring at me with blank indifference, and I was overwhelmed by the realization that their experience of life was beyond my comprehension. And, I understood in a way that I never had before why so many people in the world are not as satisfied with peaceful evolution as we are.

Seoul, is now a thriving and obviously prosperous city in South Korea, so I was too pessimistic about that country. But, anyone who travels today to, say, a hot and dusty Arab town will understand what I am talking about.

In order to give us shipboard types an idea of what a land war looked like, our Army hosts took us on a helicopter ride up to the front. The Korean conflict had settled into an almost static trench war, roughly similar to World War I. We could clearly see the way things were arrayed on our side, with storage facilities further back, parked tanks and heavy guns closer in, and finally the front line of trenches. We could also see at a distance, a similar pattern on the enemy side. Close below, there was a demilitaristic zone that continues to exist in some form today.

Inside that zone were some unremarkable looking buildings that have long since been forgotten by most people. I am not one of them, for reasons I will explain.

The buildings housed the so-called "Indian Camp", and they were there for an important reason. The Korean truce was held up for some two years because of a dispute about the exchange of prisoners of war. Over half of the thousands of Chinese captives - whom their government insisted were "volunteers" - had indicated they did not want to return to their homes on the mainland. They wanted to be resettled in Taiwan (then called Formosa).

The situation was obviously profoundly embarrassing for the Chinese overlords, but they finally agreed that representatives of a neutral government could interview all the prisoners on both sides to determine where they wanted to go. India was the most visible country that had maintained a strict neutrality throughout the War, and its representatives conducted the interviews. That's how the camp got its name.

In the end, of course, thousands of Chinese prisoners went to Taiwan. About twenty Americans chose to go to China. I was later present when some of our returning POWs were interviewed. They were of the opinion that the mavericks were influenced less by ideology than by fear. It is an unfortunate fact that some prisoners will betray their comrades in order to curry favor with their captors - it happens in every conflict - and those men who defected were likely afraid to travel home in company with those they had betrayed. (In fact, I believe that all but one of them quietly returned to the U.S. in subsequent years.)

The reason I remember the sight of the "Indian Camp" so well, and the reason it is mentioned here, is that the story behind that camp continues to affect the way I view the world. Many countries in the world restrict the liberties of their citizens in a way that we would not tolerate in the United States. I have engaged in many fruitless arguments - often with fellow lawyers - about which countries are the worst. For me, the answer is very simple. The worst of the worst are the countries that attempt to wall in their own people. And, for most of my life, those countries have been in the Communist bloc.

Case closed, by application of the "market test." But for a group of lawyers, who are the ones most likely to read this memoir, I suppose no case is ever closed.

There is another story, of less lasting significance, but nonetheless interesting. I doubt that many people realize we almost went to war in Vietnam in the spring of 1954.

When it became apparent that the six-month truce in Korea would be extended indefinitely, our focus turned South. There were two areas of interest: the Strait between mainland China and Formosa, and the war in Vietnam between the French Colonial power and the Communist-led Viet Minh. In order to understand these concerns, remember that we then believed that the Communist world was a more united force than it later turned out to be. They all seemed to spout the same jargon. The British were engaged in a prolonged war with Communist rebels in what was then Malaysia; the Philippine government, our former colony and close ally, also was threatened by an internal rebellion; and Indonesia appeared ripe for a Communist takeover.

The most dangerous events, however, were thought to involve the rebellion in Vietnam, and Red China's consistent threats to invade the island of Formosa. Accordingly, the Far Eastern port of our carrier *Essex*, our sister ship *Boxer*, and various screening and auxiliary vessels was changed from

Yokosuka, Japan, to Subic Bay in the Philippines. That way, we would be available either to reinforce the Navy's "Formosa Patrol", which was supposed to intercept any Chinese invading force, and also to keep a close watch on developments in Vietnam.

The move South was unpopular with the crew. Japan does not have the best climate in the world, but the Philippines and the adjacent South China Sea compete for the worst. The heat and humidity were close to unbearable in steel vessels, that soaked up the sun, with few air conditioned spaces. Yokosuka was considered one of the best liberty ports anywhere, while the town of Olongapo on Subic Bay was then, quite candidly, a dusty dump.

But, soon things got interesting. The Intelligence Officers on board, and the Photo Interpreters with whom we worked closely, were quietly told to gather whatever information we could on Vietnam - and particularly the area around Dien Bien Phu, where a French force had been surrounded by the Viet Minh rebels. A few days later, without advance warning or any explanation to the crew at large, our two carriers and supporting screen made a high-speed run across the South China Sea into the Northwest corner of the Gulf of Tonkin. It was then announced that early the next day we would launch carrier air strikes in support of the besieged French forces.

Along with the Photo Interpreters, our small Intelligence group stayed up all night to prepare briefing packages for the pilots who would fly the attack missions. We finished the job around 4 in the morning and, in need of some fresh air, I walked up to the flight deck and saw the crew members preparing to load bombs on the attack planes and machine gun ammo in the fighters that would protect them. A preliminary briefing for the Rear Admiral aboard, and other senior officers was scheduled for about 5.

Then, again without warning, the entire force began to sail in a southeast direction, away from the shore and out of the Gulf. The senior briefing commenced, but we were abruptly told by the Admiral that the mission had been cancelled. He offered no explanation, but was obviously mad as hell.

We all felt let down. I guess it's a natural physical reaction once a high level of adrenaline drains away, but it was more than that. I said earlier that we were not a particularly bellicose bunch, and I still believe we weren't in normal times and places. But, once you are at the scene of a looming conflict, geared up and ready to go, things are different. The order to stand down is somehow taken as a message that your country does not have full confidence in your capabilities. In fact, that actually was what the problem was, but there was no need for us to take it personally.

The very senior officers aboard might have had some knowledge of the rationale, but I'm not sure they did; and, for a long time, there was no public discussion of the incident. Some 30 years later, I read a book which explained what had happened. It seems that the idea of Naval air strikes to help the besieged French in the fortress of Dien Bien Phu had been approved all the way up through the Joint Chiefs (albeit not unanimously) and the State Department, but the mission was personally vetoed at the last minute by President Eisenhower on the grounds that it was militarily unsound.

Subsequent events have demonstrated that he was right. Relatively small carrier attack planes could only carry modest bomb loads to a battle site deep in North Vietnam. Years later, the huge B-52s dropped vastly greater loads into remote areas of the country, with little effect.

When it became clear that the United States would not become involved in France's colonial struggle in Viet Nam, there was a temporary relaxation of tension in the Western Pacific area.

The *Essex* returned to the Yokosuka base for the needed replacement of its wooden flight deck. Everything was cheaper in Japan at that time.

Whoever was responsible for overall morale decided that it would be a good idea to have an *Essex* "Cruise Book" published, and distributed to each man in our crew of some 3,000. It was similar to a college yearbook, with group pictures of everyone on the ship, scenic views of the various countries we had visited, and informal shots of people at work on various tasks aboard ship.

(There were even shots of non-fatal flight deck crashes, including the one that came so close to me.)

Along with one guy who had taken most of the pictures, I was selected by the Captain of the Essex to work on the overall format, and to write narrative text and descriptive photo captions. The two of us were detached for a week's temporary duty in Tokyo, where the book would be printed. Again, a lot cheaper there than in the U.S.

I still have the book, and it brings back many vivid memories of the cruise. But, there is one important memory that is not pictured or described.

Late one evening, after a long session with the printer, I decided that I wanted to see something of the City. Remember that Japan was still an occupied country, and the death and devastation of the War must have been still fresh in the minds of many. (More were killed in the fire-bombing of Tokyo than in Hiroshima.) There I was, a lone American in uniform among hoards of Japanese people still on the street. Yet, I felt perfectly safe, and was often acknowledged with bows and smiles.

I came to a four-way street intersection that was completely blocked with people standing silently. They were all staring up at a television set, that had been mounted outside one of the buildings. From the street, the screen looked about as large as a postage stamp, but I finally could make out the picture. It was Douglas MacArthur, speaking in English, at some function in the United States.

A lot has been written about the almost-mystical respect that MacArthur had earned while he was the real ruler of the country earlier in the occupation, and this was proof of it. But, my experience was also an illustration of something that has had lasting effects in this country. The occupation of Japan (and Germany, as well) was calm and almost friendly. I don't really know how the Japanese people felt inside, but their behavior was impeccable. I believe that those examples of successful occupation may have contributed to the recent unrealistic expectations about the way our occupying forces would be received in Iraq and Afghanistan.

Overall, my job in the Navy taught me a lot about life generally, helped to shape some lifelong views on matters of national security, and in many ways fostered the development of skills that served me well as a lawyer later on. But, before concluding the discussion of Navy experiences, I want to tell a few stories that deal with legal more matters directly.

Matters of Law

When a squadron was engaged in combat operations during the Korean War, the Air Intelligence Officer had more than a full time job. He was expected to brief pilots before they took off on a mission, and to debrief them on their return. If missions were flown day and night this meant that sleep was short. When the squadron was simply engaged in training exercises at home in the U.S., or overseas after the truce was signed, however, the AIO had time to take on some other administrative duties.

I was named as the Legal Officer in VF-123. I was not a lawyer, of course, but neither was anyone else in the squadron. At least I had a job a lot of lawyers had traditionally held, and had demonstrated some interest in the subject as an undergraduate by applying to Law School. A Manual on military justice was available, and I studied it with care.

My job was to advise the squadron Skipper on legal matters that he had to know about; to provide similar advice to any other officers or enlisted men who had questions; and to represent our men in summary disciplinary proceedings conducted by the Captain aboard ship. This last was a so-called "Captain's Mast", although the job was normally assigned to the Executive Officer, his second in command.

I developed a high respect for the system of military justice, although it differed in some significant respects from the system that is applied in the civilian world. The following stories illustrate what I mean.

One day at Miramar, a sailor in the squadron came to me for advice.
I remember his actual name, but will simply refer to him as "Gooch", the name he was known by. The nickname suited him well actually, because he was an amiable lump of a guy who normally worked hard but sometimes got mixed up in a rumble when he'd had a few too many ashore.

Gooch had enlisted for four years, and then signed up for another six. Now, he was two years into the re-enlistment period and decided he wanted out. He came to ask what his options were. My handy little Manual had a discussion of the various circumstances that would trigger various kinds of discharges. None of them seemed to fit but, if I had been more observant, I might have picked up some signal when I mentioned that an "Undesirable" discharge was available for people who acknowledged some form of sexual deviancy. We naturally agreed, however, that Gooch was a red-blooded American guy, with no strange tendencies, and just passed on.

The prospects didn't look all that promising for Gooch, but I got his permission to talk to our Skipper, John Fox, and see if he had any good ideas. I did, and he didn't, so it looked like Gooch was stuck.

Shortly thereafter, I was notified that Gooch had briefly exposed himself on the street in San Diego, before a number of surprised observers - and a convenient policeman. When I reported all this to the Skipper, he was enraged. "That SOB Gooch is as normal as anyone else; I know why he did it, and he won't get away with it!"

Gooch was sentenced to three months in the San Diego jail. I went to see him there, and he ruefully acknowledged that our little discussion had triggered the whole thing. And, because he was officially AWOL while he was in jail, he served another three months in a Navy brig after his release. And, of course, he didn't get the discharge he wanted.

Gooch returned to the Squadron, and made no more waves. A year after my tour of active duty had ended, and I had just completed my first year of Law School, my wife Stephanie and I returned to Coronado for the summer. I took a trip out to Miramar to visit with some of my old friends in VF-123. In the course of a warm reunion I asked how Gooch was getting along. The response was unanimous: "A model sailor."

There was another event that occurred well before I was formally designated as the Legal Officer.

A few days before the Squadron was scheduled to go overseas on the *Essex*, one of our young sailors went missing. It didn't take long to discover that he had decided to take up residence in Tijuana, Mexico, with a well-known lady of the evening and probably the afternoon as well.

The normal process of extradition was available, of course, but it can be time-consuming and the young man would likely miss the ship. We were told that a more expeditious process was available. The Tijuana police would take him to the border crossing and literally shove him across into the waiting arms of our MPs. After consultation with higher authority we selected that option. The "extradited" man was confined to the brig in Miramar until he went overseas on the *Essex* with the rest of the Squadron.

I grant that this may seem shocking to someone who believes in process at all costs. Initially, it did to me - but, then, I thought again. Someone who missed the ship in wartime could be charged with "desertion," and a conviction for that particular offense would literally be a life-changing event.

When this young sailor sobered up, he expressed relief that his life had not been ruined. I don't know what he actually felt, of course, but he never got in any kind of trouble again.

There is a more humorous story about military justice. One of our young sailors got in trouble on the ship because he told a Chief Petty Officer who had ordered him to do something on the flight deck to "go [bleep] yourself." The sailor was put on report, then summoned to appear at a "Captain's Mast". As squadron Legal Officer, it was my job to represent him in that process.

The proceeding before the Ship's Executive Officer started in a formal way. The Chief told his side of the story, and then I made a little speech about how our man had a clean record and had always performed well, etc., etc. The young man was then asked whether he had anything to say for himself.

He actually did a rather good job. " I had been up on the flight deck for hours in the bright sun; and you know how hot it is up there, sir; and I was just too tired to think, sir; and I'm really sorry I said those things to the Chief who has always been fair to me; and I really didn't mean anything by it, sir - it was just seaman's talk, sir, just seaman's talk."

While this was going on, I could see that the Exec was moving his mouth about, probably biting his tongue, in an effort to stay solemn. When the young sailor had stopped blubbering, the Exec gave his own speech. He said that the flight deck was a very dangerous place, and that quick response to orders was not just a matter of protocol but often necessary to save lives. This was not something to take lightly but, in light of the young man's previous record and obvious remorse, he would take no action this time.

Big relief all around. The Chief wasn't really out for blood either. The Exec was about to dismiss us all, but then had a last-minute thought: "One more thing. No more of that [bleeping] seaman's talk."

Many of those serving at that time were teenagers - just boys, really. They were away from supervision by parents or teachers for the first time, and they not only had rigorous, and often dangerous, tasks to perform, but they also were exposed to temptations in Navy ports that they had never experienced before. Those in command were seriously concerned with the welfare of these young fellows. The commanders were, in effect, surrogate parents. The military justice system took account of this reality, in ways that might not be appropriate for civilian life. In my experience, the system was sensible and compassionate.

There are many more stories that I carry in fond memory. But, the Navy narrative is coming to an end. It really was part of my education, even though I didn't fully realize it at the time. The experience that I gained in researching complex facts and summarizing them in a concise way, and the opportunity to speak to a group again and again, are of obvious value. But, there is something else equally important. I became a lot more self confident.

Allow me one final story that illustrates each of these things. In a real combat situation, one of the intelligence officer's responsibilities after completion of a mission would be to collect the available information from our own pilots, and from other sources like followup reconnaissance flights and aerial photography, and report back on the results. In simulated training missions, it was my job to collect and report back on the results of the aerial combat or bombing exercises.

The dispersion of bombs and rockets fired at ground targets, or the hits by our 20mm nose cannons on towed sleeves, could be evaluated and compared to expected performance. On one set of exercises that I remember well, our pilots had for some reason – perhaps random chance – scored well below their usual standard. When I reported the results, they seemed to take it lightly, and were much more impressed by their fine formation flying and slick landings.

So, with no notice to anyone, I started to paint a verbal picture of the resources that were devoted to their support. The base where we trained, the even larger base at North Island, Coronado, which supported the *Essex* and other warships, the initial and ongoing costs of the carrier itself and the vessels that guarded it, the advance bases all across the Pacific, the thousands of people in myriad supporting roles, and on and on. "You handful of men are the point of the spear," I said, "and if you don't hit your targets, an immense amount of taxpayer money has gone down the drain."

The initial reaction was stunned silence. My own mind was racing: "What the hell have I done?"

This kind of lecture was really the Skipper's job, or maybe the Exec's. What right did I have to lecture these guys, who have extraordinary skills that I don't?

John Fox, our skipper jumped up, shook my hand, and said to the group: "Tom has just said exactly what I had intended to say myself, only he has said it in a way that would not have occurred to me." He then went on to discuss the actual performance more specifically, and the corrective actions that he intended to take. Other senior pilots said similar things to me after the briefing was done.

I tell this story because it is such a good illustration of what lawyers also have to do. It is our job to think of things that may not occur to our clients, and we cannot be afraid to tell them things that they may not want to hear.

Some Big Decisions

Stephanie and I were engaged in the Fall of 1954, after I returned from my first overseas tour.

Engagements tended to be short then, and we married in the Chapel on the North Island Naval Air Station on December 18, 1954. It was a military wedding, with crossed swords and six ushers in Naval uniform. The Squadron Skipper Cmdr. John Fox was head usher in a group that included three other pilots from VF-123, a fellow AIO from another squadron in our Air Group, and my oldest brother, Dan, in his Naval Officer's uniform. My brother, Barrett, then in the Army, was my Best Man, and Stephanie was given away by her Godfather, a retired Rear Admiral.

After a honeymoon in San Francisco, our first home together was a bright furnished apartment close to the campus of San Diego State University, where Stephanie was in her third year and I had an easy commute to Miramar. In memory, it has the sweetness of an extended honeymoon, which couldn't last long because I had to go to sea again soon after, this time on the

Philippine Sea. And, there was a nagging uncertainty about a decision that I could not postpone much longer.

In those days, a husband was expected to assume full responsibility for the support of his wife and any children that came along. I could handle it, even as a junior officer, because provisions were inexpensive at base commissaries, medical care was free, the Officers' Clubs at a big Naval Air Station had all the amenities of a pleasant country club at a fraction of the cost. But, my active duty commitment would be up in late October of 1955, and I really didn't know what I wanted to do.

I might have been able to extend my tour on active duty. But it really wasn't an attractive long term option. The Korean War was over, and all the military services were cutting back. A Reserve Officer did not have assured tenure. In fact, the Navy was releasing people early if they had any good reason for the request.

As part of my job as an Air Intelligence specialist, I read a lot of CIA reports on areas of interest, and was impressed by them. John Fox had served a tour as Naval Attache in a European country, and it was no secret that military Attaches worked closely with the CIA. He was encouraging me to consider a career in the Agency, and was willing to help. I was tempted. As the stories indicate, I had some experiences that I thought were really important. I was a dedicated "cold warrior", and most alternative civilian occupations did not light up my youthful idealism.

Then, once again, something happened.

On my second cruise abroad the *Philippine Sea*, I was senior enough to move out of a Junior Officers' bunk room - a zoo right under the flight deck up forward, inhabited by about 30 guys, with an overall atmosphere that I will leave to your imagination. This time, I had a nice room with only two roommates, who were serving as AIOs in other squadrons on the *Philippine Sea*. Bill Millar and Gerry Ewell were both lawyers in civilian life, one from North Carolina and one from Tennessee. I mention their names because I owe them a lot.

One night, we were sitting around the room talking in our skivvy shorts because it was ungodly hot and the room was not air conditioned like it would be today. They knew I was interested in the CIA, but I had never said much more about it. In the course of the conversation, I mentioned that I once had been accepted by both Columbia and Harvard Law Schools, but didn't think I wanted to go.

That set off an explosion. For these small town lawyers in the South, the idea that I would pass up a chance to go to Harvard, in particular, was simply unfathomable. "How could I possibly be so stupid," was one of the milder comments. After my usual extended and calm reflection, I had to agree that maybe they were right. When I woke up the next day, I had decided on Harvard. That morning, I wrote four letters. One letter went to the Navy, requesting a release two months early so I would have time to get back to the States, pick up my bride and drive across country; and then go up to Cambridge, Mass., in time to begin the Fall term.

The second letter was to Harvard, informing them that I would take them up on their three-years-old acceptance. (Military interruptions were so common that they had promised they would.) I wrote the third one to Stephanie telling her what I wanted to do, and that I hoped it would be alright. The last letter was to my father because there were certain financial matters with which I was seeking help.

There was, of course, no such thing as e-mail in 1955, and replies to letters from a ship in the South China Sea typically took about a month. So, I just had to be patient. After a month the answers came back. The Navy said I could leave in August; Harvard said come on up; Stephanie said it sounds good to me; and my father said he'd pay my Law School tuition and make a generous monthly contribution for part of our living expenses. (The "GI Bill" would cover the rest.)

So, one more chance conversation set me on the path that I have now followed for 56 years.

HARVARD LAW SCHOOL

Once the decision was made, my last few weeks on the *Philippine Sea* passed in a blur of conflicting emotions. I was obviously thrilled at the prospect of a reunion with my bride a few weeks earlier than originally expected, and looked forward to a new challenge in Law School. At the same time, the men in VF-123 were like an extended family, and I knew I would miss them and the warm pride of service. Remember, I was barely 24 years old.

Some things stand out in memory, and affect me even today. The threat of war had temporarily receded, I had long since completed my part of the Squadron's Training Syllabus, and there were no free-floating AIOs in the Western Pacific. So, I spent a long time explaining the job to Pete Sherman, a pilot in the Squadron, who would temporarily take over.

Pete was then obviously a rising star in the Navy. An Annapolis graduate and nephew of the famous four-star Admiral Forrest Sherman, Pete was calm, confident and articulate. Stephanie and I had socialized with Pete and his wife Betts ashore, and we exchanged holiday messages for many years after I was out of the Navy.

Pete was a Commander, and Squadron Skipper in his own right, when he was shot down over North Vietnam in the mid-1960s. There were conflicting reports on whether he had been killed in the crash or had survived as a POW. At one point, when his survival seemed likely, Pete was promoted to the rank of Captain - in step with the leaders of his class.

Betts Sherman, who was battling serious health problems of her own, lived in limbo for some seven years. She didn't know she was a widow until the POWs were released in 1973, and Pete did not come home. Most Americans today know what the Vietnam POWs endured, and have honored them for it, but people like Betts Sherman deserve to be remembered and honored, too. I won't forget either of the Shermans.

Another "Pete" has played a big role in my life. Peter Mezey was a buddy in OCS - all my friends there had names that ended in "K", "L" or "M", because that's the way the barracks were assigned. He had stored a car at Newport, and we sometimes drove up to the Boston area when we had a 24-hour weekend liberty. Pete had gone to college at Williams, and not only knew a lot of girls around Boston, but also had some close friends at Harvard Law School. I became familiar with the Law School campus, and got some notions of student life on these visits.

Pete Mezey did his tour of active duty in the Atlantic Fleet, and we were out of contact for three years. But, in the Summer of 1955, when I was preparing to leave the Squadron and the Ship, I got a letter from him out of the blue, addressed simply to me via the "Fleet Post Office", San Francisco. Pete described his various Navy experiences, and then told me that he had gotten an early release from active duty and expected to start at Harvard Law School in the Fall of 1955. He also said that he was now married. Parallel lives.

I didn't answer because I wasn't sure whether any letter to the Atlantic Fleet Post Office would reach him in time and, besides I wanted to give him a surprise. On registration day at Harvard, I saw Pete in a line of people waiting to sign in. I was looking for him but he wasn't looking for me, so I was able to slip in a few rows behind him without his notice. I still remember his startled expression when I snuck up and tapped him on the shoulder.

Pete and his wife Caryl were our closest friends throughout the Law School years. And, we still are close friends today, even though we have lived on opposite sides of the country ever since graduation and seldom see one another. In a sense, we flipped our Navy and civilian locations: Pete and Caryl settled in San Francisco, and Stephanie and I have generally lived in the East. The reason that this friendship has a particularly important place in a memoir that emphasizes cerebral development is that Peter and I would seem to be political polar opposites. He appears to lean left to the same degree that I lean right. Yet, we have similar backgrounds, interests and values; and we almost always agree on what is important and what is not.

I have a similar affinity with a present close friend, DeVier Pierson. He will reappear in this memoir, and we naturally have even more life experiences in common at this late stage. But, history has repeated itself in this one respect. DeVier, who served in the Lyndon Johnson White House, is a Democrat and I am a Republican. Yet, we seem to agree on most matters of public concern.

Lawyers may be particularly likely to form this kind of amicable relationship. Their common legal training enables them to quickly identify the intractable value judgments that underlie any disagreement, and there really isn't any way you can argue anyone out of their value judgments. We may argue anyway, just for the sheer joy of it, but do not expect to convince anyone.

My education and life experiences have gradually made me aware of an explanation for this apparent paradox. Every public policy decision of consequence involves a choice between courses of action that have mixed - and often unpredictable - effects. It is never all pluses on one side and all minuses on the other; there are always advantages and disadvantages on both sides. There also can be common agreement on what these various factors may be. As a simple example, people might agree that increased incentives (a plus) can be associated with increased inequality (a minus). But, they may disagree vehemently on the weights they assign to the two, and therefore on the appropriate way to balance them. Disagreements like this cannot be resolved simply by reasoned discourse. The pertinent questions, then, are who will make the decisions and by what process.

As I reflect on my friendship with Pete Mezey, and so many other stories set down here, I am reminded always of that paternal injunction: "Tom, why don't you just let someone else be wrong?" Might as well, because there really isn't anything I can do about it anyway. Actually, this is a pretty good introduction to my experience at Harvard Law School.

The Lessons

A law school does not primarily teach students "the law"; it teaches them how to think about the law. At the beginning, particularly, we were not presented with statutes to memorize, or concise summaries of various decisions. Our texts were "casebooks", which contained the full text of, or extended excerpts from, actual judicial opinions. The obvious intention was to familiarize the students with the ways that various judges have arrived at their ultimate decisions. For this purpose, the reasoning *process* was as important as the *conclusion*.

When a professor asked a student to summarize and comment on a particular opinion, there really was no "right" or "wrong" answer. The professor didn't really care whether the student expressed agreement or disagreement with a particular outcome, either in class discussions or when answering questions on an exam. The focus was on how well the student could identify issues and defend a particular point of view. If students thought they would have an easier time by mirroring the professor's own philosophical preferences - perhaps as disclosed by published articles or even the drift of a previous class - they might get a very unpleasant surprise. A professor could savagely question a conclusion today when the opposite had been challenged just as vehemently yesterday.

This method of instruction, based on a so-called "Socratic" dialogue, captured the dominant intellectual tenor of the School at the time. The most respected judges were men like Oliver Wendell Holmes, Learned Hand and Felix Frankfurter. Each had close associations with the School, but they were principally admired for their recognition that there are no simple answers. They did not believe that judges have a unique pipeline to Divine wisdom. They advocated "judicial restraint" and respect for popular sovereignty. This restraint was considered "liberal" in the days when conservative courts were standing in the way of progressive reform, but later identified as "conservative" when liberal courts began to lead the forces of change.

The common thread was a certain skepticism, best summed up in Judge Hand's famous speech on "The Spirit of Liberty". The speech was delivered in New York's Central Park in 1944, smack in the middle of World War II, when we in the U.S. probably had greater unanimity about what was right and what was wrong that we ever have had before or since. In his speech, Learned Hand said "The spirit of liberty is the spirit which is not too sure that it is right; the spirit of liberty is the spirit which seeks to understand the mind of other men and women …" Later in this memoir, I will describe a memorable occasion when I heard Judge Hand revisit this theme at length in a series of lectures at the Law School.

Personal Interludes

Stephanie and I lived together in a Cambridge apartment that consisted of one room about fourteen feet square (albeit with a nice bay window), a "kitchen" that might have measured four by six, and a bath of roughly equal size. We weren't deprived because some of our married friends lived in boarding houses, with a communal kitchen, a single bedroom and a bath down the hall. My parents (who had been given an eight room house as a wedding present from my maternal grandparents) were somewhat aghast at the arrangement, but I wasn't at all defensive about it: "I've lived in a lot closer quarters for several years with far less appealing roommates." Lawyers will here recognize the use of precedent and argument by analogy.

This so-called "apartment" which we rented for $75 a month, furnished, was also conveniently located. It faced on a small park, so it was always easy to find a place for our car on the street, and close to the bridge that led to Boston University where Stephanie completed her own undergraduate education. After graduation, Stephanie got a job as assistant in a pediatrician's office. The added income later allowed us to upgrade to a three-room place, where we felt like plutocrats. Everything is relative.

The married students tended to socialize together, and we were not conscious of our relative poverty because none of us had much money to spare. Our "dinner parties" were potluck; we bought beer in quart bottles because it was cheaper; and there were myriad free entertainment options in a University town. Perhaps the most significant advantage for married students was the fact that we lived off campus and were not much affected by the panicky competitiveness of dorm life, so vividly portrayed in the 1973 film, *The Paper Chase*.

In fact, I really had no idea how well I did on my first-year exams until the grades actually were circulated some weeks later. It is always difficult to tell how well you have done on an essay-type examination, and this is particularly true when you don't really know what a "right" answer might be. Moreover as a matter of principle - then and later - I refused to discuss any exam with anyone after I was finished. My theory was that someone else would always have had an insight that I didn't, and my annoyance with myself would distract me from the necessary preparation for the next test.

Fortunately, in retrospect, there were almost no legal internships available for students who had completed only one year, so Stephanie and I drove across the country once again and spent our first summer vacation together in her mother's home in Coronado. I needed to earn some money over the summer, and my mother-in-law got me a job on the City's "street and sewer" gang, where I earned $1.25 an hour. The "street" part was thoroughly enjoyable; I swung a pick, shoveled and graded asphalt all day in the magnificent Coronado weather. (The "sewer" part was fortunately infrequent.)

In the course of my work on the gang, I also got to know a remarkable man, Bruce Muirhead, our foreman. My memories of Bruce may seem wholly unrelated to the practice of law, and they probably are. I suppose I could argue that Bruce was one of those ordinary people with good common sense, on which so much of our legal system relies. The truth, however, is that I just like to tell his story.

Bruce was tolerant and fair, and his amused smile evidenced a keen appreciation of the light side of life. He was both sensible and pragmatic - boy, was he! Let me give an example.

One day, we had a sewer break near the Bay side of the town. The general location of the break was easy to identify, for reasons that do not need to be mentioned. It was, however, critical to pinpoint the exact spot and plug the ongoing leak because entire blocks of buildings can otherwise subside in the sodden earth. Our crew brought in a big machine to help dig a large hole where we thought the break was, and we hit water about ten feet down. This could mark the source of the problem, or it might just be groundwater from the Bay nearby.

Closer analysis was required, and there was talk of running samples over to a laboratory in San Diego - which obviously would take up critical time. "Chemical analysis [bleep]" was Bruce's pithy response. Whereupon, as befits the man in charge, he clambered down into the hole, scooped up a handful of the liquid in question, swirled it around in his mouth, and finally spit it out with authority.

"It's sewer", said Bruce. Another case closed, with expedition.

You can see why I loved the guy. He lived well into his 90s, and in recent years I ran into him sometimes at lunch in a little café that Stephanie and I also frequented. Bruce was a celebrity in town because a local magazine had pictured him on the cover to illustrate a story on "Coronado's Unlikely Millionaires." Bruce had been a manual laborer all his life and built his own small house in downtown Coronado, largely with his own hands. The inflation of real estate in this California seafront town meant that his property was worth over a million.

Bruce took it in stride. When I congratulated him on his apparent wealth, he laughed and said: "Well, it doesn't mean much, because I like it here and if I sell my house I'd have to spend almost all of it on another place. I'd be right back where I started from." Some basic economic understanding here that might have been useful for those wiped out in the real estate bubble a few years later.

Some Great News

One day, when I was out with the gang, Stephanie appeared on the scene, waving a piece of paper in excitement. My first-year grades had arrived! Averages were calculated down to the last decimal point, and it seems that I had a solid "A" average that placed me 10th in a class of over 500. That meant I had earned a place on the Law Review, which automatically took the top 25 in a first year class. (The rigid system was modified a few years later to accommodate "diversity" concerns.)

The immediate effect was that we had to cut short our summer holiday by a few weeks because the Law Review people had to start work on the magazine well before the second year classes began. The intermediate effect was that I worked longer hours that I ever have before or since, and with some really interesting people. The long term effect was that I acquired a credential that has eased the way for me throughout my professional life.

The People

The Navy experience was high adventure, of one kind; the Harvard experience was an adventure of another kind. Never, before or since, have I been surrounded by so many really smart - albeit often quirky - people. It felt like I was opening the window shades of my mind. The roster of professors and fellow students that are listed below is necessarily incomplete, and the stories are inadequate. I owe a lot to each one of them, and to many others who are not mentioned.

The faculty members were, for the most part acknowledged giants in their chosen field of study, but what I remember best are their individual idiosyncrasies. Some examples:

Benjamin Kaplan, later a judge on the Massachusetts Supreme Court, taught the Law of Contracts in my first year. His benign, almost avuncular, manner overlay a sharp wit that could demolish almost any argument advanced by us eager neophytes.

Early on, I was injudicious enough to raise my hand and volunteer what I thought was an original idea. Prof. Kaplan started off by saying "That argument is very similar to one offered by the great Benjamin Cardozo when he was Chief Judge of New York's highest court." I was allowed to enjoy the comparison for a few seconds, before he added: "But, this was one of those rare occasions when his view really doesn't make any sense." There followed a neat evisceration that shrank me down to appropriate size.

Calvert Magruder was the Chief Judge of the First Circuit Court of Appeals, who taught a first year Torts class as a sideline. He was a salty, no-nonsense sort of guy.

He once said something that I remember, and often quote to this day. We devoted a number of sessions to discussion of cases that parsed the fine distinctions between, and varied consequences of, simple "negligence", "gross negligence" and something called "wanton misconduct". At the conclusion, he summed up all the hair-splitting by observing that "You can't really draw firm conclusions about these things because so much depends on the eye of an individual beholder. Just think of it as the difference between a fool, a damn fool, and a goddamn fool." Many technical distinctions in other areas of law have a no better rationale.

Henry Hart was one of those rare individuals who cared passionately about process and matters of jurisdiction. I can still picture the anguished expression on his face deeply lined by the smoke from the cigarettes that killed him before his time, as he discussed the landmark case of *Erie v. Tomkins* [3] This case, familiar to all lawyers, spelled out the circumstances when Federal Courts were obliged to apply State Law. "The *Erie* case is just wrong," he would say, "for eight separate reasons." It was amazing and amusing, almost medieval.

Al Sacks was later Dean of the School before he also died too young. He plowed much the same ground that Hart did, with a focus on the interaction and possible conflicts between statutes, administrative regulations and common-law principles. Unlike Hart, he approached the subject in a light-hearted way, with engaging self-deprecatory humor. (A very rare quality on the Harvard faculty.)

Some years later, when Sacks was Dean, I got a mass mailing from him, asking alumni to respond to some kind of material that was "attached herewith". I responded with the requested comment (or donation) and then took him to task for the unnecessary redundancy in the cover letter. "Where could the material be possibly attached," I wrote, "if not herewith?" By return mail, he apologized for an expression that, however common, reflected poorly on the School, and promised that he would never use it again.

By contrast, it was not possible to imagine that **James Casner** would ever joke about himself or apologize for anything. He was such a scary martinet that many of us who took his class in Estate Planning just assumed he was the model for the tyrannical professor in *The Paper Chase*. He was, however, so damned good at what he did that the classroom was always packed with auditing students who came to see the show.

At the conclusion of the term, he said with a perfectly straight face: "This is my farewell to you all. I hope you realize that - for a relatively modest share of your tuition - you have had the privilege of learning this subject from someone who knows more about it that anyone alive. I will be pleased to advise you on these matters when you are in private practice. but I must warn you that then I will be a great deal more expensive."

He exited to deafening applause. And, he deserved it, as most of his colleagues did.

Incidentally, I did not evidence any particular interest in Antitrust Law at that time. Instead of the full-year course taught by Donald Turner, a recognized specialist who later was head of the Antitrust Division of the Department of Justice, I took the half year-course taught by Kingman Brewster, later President at Yale. The course did not make a particularly strong impression. It was only later, in private practice that I decided to become an antitrust lawyer - by accident of course.

Some of my fellow students also made a lasting impression, particularly those with whom I served on the Law Review. That publication consumed more of my time than any other activity. We were expected to put in about seven hours a day, six days a week - all this, of course, in addition to normal class work. The workload was so intense, in fact, that we rarely were able to prepare for any given class. Fortunately, the professors - most of whom had served on a Review themselves - were familiar with the pressure and usually would inquire whether we were prepared to answer before calling on us. One Review Editor was assigned to prepare an outline for each course, which was circulated to all so we could cram for an exam.

An adequate summary of the things I learned from my peers would go on forever, so I will just mention a few names.

Dick Goodwin, the top-ranking guy in my class, was also the President of the Law Review. He had, without question, the finest legal mind of anyone I knew in the School, excepting some members of the faculty. He had an uncanny ability to see deep connections between diverse areas of law that appeared to be totally unrelated. And, he had a keen sense of what conclusions were supported and what were not. No glittering generalities.

He was also an engaging companion, and I had immense respect for him. Sometimes, we would talk, half seriously, about a joint practice after we graduated. We figured we couldn't miss because we covered the religious bases (Jew and Catholic) and the political ones (Democratic and Republican). My father, who was not easy to impress, met Dick at a Law Review banquet, and later said: "If you two are serious about practicing together, I'll stake you to a start." But, we really weren't.

Dick actually had his mind on other things and so did I. While a student at Law School, he already was an advisor to then Governor of the State of Massachusetts, and he later had a prominent role in both the Kennedy and the Johnson Administrations. He also is married to an even more famous writer and baseball fan: Doris Kearns Goodwin.

Something has happened to Dick Goodwin, and neither I nor any of his other close Law School friends can figure out what it is. In recent years, he has simply dropped out of sight. He published a couple of books some time ago, which were well written but larded with unsupported generalities that he never would have condoned as President of the Review. So much early promise.

In contrast, **Ruth Ginsburg** is a star who seems to have risen steadily since her Law School days. Ruth's husband Marty was a classmate of mine, and Ruth was a year behind. Stephanie and I had known them both outside the orbit of the Law Review because, as mentioned above, the relatively small group of married students tended to hang out together. When Ruth came on the Law Review a year after I did, I came to appreciate her intellectual power, and her strength.

You would never guess she had those qualities at first glance. She was tiny and looked rather like a pretty girl in high school, with a quiet and unassuming manner. She followed Marty to New York when he took a job there after graduation, and finished her third Law School year at Columbia - just as wives were expected to do in those days.

The rest is history. Ruth Ginsburg is also someone who has taken public positions that I do not necessarily agree with, but she is a gracious and warm person. I have followed her career with interest, sometimes quietly tried to support her in ways she probably does not know, and am proud to have known her.

Before taking leave of the Law Review, and the people I worked with there, I would like to add a general comment. The demographics of the group overall were very different from what I had experienced before. The editors were disproportionately Jewish and politically "liberal", and the people I knew at Princeton and in the Navy were mostly Christian and "conservative".

At first, many Law Review editors seemed a little odd to me, and I'm sure that I came across as a little odd to them. But, in a short while, I began to feel completely at home in their company. The differences became less and less important; we were "explorers" together in new territories of the mind. We worked very hard to submerge our differences, in aid of our common enterprise.

In 1987, almost 30 years after I had graduated from Law School, the Review published a Centennial Album to mark the 100th Anniversary of its founding. The book listed the names, and brief biographical information on every editor who had served, along with some personal reminiscences of those who chose to include them. I concluded my own contribution with the following observations at a time when the Review seemed to have become a lot more "politicized" than it had been when I was there.

> "The idea that legal analysis can be value free sounds hopelessly naive today, and I suppose Gannett House [the Review's office] was an artificial world. But our almost monastic detachment also gave the *Review* a timeless quality … We really were concerned about the traditions and standards of the institution; we felt a strong bond with the editors who had preceded us; and perhaps most important, we recognized that there were good arguments on both sides of most questions and were therefore inclined to be civil to people who disagreed with us."

With the exception of the "monastic" part, which is a bit impractical outside an academic setting, I'll stand by that comment. And, add one more thing. The 2008 Presidential election matched a veteran Naval Aviator against a veteran of the Harvard Law Review. There cannot be many others who have lived in close association with people in both groups, and bonded with both. All I can say is that a comparison of the very different experiences did not drive my vote. And, I also still treasure my brief association with the Street and Sewer Gang.

There is one other Law School classmate who deserves mention even though he was neither a Law Review colleague or a close personal friend. **Ralph Nader** is, however, by far the best known, and for a time had more influence, than any other member of the Class. His name is likely to pop up again in this memoir, and a little story about him may be of interest to those who have followed his later career.

At the beginning, the story has nothing to do with Ralph Nader, but bear with me. As I approached the completion of my second year of Law School, I had to decide what to do with the Summer. Some large firms did have a limited number of interns after the second year, but the programs were nothing like the designedly varied and interesting experiences that firms provide today as part of a recruiting effort. The intern was typically assigned some tedious research projects that the full time Associates had neither the time nor the inclination to undertake. (One guy, a year ahead of me, had spent his entire summer researching the Lottery Laws of all the States.)

This was an unattractive prospect, and I really did not welcome another summer of streets and sewers. Then, as usual, a much more appealing opportunity appeared, and I jumped at it.

The Ford Foundation had offered a modest grant of travel money to the Review, in order to fund a study of censorship laws in various states. Dick Goodwin offered the job to two of us on the Review: Roger Noall, a native of Utah, would cover the Western part of the country and I would cover the East.

Stephanie and I had a wonderful time on what we have always referred to as the "smut" trip. Some states, including Virginia and Maryland, actually had formal boards of censors, who reviewed every film that exhibitors wanted to show in the state, and granted the necessary licenses only after any objectionable material had been cut out. They came across on interviews as very earnest citizens, who were concerned that the general public needed to be shielded from moral contamination by material that they, the censors, could presumably view without harmful consequences.

We interviewed similarly serious local prosecutors who occasionally raided newsstands and confiscated "girlie" magazines that were deemed to be pornographic. (This was what is called "soft-porn" today; no hardcore scenes were publicly sold anywhere.) We also interviewed magazine distributors and proprietors of movie theaters to get another side of the story.

There was an amusing side to all this. When we were talking to one local prosecutor, I asked him what kinds of stuff he was particularly concerned about. He called in an assistant and said "Miss _____ , would you bring in the file?" She returned a few minutes later with an armful of empty folders. He said, "What happened to the exhibits?" And, she said, "You know how it is, sir. People keep borrowing them, with some excuse, and never bring them back."

After the interviews, and a lot of legal research was completed, Roger and I wrote a rather lengthy Law Review article. We took the predictably libertarian view that adults should be able to buy whatever they wanted for their private entertainment, and that laws should only restrict public displays that offend people who do not want to see them. That is pretty much the way the law has since evolved, only that this freedom now extends beyond anything that we contemplated. However, it is still deemed necessary to intervene when there are depictions of scenes that involve minors - something beyond our imagining in a more innocent era.

Enter Ralph Nader. He was then an Editor of the Law School Record, a newspaper that published news of events on the campus, including published articles of interest. Ralph was particularly interested in the Law Review study that Roger Noall and I had written. We spent an afternoon in discussions with him; and late in 1957 the Record published a full-page article by Ralph Nader, about our Law Review article.

I was not particularly happy about the Nader piece, although it was generally larded with compliments about our work. There were expressions of hysterical alarm that I did not think were warranted; after all, there were a lot more serious intrusions on human freedom extant in the world.

Consider these passages from the article, which I still have after all these years:

> "Much regulatory action is incited by non-responsible voluntary groups or prominent individuals …"

> "Leary and Noall found overwhelming paternalism, self-righteousness and shallowly conceived concepts of protecting the public (generally pictured as on an inferior level) …"

> "In this area, paternalism is dangerous to democracy in the broadest sense in contrast to its more appropriate role in family, church, school and mental institution."

These harsh words about self-appointed pressure groups seem particularly odd, in light of Ralph Nader's later career. He has devoted his life to encouraging the formation of self-appointed pressure groups. And, many of his crusades are based on the paternalistic notion that individual consumers cannot be trusted to make sensible or socially responsible choices.

Ralph Nader is a very curious individual. In face-to-face conversations he comes across as personable and pleasant. Almost mild. But, people who have the temerity to disagree with him are publicly excoriated in harshest terms. I once heard someone, whose name escapes me right now, sum it up this way: "The trouble with Ralph Nader is that he always acts like he's the only honest man in the room."

Ralph Nader has directly, or indirectly, tried to harm the reputations of a lot of people whom I respect. He has often trashed Harvard Law School, as just a training ground for business apologists. (I suspect his real problem is that Harvard taught us that there were usually two sides with plausible positions in most disputes – anathema to those who believe they have a unique pipeline to wisdom.) In the role of "consumer advocate", he has supported paternalistic government measures that actually diminish consumer sovereignty.

And, yet, I cannot bring myself to dislike Ralph Nader. I don't think he can really help himself. He reminds me of Giralamo Savonarola, the Florentine friar, who denounced the frivolous pursuits of the society in which he lived and lit the original Bonfire of the Vanities. Savonarola sometimes had a valid point, too, but shouted so loud and so long that he grew tiresome, and was burned at the stake in 1498. Ralph Nader seems burned out today. He also has attacked and alienated too many people, and no one pays attention anymore.

The saddest thing is that I don't think he has had much joy in his life.

The most memorable experience in my final year was the so-called "Holmes Lecture", delivered over a three-day period by **Learned Hand,** who by that time was probably the most respected judge in the country, and someone ideally suited for a lecture series in honor of Oliver Wendell Holmes. The room was packed with people seated in the aisles and standing by the walls.

Hand was 86 years old, and bent with age. But he still had that look of a lion and a booming voice, too. "Fellow students of the law," were his opening words to us awestruck neophytes.

The talks elaborated on his familiar theme of "judicial restraint", elaborated with specific examples. His view was based on the idea that many policy decisions involve value judgments, which cannot be resolved by simple logic; that judges have no special competence to make these judgments; and that, under the U.S. Constitution, value judgments are the business of the people's elected representatives. Accordingly, their laws should be given a high level of deference.

The talk was widely interpreted as criticism directed at the Warren Court which had already begun to show signs of judicial activism. But, it was not really a political attack because Judge Hand had said the same things when conservative courts had overturned laws passed in the early days of Roosevelt's "New Deal".

This part is actually not what I remember best now. I was already sold on his basic theme, and obviously have continued to be sold. It is Judge Hand's concluding words that I have never forgotten. At the end, he closed his lecture notes, and addressed us once more in a personal way, this time with tears in his eyes. He must have realized that this would be his last visit to a place he had loved so much, and he wanted to say farewell. This peroration was not included in the printed lecture but is quoted in a biography, published in 1994.[4]

> "More years ago than I like to remember, I sat in this building and listened to - yes, more than that, was dissected by - men all of but one of whom are now dead …
>
> I carried away the memories of a band of devoted scholars; patient, considerate, courteous and kindly; whom nothing could daunt and nothing could bribe … From them I learned that it is as craftsmen that we get our satisfaction and our pay. In a universe of truth they lived by the sword; they asked no quarter of absolutes and they gave none."

A pause, then, somehow standing taller, he said in a voice like thunder: "Go ye and do likewise!"

My classmates and I just looked at each other, speechless in a daze, and stumbled out.

My Law School experiences are almost as remote now as Judge Hand's memories were when he spoke those words. But, they are still vivid in my mind. And, that is one reason why I personally cannot - will not - treat our calling as just another business.

The Next Step

I realized that my educational record would enable me to compete for almost any job after graduation, and a multitude of choices can complicate the decision process. Contrary to my usual practice, I approached the task in logical steps. Like many other law students, the first decisions that I had to make were: "what kind of lawyer do I want to be;" "where do I want to settle;" and "what kind of employer do I want to work for."

By the "kind of lawyer", I do not necessarily mean choice of a substantive specialty. I think of it as a binary choice between so-called transactional lawyers and advocates. Transactional lawyers, which include lawyers who advise on contracts and wills, tend to be a very different breed from advocates who argue on clients' behalf before courts or government agencies.

Transactional lawyers draft documents, which attempt to identity and deal with every event that could lead to dispute down the road; advocates typically represent clients when disputes have finally ripened, and the job is to argue for a particular result. In England, the two jobs are roughly captured in the separate labels of solicitor and barrister, but we have no such formal distinction in this country. In irreverent moments, I have sometimes said we are talking about the difference between people with the souls of accountants and those with the souls of poets. You can probably guess my choice. I really would be an incompetent transactional lawyer.

The question of location was not much more complicated. I argued half heartedly for San Diego, where living conditions seemed ideal, but had to agree with the hometown girl I married that then San Diego offered a more "small town" practice than I really wanted. And, among the big cities, New York was then the Major League town. It was also a town that I already knew well. If I was going to aim high, I wanted to play for the legal equivalent of the Yankees, and that meant one of the major Wall Street firms. There were a lot of them, but the number with active litigation practices was surprisingly small. Some of the stuffier downtown firms acted like litigation was a somewhat sordid calling of ungentlemanly types.

Thomas Kiernan, a family friend who lived right across the street from my parents, was a senior partner at White & Case, one of the firms with a recognized strong litigation practice. We had a number of conversations when we were visiting my parents' home, and he gave me some pithy descriptions of the varied firm personalities. It may seem odd to attribute different "personalities" to firms, which at that time seemed to hire people of similar backgrounds from a limited number of the same schools. But, they were different then and they are different now; you can still sense it if you walk down the halls.

Tom Kiernan would be pleased if I interviewed at his firm, of course, but he advised me to visit all of the five or six firms on my narrowed list. I did just that, and got offers from all of them, but I genuinely felt more comfortable with the people I met at White & Case. They seemed to share the same buoyant good humor, which appealed to me. So, I accepted their offer and that was that.

I really don't remember much about my final months at Harvard. Once I decide to make a change, whether it be a job, or a house, it seems that I psychologically make the move. I may still seem to be present in the same place, but I'm really gone.

A WALL STREET LAWYER

Stephanie and I drove down from Cambridge to New York City in early June, 1958, with our month-old son secure in the back seat and a small Hertz van with our meager possessions towed behind. We were lucky enough to get a relatively large apartment, with two bedrooms and two baths, in Peter Cooper village. The Village is a complex of multiple buildings on 23rd Street and the East River, and it was our home for the next 54 months.

My starting salary at White & Case was $6500 a year which is perhaps equivalent to $40,000 in today's dollars, but still far less than first year Associates get now. The rent for this spacious and convenient apartment was only $190 a month, however, and my parents were generous. There were a substantial number of similarly situated young couples in the complex, and our social life did not differ much from what it had been in Law School.

I did not actually start work until late July because I first had to spend several hours a day in a "Bar Review" course, and then take the exam which lasted a day and a half. The Bar Review course was not really a recapitulation of things I had already been taught, but rather an introduction to those idiosyncratic features of New York law and practice that I would not learn in a national school like Harvard.

Like many other law firms, including the HoganLovells firm with which I am affiliated, White & Case had a "rotation" program of a year or so, where new associates were given a taste of various different practice areas before they settle into one of them. For some time, it has not really been possible to survive as a legal generalist in a big city, and rotation programs are one way to find a fit between the wishes of the lawyer and the needs of the firm.

A system like this seems to work better than you might expect; in most cases it is possible to find a match that satisfies the individual and the organization. I think this apparent anomaly can be explained by a simple analogy - which I have often used to reassure nervous potential recruits. When a man and a woman marry, they may each have had a number of more-or-less serious relationships in their past that did not survive. It might seem that the odds are against a mutual lifetime commitment, but it happens all the time. The answer, of course, is that it is not a matter of random selection. People are particularly attracted to potential mates who are also particularly attracted to them.

If young lawyers enjoy the work in a certain area of practice, they are likely to perform well, and this will increase the chance that partners in the practice will want to keep them there. It also can work the other way. If partners in a practice area want to retain particular young lawyers, they will go out of their way to give them interesting assignments.

I think both of these factors were responsible for the series of decisions that ultimately made me an antitrust lawyer. It just so happened that Tom Kiernan, who originally recruited me, had an uniquely interesting assignment for me almost as soon as I walked in the door.

Panagra

Pan American World Airways pioneered in the development of airline service outside the United States. W.R. Grace was a shipping company with long experience in providing service up the West Coast of South America. It was therefore natural for them to form a joint venture in 1928 called Pan American Grace ("Panagra") to initiate air service in this area. For many years, the joint venture worked well but, as so often happens, friction developed because Grace wanted to expand Panagra's service, which then terminated in Panama, into the United States, in direct competition with service provided by Pan American alone. Pan American, not surprisingly, resisted.

In the late 1950's, the U.S. Department of Justice sought to break the impasse by bringing an antitrust action against the two owners for restraining the growth of Panagra. The complaint also took a carom shot against the owners with a claim that Panagra itself had unlawfully stifled competition in

South America by acquiring its local rivals and engaging in various predatory tactics.

The Panagra claims were obviously a sideshow, and would probably be dismissed summarily today because there was no significant impact on U.S. commerce. But, the jurisdictional limitations were not as clear then as they are now, and Panagra had to be defended. Counsel for the owners selected White & Case to defend Panagra. Tom Kiernan was the partner in charge, but the matter really did not justify the services of more than one associate.

I had initially been assigned for a rotation through the Corporate Department of the firm, and I did do some work there - enough to know that I really wouldn't have been very good at it. But, I guess Tom Kiernan was senior enough to override the system and he chose me for the Panagra assignment, which was my major assignment for most of my first year.

Anyone who has worked as a junior associate on an antitrust case will understand what a dream job it was to be the *only* one. I was able to frame the defensive arguments, select the witnesses and documents in support, prepare a draft trial brief (which survived almost unchanged), help my senior prepare our witnesses and his own cross examination of government witnesses, and second-chair the trial. To make things even better, the subject matter involved significant events in the history of aviation; the President of our client Panagra, was Douglas Campbell, the first American Ace in World War I; and the principal liaison within the client was a man named Ed Farrell, who had served heroically and been wounded in Korea.

My initial exposure to the case seemed forbidding at first. Tom Kiernan called me into his large office, where it seemed that every available flat surface was covered with copies of documents produced in discovery. In those pre-Xerox days, the copies were negative photostats, stiff and hard to read. They were jumbled in total disorder. He gave me a quick review of the case and a copy of the pleadings. He then announced that he would be out of touch for a month on a European vacation, something possible in those halcyon days before the invention of cell phones. In the meantime, I should feel free to use his office, and try to make sense out of the jumble.

By the time Tom Kiernan returned from Europe, I had ordered the jumble, selected material that could be helpful and potentially harmful material that would have to be explained. No big surprises. Then, Ed Farrell called and said he had discovered an old storage room in the basement of the New York building where Panagra had an office. No one had been in there for years, or remembered what was in it. I was asked to take a look.

At first, it did not look at all promising. The place was lit by a single bulb on a wire, and the files were so dusty that I had to take frequent breathing breaks out in the hall. Most of the stuff stored consisted of routine maintenance records, schedules and collected passenger comments about the service. Buried in all this trivia, however, was a letter with the impressive seal of the U.S. State Department. The letter expressed the gratitude of the United States for Panagra's cooperation in a program to eliminate Nazi influence in South American aviation. The multiple acquisitions of local airlines, which the Justice Department was attacking as a scheme to monopolize, had been encouraged by the U.S. government in the 1930s because the acquired airlines were secretly controlled by German interests.

I have conducted a lot of file searches and supervised a lot more in later years, but I don't remember any document as helpful as this one - and it happened in my first case!

I also found an old album of photographs from the earliest days of Panagra's service. One of our defenses was that Panagra enjoyed a large market share because it had been a pioneer. The shots of grass landing fields, terminals that were just small sheds, and the old Ford Tri-motors in flight over the High Andes were a more vivid demonstration of what it meant to be a pioneer than any testimony could be. I attached selected photos from this album as an Appendix to our trial brief, and some time later I heard the trial judge say that these pictures were the most impressive part of the case we had presented.

The trial itself was not particularly dramatic, but it was a great education for me. The trial judge was Thomas Murphy, an imposing man with a booming voice who dominated the courtroom. As a U.S. Attorney, he had successfully prosecuted Alger Hiss for perjury, which impressed me a lot, but I was even more impressed by the fact that he was the brother of Johnny Murphy, the premier relief pitcher for the New York Yankees in the 1930s, and early 1940s when they won seven World Series. (I will refrain from an extended narrative of my lifelong infatuation with the New York Yankees. Another story for another time.)

Overall, this case is not particularly important in antitrust history. Judge Murphy dismissed the charges against W.R. Grace and Panagra, but held that Pan American's refusal to allow Panagra's route extensions violates Section 2 of the Sherman Act. The U.S. Supreme Court dismissed the charges against Pan American, as well, on the grounds that the Civil Aeronautics Board had primary jurisdiction of the matter. [5]

In addition, some arguments in the case seem primitive in retrospect. I do not recall that we consulted an economist, and we certainly did not offer economic testimony at the trial. Arguments consisted of an appeal to "common sense," rather than economic principles. For example our defense against the claim that Panagra's sometimes aggressive pricing had stifled local competition was that these competitors should have realized it was suicidal to start a price war against a much larger competitor. Our trial brief assumed it was common knowledge that price wars were a "chronic disease" in the airline business, and that the disease could be "very serious" because the competitor that had started the war "died of it." The pungent language was enough for the trial judge, who quoted it with approval. Today, of course, we probably would have expert testimony about the economics of competition in a business with high fixed and negligible variable costs. And, much more high-falutin language.

The case was important for me. I was able to make what I believe was a significant contribution to a successful outcome in my very first case. The factual background case was fascinating for me. The overall experience - which I was able to enjoy simply because I happened to be in the right place at the right time - was the decisive event that set me on a career path I have followed ever since.

I also learned some lessons that have been retained over the years. You may strike gold in the middle of the most dreary search. Vivid illustrations can be more persuasive than prose. Joint ventures with control split 50/50 are a recipe for later litigation. Most important, perhaps, was something Tom Kiernan said to me close to the end. The trial was over; final briefs had been exchanged; and the judge had the case under advisement. Even though I had moved on to other matters, I was upset by the delay and fretting about the outcome.

Tom Kiernan took note of this one day, and said to me: "We've all done the best we can, but our job is over. There isn't one more thing we can do that will affect the result. Take the lessons you've learned, and don't torture yourself with worry about the outcome."

This advice is, of course, identical to my paternal grandmother's recipe for serenity.

The Tire Case

Shortly after the *Panagra* case ended, I was asked whether I would be willing to work on another antitrust case, involving a different industry and different issues. Naturally, I said that I would.

This case was an antitrust action brought by the Federal Trade Commission against all of the domestic tire manufacturers. The client was the B.F. Goodrich Company, which today is principally a chemical manufacturer but then was one of the major suppliers of tires. Once again, I was the only associate assigned to the case, but responsibility at the "working level" was shared with associates in firms that represented the other major tire companies: Goodyear, Firestone, Uniroyal, and General. We were operating under what is known as a "Joint Defense Agreement", which enabled us to share client-privileged information without waiving it, and we worked as a single team.

The core of the case was an attack on so-called "basing point" pricing, an industry-wide system in which freight charges to end-users were calculated as if the shipment had originated from a common "basing point" rather than the actual plant location. The complaint charged that this system made it easier for industry members to avoid price competition - what we would today call a "facilitating practice".

Tire companies had powerful incentives to avoid price competition. Their products were not highly differentiated, and their principal customers for so-called "original equipment" sales were the "Big three" domestic auto companies: General Motors, Ford and Chrysler. These much larger companies had enough bargaining power to drive prices below cost, and the tire companies relied on the profitable "replacement" market to survive. (Tires had to be replaced a lot more frequently than they are today.)

I was fascinated by the opportunity, and the need to learn about the fundamental economics of another industry, and this became one of the things that I always enjoyed most as an antitrust lawyer. Ideally, you want to acquire enough knowledge of competitive dynamics in an industry to articulate them better than the business people themselves can. That is what lawyers are hired to do.

In this case, the partner-in-charge was a man named Edgar Barton, who became another mentor in my early days as a lawyer. (I later served as his associate assistant when he was Chair of the Antitrust Law Section.) The case did not have the same dramatic clashes as the *Panagra* case, because it was settled before trial and it had no lasting effects as a precedent. It was significant for me, nevertheless. It was the first experience that I ever had with the

Federal Trade Commission, and I also learned some things that I have used all my life.

Ed Barton maintained that litigation with the government was fundamentally different than litigation generally. "Never make an argument that you don't really believe in", he would say. "It's a mistake to think that you can improve your bargaining power by fighting over every little point. The government has a deep pocket, and you can't wear them down. If you try, you'll just undercut your credibility, and credibility is your most important asset." This is particularly true when you are repeatedly appearing for different clients before the same people in a government agency.

This approach to litigation strategy is not just a choice, but a matter of principle for me. In later years, I have taught it to people that I have mentored. And on those rare occasions when clients asked me to make an argument that I thought was frivolous, I have refused to do it. Clients have almost uniformly taken it well when I explained the rationale; once, a client fired me and hired a more complaisant lawyer. I didn't mind a bit.

When I was a Federal Trade Commissioner, and therefore on the receiving end of lawyer advocacy, I am pleased to say that most lawyers did not waste my time with silly points; I remembered those that did, and was more skeptical thereafter. And, I can assure you, I was not alone.

If I may digress for a moment, I do not necessarily blame the lawyers when this happens; they may be victims of present competitive realities in the profession. Prospective clients, subject to competitive pressures of their own, are tempted to hire lawyers who display the greatest fighting spirit, and these lawyers may feel that they then have to do battle over everything. I'll have more to say on this later.

An amusing incident marked the end of the Tire Case. The settlement process was rather lengthy because there were so many respondents who had to agree. We spent more time on negotiations with our own side than with Commission counsel. But, once we got our own act together, things moved smoothly. (I can pinpoint the time as late September, 1961, because the first agenda item was always a discussion of whether Roger Maris would break the Babe's record.)

Anyway, when it was all done, we had a little party in one of the Commission's courtrooms. Toasts and speeches all around. Joe Sheehy, a legendary career lawyer and the chief negotiator for the FTC team brought down the house.

> "I want to express my appreciation to respondents' counsel for the graciousness with which they received all the major conces- sions that I made in the course of these discussions, and I want to assure you that - had you made any concessions at all - I would have received them with equal grace."

A Cascade of Cases

With these two cases behind me, it was tacitly understood that I was a member of the antitrust group in the firm. And, the assignments came thick and fast. At one period, I was actively involved with five matters in litigation before the Federal Trade Commission. (In those days, almost all FTC matters were handled in Administrative trials.)

One case, in particular is still cited today - not with approval, but as the nadir of now-discredited populist antitrust enforcement. In *Foremost Dairies*[6] the Federal Trade Commission challenged a series of acquisitions that trans- formed Foremost from a local company in California into one of the largest multi-state dairies in the country. The complaint was based on the theory that the cumulative effects of multiple acquisitions was anticompetitive, even though individual transactions may have been benign. The problem, however, was not with the decision to view the transactions collectively, but rather with the complaint's assumption that it was anticompetitive to acquire a "competitive advantage" by acquisition. Put bluntly, the claim was that a series of mergers was harmful if the resulting enterprise was *more* efficient.

I would like to say that we on the defense team attacked this strange idea head on. But, economic learning that is accepted almost universally today had not yet percolated from the academy into the legal profession. In the early 1960s the main thrust of our defense was that the mergers would not confer any advantages at all. One big problem, of course, is that this defense was flatly contrary to the usual claims that the client had in Annual Reports.

The "Hearing Examiner," who would be called an Administrative Law Judge today, ruled against Foremost, and imposed a massive divestiture order. Our litigation team was troubled by the variance between the real facts and the arguments that had been made in response to the theory of the complaint. However, we did not have either the precedents or the economic tools to challenge the "competitive advantage" theory head-on.

When I prepared a draft of the appeal brief to the full commission, I did include a sarcastic comment that called attention to the inherent absurdity of the complaint. My seniors approved it. I don't have a copy of the final brief now, but the sentences read roughly as follows:

> "Commission staff argues that these multiple acquisitions have given Foremost the ability to engage in research and develop new products. This is obviously a very bad thing, and Foremost should be dismembered to ensure that it doesn't happen again."

The statement had no visible impact on its intended audience. The Commission did scale back the scope of the order - and avoided an appeal - but my little contribution was ignored. Nevertheless, I'm still proud of it after some 50 years.

Another case of no lasting impact is memorable for me because it gave me the opportunity to meet someone who was then the most famous man in the world, and also learn a lesson from a master that I have never forgotten.

The American Broadcasting Company ("ABC") was a longtime client of the firm. Their programming schedule featured three popular Walt Disney productions: "The Mickey Mouse Club", "Walt Disney Presents", and "The Mask of Zorro". ABC had a seven-year exclusive.

About five years into this mutually profitable arrangement, the CEO of ABC was hired away by the Rival NBC network. Walt Disney himself had a particular rapport with this particular executive, and wanted to move his programs over to NBC. His problem was that ABC was standing firm on its exclusive rights.

The Donovan Leisure firm, which represented Disney, came up with a novel solution. They brought a private antitrust action against ABC on the ground that Disney programs were so unique that they should be considered a monopoly, and it was illegal to contract for a seven year exclusive right to the offerings of a monopoly. The idea that it is possible to "monopolize" a slice of the diverse entertainment industry seemed like a stretch then, and it does now. (If, however, you were to apply the test for market power that is sanctioned by recent merger guidelines, I suspect Disney would meet the standards. Harry Potter would, too.) This interesting legal issue, however, is not what made the Disney case memorable for me.

Walt Disney came to New York for a pretrial deposition. Polls showed that more people throughout the world recognized his name than the names of any national leaders or other celebrities. I was one of the curious who packed the room, even though I was pretty low on the ladder of ABC's defense team. Orison Marden, a senior White & Case partner, was conducting the deposition. This was to be what is called a "hostile" or "adversarial" examination because the lawyer was questioning a representative of the opposing party. Yet, Orison Marden was a model old-fashioned gentleman, who was literally incapable of rudeness to anyone.

He began with the usual preliminary questions: name, address, relationship to plaintiff company, etc. Then, he smiled and asked: "Are you the same Walt Disney who has given so much pleasure to so many children around the world?" Disney first lowered his head, then smiled back and said: "Yes,

I suppose I am." This established a mood, and Disney responded openly and candidly to every question that he was asked. At the end, Disney and Marden walked out of the room, side-by-side, patting each other on the back, as Disney's own lawyers stood stupefied.

This was not an act. Disney and Marden were both fundamentally decent people who happened to be on the opposite sides of a business dispute. That's all. Shortly after the Disney disposition, the case was amicably settled.

I have remembered this incident and applied the lesson I learned throughout my professional life, because many antitrust cases are similar. Witnesses for the opposing side usually are not "bad" people, and the objective is not to trap them or expose them as liars. The objective is to make them willing to talk freely about facts that will help your case. To be successful, it is necessary to establish some rapport with the witness, and you can't do that if you come across as an ill-tempered bully.

Over the years I have found that the most responsive adverse witnesses are sales people, because they love to talk and instinctively bond with anyone. Expert witnesses - particularly the most eminent ones - tend to be responsive for a slightly different reason. They are retained, obviously, to support a particular conclusion, but they have to acknowledge qualifications in order to preserve their professional respectability.

Accountants and other "financial" people are the most difficult. They are not naturally talkative, and it's hard to get them to be definite about anything - even if they're on your side.

While we're on the subject of litigation tactics, let me digress for a moment and talk about David Hartfield, another White & Case partner who specialized in matters that were not at all like antitrust cases, and required a very different approach. David suffered from some crippling ailment that forced him to shuffle painfully, bent over double, and ultimately confined him to a little electric scooter. Yet, for reasons I cannot explain, he had immense personal force. I sometimes worked for him on general litigation matters when the antitrust work had temporarily slackened off, and it was a demanding experience. When he smiled in approval, it lit up the room; when he frowned, he scared me to death. And, he had the same effect on opposing witnesses.

David Hartfield specialized in litigation where the adversaries often really were scoundrels, rather like Bernie Madoffs of the day, and he was delighted when he found innovative ways to torment them. "We'll get to the merits only in extremis," he would say.

His general approach has not been particularly helpful in my later life because my work has been focused elsewhere, but he did give me one set of tools that I have consistently used and passed on to others. David Hartfield would not tolerate "legal" jargon of any kind. The first time I worked for him, he asked me to draft an affidavit for submission to the court in support of some preliminary motion. I had no problem with the factual part, but had no notion of the appropriate form because I had never drafted one in Law School.

The firm library had a reference book that contained samples of various legal documents, and I found a sample affidavit. It had a heading that read: "John Doe, being duly sworn, deposes and says." So, I drafted an affidavit for David's approval that began with what I thought were necessary words.

He looked at it and scowled. Chills went up my spine. "Tell me," he said, "what is the difference between being sworn and being 'duly' sworn?" Of course, I didn't have the slightest idea. He said "Out it goes." Next, he asked "What is that 'deposes' word in there for?" I couldn't answer that one either, so "deposes" went out, too. It is quite enough to begin with "John Doe, being sworn, says."

"The reason I am making a point about something so trivial," he said, "is to teach you that unnecessary legalistic terminology is distracting, and interferes with the flow of what you are trying to say." This is a lesson that I have been able to apply, and to teach, all my life. Legal briefs are not contracts; they should have a narrative flow. Unnecessary details should be omitted. Precise dates or place names should be avoided unless they are relevant for some reason. Expressions like "regarding" or "with respect to" are jarring, because they aren't used in ordinary conversation.

I advocate a simple test for good legal writing. When you think you have a final draft of a brief, an affidavit or an opinion letter, read it out loud to yourself. If it doesn't sound like the speech of a normal human being, rewrite it until it does. David Hartfield taught me that.

There were other cases outside the antitrust field that contributed to my legal education. In the next two stories, the cases are not important, but I think the lessons are.

One of the advantages of an apprenticeship in a large law firm is that you get to work on significant matters and learn from recognized leaders of the Bar. One of the disadvantages is that you have less opportunity to handle matters on your own.

The first, and I think the only jury trial that I ever handled on my own was a dispute over the grand sum of $700! That's not much, even if you multiply by five or six to account for inflation in the meantime. My client was a woman named Loretta Howard, whom the firm represented regularly on other matters that involved a great deal more money. Mrs. Howard was a widow who lived alone in a large New York townhouse, attended by five or six servants. She was not a social airhead, however, but someone with intellectual curiosity. I thought she was charming and interesting - actually, like a richer version of my own mother.

She was also someone who was easily hurt, and naive in many ways. I still remember an amazing exchange in the Summer of 1964. We were in the middle of a discussion about the general state of the world, and she said: "I like Mr. Goldwater. Do you think he will win?" I indicated that I liked Mr. Goldwater, but I really thought that President Johnson would beat him by a large margin. "I don't think so," she said, "everyone I know is going to vote for Goldwater." I changed the subject because I didn't want to tell her that her circle of friends may not be a true sample of the electorate.

The $700 lawsuit I was defending for her involved a claim for unpaid over-time by a former cook in her household. The money was not the point for her; she obviously would spend a lot more on lawyers than the amount in dispute. But she was hurt and angry: "I had treated this woman very kindly, but she abruptly left me, without explanation, when I was expecting a house-ful of guests." Compromise was out of the question. The plaintiff's counsel, needless to say, was not a partner in a major law firm. He was a middle-aged single practitioner, obviously hanging on by his fingernails and without the resources to manage his calendar.

I was increasingly impatient and irritated by his failure to meet deadlines or return my calls. One day, I did reach him and exploded over the telephone. "Don't be so mad at me," he said. "I'm just another lawyer, trying to repre-sent a client as best I can." I suddenly felt about two feet tall. Here I was, an arrogant young twit - who had been handed everything on a platter - bawl-ing out a guy who had come up the hard way.

I apologized; we smoothed things over; and eventually went to trial. He was every bit as good as I was in court, maybe better. My client and the plaintiff each did well on the stand. I actually believe they both were telling the truth, as they saw it. The plaintiff was a recent immigrant from Eastern Europe, who did not speak English very well, and it was likely that the language bar-rier resulted in a genuine misunderstanding over the terms of employment.

The six-person jury deliberated for a surprisingly long time, and came back with a plaintiff's verdict for $350, exactly half the amount claimed. It's easy to guess how that happened. And, everyone appeared satisfied. Even the judge, who initially could not understand why such a small case had to go to trial, went out of his way to tell me later that he had come to admire Mrs. Howard's willingness to trust the judicial system.

The opportunity to be heard in court seemed to have lanced a boil for each of the warring parties. Along with the lesson in humility, this experience taught me how much people value the simple opportunity to be heard - win, lose or, as in this case, draw.

Another case had a similar pleasant conclusion. The firm also handled financial matters for a very substantial real-estate investor, who owned buildings all over New York City. Our client was sued for an unpaid commission by a real estate broker, who claimed that he had produced a willing and capable buyer for an apartment house at the advertised offering price. Under New York law, a broker was entitled to his commission in that situation, even if the sale was never consummated.

The problem was that our client stoutly maintained that he had never heard of the buyer or the broker, and refused to pay. (I don't remember whether written evidence was lacking or ambiguous.) A $50,000 claim was still small enough to be entrusted to a youngster like me, and the senior responsible partner just instructed me to keep him informed.

Our client was a dignified gentleman in his late 80s. In deference to his years, his deposition was held in his New York apartment, and the broker, his lawyer, the court reporter and I gathered there.

In the midst of the preliminary questions, the elderly gentleman kept looking quizzically at the plaintiff broker. Finally, he broke in and said: "You look familiar to me. Do I know you?"

Needless to say, this is a bit unusual in a deposition. The plaintiff's lawyer, a courteous guy, looked at me as if to say "do you mind?" I shrugged and said something like: "OK, let him answer." Whereupon, the broker answered: "Yes, sir. Don't you remember? I met you with a buyer in hand when you wanted to sell the building at [some address]."

The old gentleman brightened, and said "Of course, I remember you now. I think I owe you some money." Well, we settled the case right then and there.

Handshakes all around. Our client, embarrassed now, wrote a check on the spot, and then proceeded to give us all a tour of the art works in his vast apartment.

I was a bit nervous when I reported back to the senior partner, but he was simply amused. This time the misunderstanding had been resolved promptly in an efficient way, probably because there was no great emotion involved on either side.

The fact that I remember this incident with pleasure also says something about my general approach to litigation and to life. I genuinely believe that most people - whether they are adversaries or not - are decent human beings who are doing the best they can to cope with the world as they see it. In business disputes, particularly, the best outcome may not be one where the opponent has been vanquished but rather one where both sides walk away partly satisfied. It's only money.

The Electrical Cases

The so-called "Electrical Cases" deserve particular mention because they were in some ways, the most significant events in the history of antitrust. There were literally thousands of them. It all started in the late 1950s with a series of criminal indictments for pervasive price-fixing in the electrical equipment industry. In the end, there were guilty or nolo contendere pleas in 19 product lines. They ranged from multimillion dollar pieces of equipment like turbine generators or transformers, which were designed to order, down to off-the-shelf items like insulators.

The legal issues were relatively simple. In a price-fixing case, the key questions are who did what and when. But, the defendants had admitted their guilt in the most significant product lines. Damages are always an issue in private litigation but, when liability is clear, plaintiffs do not have a heavy burden of proof. The biggest problems were simply administrative.

Most of the customers for this electrical equipment were regulated utilities, and they really were forced to seek antitrust treble damages for overcharges, even though they most likely had been passed on to the ultimate customers. Myriad antitrust cases - some of them class actions - were filed in federal courts throughout the United States. The most pressing initial question was how to deal with this litigation that threatened to swamp the court system. Today, there is a Judicial Panel on Multidistrict Litigation[7] which has a familiar procedure to deal with these litigation explosions, but then the judges had to make it up as they went along.

The defendant companies also had to figure out ways to coordinate the activities of the hoards of lawyers that they had to hire across the country. The largest of these companies, in the most significant product lines, was General Electric. White & Case, then the third largest law firm in the world, had a long time relationship with GE, and was chosen to represent the company in all litigation in the State of New York. The firm was also asked to lend assistance in turbine generator cases throughout the company.

Because the litigation was so large, White & Case had to put together a large team, which included my two most important original mentors Tom Kiernan and Ed Barton. With all that firepower, I was only a junior member of the group. These cases are memorable for me not so much for what I did, but for what I observed. I really was more of a roving reporter than a player.

In some ways, work in the Electric Cases was a dispiriting assignment. I think that most of the myriad lawyers on the defense side realized that we would lose every battle and ultimately lose the war. We had to engage in some preliminary skirmishes before our clients were willing to accept the grim realities of their situation. We also needed to make our adversaries aware that there were some legitimate economic disputes over damages, so they would temper their settlement demands.

It was, however, a fine educational experience for a young lawyer. One of my jobs was to monitor the situation in those locations where the turbine generator cases were most active. I was able to see some of the finest lawyers in the country at work. In fact, one of the lifelong lessons that I learned from this experience is that general litigators, who are familiar with local judges and juries, can often do a better job than antitrust specialists who are brought in from the outside.

There were so many great lawyers involved that I cannot do justice to them all in this memoir, and whole books have been written about the Electrical Cases anyway. Let me just mention two of the best, one on our side and one a respected adversary.

The turbine cases were moving faster in Philadelphia than anywhere else, and Henry Sawyer was General Electric's top lawyer there. Henry was a generalist rather than an antitrust specialist, and he was a maverick member of the Philadelphia establishment. He had argued some high-profile civil rights cases, and actually defended some accused Communists in the 1950s and 1960s. Unlike most lawyers who defended political radicals, however, he had no sympathy whatever for their ideology. "They're the most humorless and silliest people in the world," he told me once, "with their endless drivel about the proletariat." But, Henry believed passionately in people's right to say silly things, and he loved to puncture the balloons of the pompous.

Henry and his wife once invited me to dinner in his home. The entry was a glassed-over patio with genuine Roman statuary. Apparently, some ancestor had brought them back in the days when it was legal. Henry was himself a gifted amateur sculptor. The living room was dominated by the immense black head of a prizefighter, and female figure studies were scattered about the room. It was obvious that the model had been Henry's very attractive wife. This dignified mainline matron did not seem remotely embarrassed by the presence of her bronze doppelgangers cavorting in the altogether.

Henry did not hesitate to speak bluntly to our mutual client and others on our side. Early on, counsel for the principal plaintiffs in Philadelphia made a settlement offer. "Perfectly ridiculous," was the consensus of the other inside and outside lawyers. (No one cared what I thought.) Henry said: "I don't think it's ridiculous at all; I think we'll ultimately have to pay more." In the end, we did.

Henry could be even more blunt. When the turbine cases were actually tried in Philadelphia, a lead defense witness was a major executive of our client. He was an intelligent man, and he had responded well in the prep sessions. But, for some reason, he was in arrogant executive mode when he took the witness stand. He seemed to assume that he could tell his story his way, and only answer questions that he felt like answering. The inevitable result was a series of loud gavel bangs and admonitions from the bench - all in the presence of a jury.

During the first recess, Henry wrapped his fist around the executive's necktie, slammed him up against the wall, and said: "Listen to me, you [bleep bleep]. You're not the boss in there; that man in the robe is. If you don't behave yourself, I promise you there will be some very unpleasant personal consequences." I've never seen anything like it, before or since. The man ate humble pie when he got back on the stand, but the damage had been done.

Another lawyer who made a strong impression on me was Harold Kohn, lead lawyer on the plaintiff's side. Harold was honest and kept his word. He was also a pleasant person in private conversation, but the most vicious cross examiner that I have ever seen. If you read a transcription of his questions, they seem perfectly ordinary, but they were spoken with a sneer that seemed to say: "I know you're a liar, but I want to hear what tall tale you're telling now, so I can tear you apart." Harold exuded menace.

As I said before, I don't think this approach is at all effective with most witnesses. But, these were not the usual witnesses; these were witnesses who had actually been convicted of a crime or who had arguably failed to intervene when others did so. Harold's object was not to draw them out, but to destroy their credibility and the credibility of their employer.

He infuriated me, of course, but I had to acknowledge that he was doing a good job for a client in this particular setting. At the same time, I realized that I could never do the same thing. I just don't have it in me. It's not something to be proud of or ashamed of; it's just a fact. So, in a way, Harold Kohn was one of my teachers too.

Harold Kohn and Henry Sawyer both died in the same year, 1999. They were worthy adversaries, and knew it. RIP.

As part of my job as a roving reporter on the team, I also was assigned to help the GE witnesses who came to New York to testify, and to "babysit" them and hear what they might say over dinner in a one-to-one setting. I believe I have eaten more meals and drunk more whiskey with confessed price fixers than anyone other than another price fixer. It has given me some insight into the way that they think.

For the most part, they were unrepentant old pirates, who were bitter about the discipline that their employer had imposed. One former high-ranking officer was particularly outspoken. When he was preparing for testimony, he freely admitted that he had met with competitors to discuss prices of turbines and some other large products that he had responsibility for earlier in his career. But, when we asked about some of the smaller products subject to indictments, his denials became increasingly vehement. "Do I look like someone who would fix prices on a pissant product like Open Fuse Cutouts," he shouted indignantly. Beneath his dignity, apparently.

Once I asked him what conclusions he had drawn from the loss of his job and his 30-day stint in prison. "Never talk prices with more than one other guy in the room," he said. I suspect that this attitude is not particularly uncommon, and it helps to explain why I have been particularly dubious about 3-2 mergers in later life.

Today, I suspect that this proud man was covering his personal embarrassment with bluster, but I also believe that he, and many others like him today, really do not think that price fixing is a serious offense. The penalties are more severe today than they were then, of course, and I am sure offenses are less common. But, this is simply because the risks are higher.

In speeches, I have sometimes said that many business people equate price fixing more with "speeding" than with "stealing". Like most of the people who may read this memoir, I think of myself as a law-abiding person but I have often driven faster than the posted speed, particularly when I am reasonably sure that I can get away with it. And, I don't even have strong economic incentives to do so. Price fixers can have powerful incentives, depending on how they are compensated, and they can develop strong bonds with their co-conspirators. This is something that most corporate counselors need to keep in mind, as they frame their compliance programs.

I'll close this remembrance of the Electrical Cases with a story of no particular relevance other than as an illustration of one price fixer's insouciant disregard of rules. It's all a matter of public record.

Johnny Peters was a relatively low level engineer in GE's large turbine business, but he was a recognized expert in the rather complex process of pricing out the components of these complicated machines. He was so skilled, in fact, that his competitors thought it would be a good idea to let him set prices for their machines, as well, at their frequent industry meetings.

Counsel for various plaintiff utilities wanted to pinpoint the precise dates of these meetings, and compare them with order dates, in order to support an inference that bids for their particular orders had been discussed. They tried to establish dates by comparing the travel expense accounts of the known participants. When our big turbine trial was held in New York, Milton Handler - a well respected and veteran antitrust scholar - was examining Johnny Peters. Mr. Handler placed a stack of expense accounts in front of the witness and said: "Mr. Peters, I want to save time. Could you look through these accounts to confirm that they are yours and that they are accurate?" Peters looked perplexed. So, Mr. Handler said: "Mr. Peters, it's really a simple question - to the best of your knowledge, are these expense accounts accurate?"

The light finally dawned, and Johnny Peters answered, as if he were patiently explaining the obvious to a small child: "Of course they're accurate, Mr. Handler - about everything except the numbers." The courtroom erupted in laughter, and the presiding judge was so convulsed that I thought he would fall off the bench. We found amusement where we could in the midst of a saga that otherwise would have been profoundly demoralizing.

The *Electrical Cases* were a unique experience in many ways, but I did learn something that has had a profound effect on the way I practiced law ever after. It has to do with witness credibility.

In these cases, as with many others that involve claims against a number of competitor companies, counsel for defendants generally cooperated. We did not prepare witnesses jointly, but we shared information about what our clients' witnesses would say on the stand. Even when witnesses from different companies agreed on the time, place, and subject matter of various conspiratorial meetings, they sometimes differed on what was said at the meetings. An individual witness was likely to emphasize that someone else from another company was the dominant actor, but the witness from that other company was claiming just the opposite in preparation. Obviously, both versions could not be correct, but was one or the other consciously telling a lie?

I didn't think so then, and I don't think so now. Most of these people had already suffered whatever consequences the legal system or their own companies would impose. They had an affirmative incentive to cooperate with company counsel, and had been made aware of the consequences of perjury. I think the explanation for these conflicts may often flow from the natural human tendency to put the best possible "spin" on what we may have done in the past, and over a period of time the spun version crowds out a more dispassionate memory.

Counsel should be aware of this unconscious tendency. In trial preparation, witnesses need to be cautioned about the dangers of a rigid insistence on details that may be challenged by someone else or, much worse, proven wrong by some unassailable objective evidence. A skilled cross-examiner can destroy a fundamentally honest witness who is demonstrably wrong about a detail.

In counseling, it is also prudent to caution clients about the possibility that other people may be affected by the same unconscious tendency to "improve" the general tenor of conversations. Assume, for example, that you are counseling a client on the appropriate way to discuss resale pricing policies with the company's dealers. It is legal to "unilaterally" announce company policy on the question or to give general "advice," but it can be illegal to seek "agreement". The distinction can be subtle. This is the reason why some things should only be conveyed in writing by a well-advised employee, or at least memorialized in a contemporaneous business record.

Subconscious self-justification can also distort the accuracy of memoirs like this one, even though I have tried hard to be objective. This is why I have not hesitated to use the first person in the narrative. These are conversations as I best *remember* them; and what I remember is what has influenced my later views on life and law - which is the whole point. I don't claim that these views are immutable truths; readers can take what they find useful and leave the rest.

Life After The Electrical Cases

The Electrical Cases finally were concluded with multi-million dollar settlements, far larger than anything that had ever been seen before. The public utility plaintiffs actually might have been able to demand even more, but they really did not want to cripple their essential suppliers. Everyone seemed to be tired of the battle. (Like veterans of the Civil War - another conflict that exhausted both sides - counsel for the opposing plaintiffs and defendants held convivial reunions for several years thereafter.) For me, personally, the end of these cases seemed to mark the end of my apprenticeship as an antitrust lawyer. I still had a lot to learn, but I had begun to operate with some autonomy and even to supervise a group of younger lawyers.

Like most of my peers, I had also moved out of the city. In December, 1962, Stephanie and I bought a beautiful home in the suburban town of Chatham, New Jersey, where we thought our two sons, Tom and David (then 4 and 2) would have a better life. The birth of our daughter Alison in April, 1964 completed the family, and we began to do the usual suburban things. I soon was able to hold my own in the intense discussions of the relative merits of various lawn nutrients, and the optimal deployment of metal or wooden garden rakes. We even acquired a dog, an English Cocker Spaniel named Beauregard. Despite his impressive lineage, as the scion of champions, "Beau" was not very bright, but he was loyal and loving - which is what counts in a dog.

The memorable Friday, November 22, 1963, started out for me with an experiment in home improvement. I had decided to take a day off and lay tile in the entrance hall. At that time, you had to cover the floor with some dark gunk, and then you had a limited period of time to cut and lay the tiles while the gunk was soft. While I was immersed in the process, a neighbor from across the street ran over and said: "Turn on your TV; the President has been shot."

My experience of that day's bizarre events was limited to oral reports from the other family members, as I struggled to fit tiles on my hands and knees. (Oddly enough, for very different reasons, I had to rely largely on oral reports during another memorable day, September 11, 2001 - a story that will be told later in this memoir.)

There was a chilling sequel. Tom, our first child, was old enough at five to have a glimmer of what had happened. He was particularly intrigued by the flags at half mast everywhere. About a year later, the flags were at half-mast again, and he asked why. I told him that this time it was to honor former-President Hoover, who had just died. Young Tom's response was immediate: "Who shot him?"

I will digress for a somewhat more pleasant story, linked to the suburban experience and that tumultuous time. I had to learn the etiquette of the commuter train: total silence with eyes focused on the morning paper, folded lengthwise in quarters. The country had barely recovered from the shock of President Kennedy's assassination when in 1968 Robert Kennedy and Martin Luther King were also killed. The social fabric of the country seemed to have fallen apart.

One day, an older dignified gentleman wadded his copy of the N.Y. Times into a large ball, threw it into the aisle, and announced to the car at large: "I've been reading this goddamn paper all morning and there isn't one word of good news in it! The hell with it!"

Whenever I saw him on the train thereafter, he was happily reading detective stories.

My training in big antitrust cases was particularly suited for non-antitrust matters that involved complex economic facts. I worked on Texas Gulf Sulphur matters, for example. There was a government case, followed by several private class actions. The government case, brought by the SEC, clarified that it was illegal for a corporate insider to trade non-public information. I really didn't need to know much about securities law to work with U.S. and Canadian witnesses against a factual background that involved drilling for minerals in frozen regions of Canada. Real Wild West stuff.

I also worked on a major tax case for United States Steel. It was a long-running dispute with the U.S. government over Excess Profits Taxes that had been imposed during the Korean War. The case did not turn on technicalities of tax law, but rather on the economic question of whether U.S. Steel's profits in the years immediately preceding the Korean War had been abnormally depressed for reasons outside the company's control. If they had been so depressed, the baseline for calculation of any Excess Profits Taxes had to be adjusted upward. Our argument was that U.S. Steel's profits had indeed been artificially depressed during the baseline period because the company had mined out all its high grade coal and iron reserves, in order to maximize production during World War II.

It is easy to see why an antitrust background was useful in this dispute, which involved the totality of the company's business. In order to understand the fundamental relationship between the quality of raw materials and the ultimate volume of steel produced, I went down into coal mines in West Virginia and I visited the great open-pit iron mines and refineries on the Mesabi Range in Northern Minnesota. I visited Coke Ovens, Blast Furnaces and Steel Mills in Pennsylvania.

There were also a lot of courtroom experiences, and high strategy discussions. The case, which had already dragged on for years, lasted for several more after I had worked on it. Ultimately, it was settled for about fifty cents on the dollar amount of the dispute. Essentially a draw.

The principal legacy of the case for me was to solidify my growing respect for people who know how to design and operate vast and complex production facilities: Plant Managers or Chief Engineers, or some similar title. They work in relative obscurity, and they usually are not the most highly compensated executives. Yet, they are the people who actually create wealth in this country. We lawyers do not create wealth. At our best, we lubricate the wheels of commerce, and that is an essential contribution. However, I believe we should also give due credit to the people who design, build and run the wheels.

The partner in charge of the *U.S. Steel* litigation was Haliburton Fales, another old-fashioned gentleman and role model. I also worked for Hal Fales on a matter for a company then known as the Arabian American Oil Company ("Aramco"). This company, now wholly owned by the Saudi-Arabian government, was then owned by a consortium of four U.S. oil companies: Standard of N.J. (now Exxon Mobil), Standard of California (now

Chevron), Texaco (now also part of Chevron), and Socony (now also part of Exxon Mobil).

There was some dispute over the concession terms between Aramco and the Saudi government. I really don't remember what the dispute was about, but one of my jobs was to review the "history" of the concession to see what bearing it might have on the current dispute. I spent some weeks in Aramco's library, poring over historical documents, which were fascinating then and would be even more fascinating today. A few tidbits:

The present country of Saudi Arabia was created by King Abdul-Aziz Ibn Saud, a giant of a man straight out of the Middle Ages, who consolidated his power by marrying the daughters of rival chiefs. He is supposed to have sired some 40 sons by multiple wives (no more than four at a time) and probably an equivalent number of daughters whom no one has apparently bothered to count. The five kings who have succeeded to the throne upon Ibn Saud's death in 1953 are all his sons, and more sons are still left.

The original concession, granted in 1933, called for a royalty on each "ton" of oil produced, but the government got ever more generous terms in succeeding years, and has owned the company outright since 1980. But the history of the early negotiations was fascinating. For one thing, the Westerners had to wear Arab dress in the presence of the King, and the pictures of oil-men dressed like sheiks were hilarious.

The original royalty payment was fixed as a certain number of English Gold Sovereigns, because the King was not interested in pieces of paper. He wanted the gold coins. The problem was that most of the Gold Sovereigns in circulation carried the image of Queen Victoria, and this image was, of course, not acceptable in Arabia. Soon, Aramco was forced to scour the world for acceptable Sovereigns from private collections. The King ultimately agreed to settle for pieces of paper from banks, but only for a substantial increase in the royalty rate. All of which suggests that the Westerners may have underestimated him.

But the most entertaining parts were the transcripts of actual negotiations. The lead spokesman for Aramco was an Egyptian Arab, who knew how to negotiate with his counterparts in ways that they would accept. Apparently, it was not acceptable to ask the representative of royalty to compromise; any concessions that the Saudis made had to expressed as a free gift. The discussions would proceed as follows if, for example, there was a dispute that involved $100 million.

Aramco guy: "I love you like a brother. Do you love me like a brother?"

Saudi guy: "Yes, I love you like a brother."

Aramco guy: "Are you willing to give your brother a gift out of the goodness of your heart?"

Saudi guy: "Yes, I will give you a gift out of the goodness of my heart."

Aramco guy: "My brother, will you freely give me $50 million?"

Saudi guy: "Yes, I will freely give you $50 million."

I have deliberately telescoped the flowery expressions of mutual esteem, and omitted the pious appeals for Divine mercy that closed these discussions. I wonder if some of our present-day problems in the Arab world result from the fact that we really don't speak the same language in every sense of the word.

As an outside lawyer at that time, I was also particularly appreciative of the way Aramco approached litigation. The General Counsel used to instruct retained counsel as follows: "Just claims, we pay promptly. Arguable claims, we settle. Unjust claims, we resist - whatever the cost."

I learned later on that this principled stand is much easier to maintain if you are a highly profitable company and the litigation does not threaten its survival.

I also had the opportunity to participate in two additional, well-publicized antitrust cases.

The first of these, *U.S. v Grinnell Corp.*,[8] a split decision of the Supreme Court, was briefly famous for the colorful language in a dissenting opinion by Justice Fortas. I also include the case here for other reasons.

Our client was the American District Telegraph Co. ("ADT"), the well-known provider of home alarm systems, then an affiliate of Grinnell. One of the issues in the case was the question of whether ADT was a monopolist. In a dispute of this kind, a critical issue can be "market definition", and it is much easier to find that a defendant has monopoly power if the market defi-nition closely traces the parameters of its own business. (Right now, I prob-ably monopolize a "market" defined as the memoirs of a part-retired antitrust lawyer with experience in the military, in law firms, on a corporate staff, and in government.) In the *Grinnell* case, the majority opinion by Justice Douglas defined the relevant market as: "insurance company - accredited central station fire and burglary protection services." Needless to say, there are many alternative ways to provide fire and burglary protection.

Justice Fortas' dissent, joined by Justice Stewart, focused on what he thought was a gerrymandered market definition. In his words, it was like a market described as a "red-haired, bearded, one-eyed man with a limp." How many can there be? This sally was the source of considerable amusement for years, but is not really important today. Market definitions are so fact-specific that precedent doesn't mean much. I particularly remember the *Grinnell* case for some other things that happened.

The partner in charge of the ADT representation was Macdonald ("Don") Flinn, not only my senior on this case, but a staunch personal friend. We were neighbors in Peter Cooper Village for a number of years, and he always gave me sound advice on personal and legal matters - in good times and in bad. I owe him a lot.

I was sworn in as a member of the Supreme Court Bar on the day the case was argued in early 1966. People are sworn in as a group today, in a scripted ceremony because there are so many, but in 1966 Chief Justice Warren personally welcomed each new member. It was a big thing for me then. But, the most memorable events came later.

In the course of an argument, it is not unusual for a Justice to discreetly summon a page, who will slip through the curtain behind the bench and either take a note from, or deliver a note to, the Justice. These notes are presumably occasional reminders to and from people who work in the Justice's office. But, during the *Grinnell* argument, Justice Douglas sent and received notes throughout.

When we left the courtroom at the end of the argument, the CEO of our client could hardly contain his astonishment. "You guys up front couldn't see it," he said, "but I was at the back of the room right behind a very pretty young girl. Justice Douglas was exchanging notes with her all morning!" This was amusing, but hardly surprising or distressing. The Justice did have a reputation as a ladies' man, and we doubted we'd get his vote anyway.

Shortly thereafter, however, the client called in an even more agitated state. That morning a New York newspaper had a picture of Justice Douglas, then in his late 60s, with a new wife some 45 years his junior. I think she was number four. "Do you remember what happened at the argument, when Douglas was writing all those notes to a pretty girl in front of me," he said. Of course we did. "Well, I just saw his picture in the paper with his pretty young wife. It's not the same girl!"

The two Supreme Court opinions on the Fortner[9] **case** are also well-known among antitrust lawyers. My experience in this one is probably of greater relevance today. Again, my senior was Don Flinn.

U.S. Steel, a reliable firm client had diversified into the manufacture of pre-fabricated houses, of steel construction. Fortner Enterprises was a real estate development company located in Kentucky. Fortner claimed that the U.S.

Steel prefabricated houses, which he had erected on one of his developments were defective. He may well have had a valid claim for breach of warranty. But, an imaginative antitrust lawyer persuaded him to bring an antitrust case, which would of course allow a recovery of threefold damages.

In order to induce Mr. Fortner to buy U.S. Steel's prefabricated houses, the company's financing arm had loaned money on unusually favorable terms. The theory of Fortner's antitrust case was that financing and houses were two separate "products". When U.S. Steel conditioned the offer of one "product" (the money) on the purchase of another "product" (the houses), it could be called a "tying" arrangement and illegal under familiar antitrust principles. A key element in any tying case is whether the seller has sufficient market "power" over one product to compel a buyer to accept an unwanted "tied" product.

In the first *Fortner* opinion, issued in 1969, the Supreme Court held that uniquely favorable finance arrangements could indeed suggest that U.S. Steel had enough power in the market for money to force Fortner to buy an unwanted product. The claim should not have been summarily dismissed by a lower court, and the issue would have to be tried. My assignment was to sit at the side of local counsel at that later trial, in Louisville, Kentucky, and help him with the technical antitrust issues in the case.

Our local counsel, his partners, and our local witnesses were all bright and engaging people. So was the judge. The trial had an old-fashioned feel to it - informal Southern courtesy and slow Southern drawls. I enjoyed every minute of it. The more I heard of the plaintiff's case, however, the stranger it seemed. Mr. Fortner was an honest witness, who testified at great length about how well he had been treated, how money was tight, and how generous U.S. Steel's people had been. Without them, he couldn't have gone forward. Yet, these are the people he had sued!

In the laid-back atmosphere of the trial, the parties and their lawyers mingled freely during recess periods. One day, Mr. Fortner said to me: "You know, I don't understand any of this antitrust stuff you lawyers are always talking about. All I am complaining about is that the houses were no good."

That is what his case should have been all about, of course. Fortner may have recovered quickly on his warranty claims, but the Supreme Court dismissed his case in 1977 on the second appeal - about ten years after it had been brought. The Court decided this time that there just wasn't enough evidence that U.S. Steel had market power in the finance market.

Today, this prolonged dispute would have been cut short. The only reason Fortner wanted financing was to buy houses. U.S. Steel's unique financing arrangements were just a way to induce Fortner to buy something that he really wanted from U.S. Steel rather than some other company. The special financing was really equivalent to a deep discount on the houses; it wasn't really a tying case at all.

Advances in economic understanding over the last 35 years would make this reality immediately clear, and the Fortner case would have been argued and decided differently. At the time, however, none of us on either side, or the judges on the bench, knew enough economics to articulate the real reason why Fortner's antitrust claim should fail. All I had at the time was a strong intuition that there had to be something wrong when the core of a plaintiff's case is a recitation of the defendant's unique generosity.

I worked on many additional cases during my thirteen-year service at White & Case, but these were the big learning experiences. Before concluding the narrative of this interlude in my professional life, I need to mention two things - unrelated to any specific case - that marked both the high point and the low point of my experience as a Wall Street lawyer.

The Partnership and the Crack-Up

In the Fall of the year 1968, I was informed that I was one of four lawyers who had been elected to the partnership. The competition was pretty intense in major Wall Street firms at that time, and I assume it still is. I was immensely relieved that the race was over.

"Congratulations, you've had your last promotion," was the way one senior partner characterized what had happened. And, it appeared to be really true at the time. In the firm partners were not in competition with one another. Compensation was in lockstep depending on years as a partner, but changes were slow because the ratio between the compensation of the most senior and the most junior was only about 4 to 1. Each partner had one vote, not votes weighted by shares. There were no annual budgets or goals; whenever the cash balance of the firm exceeded a certain minimum figure, a partners' dividend was declared on the spot.

Partners kept track of their time for billing purposes, but the time was not aggregated as a measure of overall workload. There also were no statistics on the work that individual partners had attracted to the firm; the theory was that it is the firm name and reputation that attracted clients, not the talents of any individual partner. In fact, self-promotion of any kind was frowned upon. I remember that a partner was once pictured in Fortune magazine for some accomplishment; there were mumbles of disapproval; and he went out of his way to explain that he had nothing to do with the article.

There are advantages and disadvantages to a system like this, but I doubt that it would be viable in many firms today. One obvious advantage is that no partner had a financial incentive to keep control of a matter when another partner might be better qualified to handle it. The obvious disadvantage is that there was no objective way to ease out partners who had lost their desire or their effectiveness as they aged. However, it suited my temperament. As mentioned before, I have never been much interested in or motivated by money, and really did not want to "compete" with my law partners, for bigger pieces of the pie. There was plenty to go around.

Before I take up a serious and unpleasant memory, I want to tell a funny story that actually dates back to my early years at the firm. I mentioned that

White & Case did not maintain any records on client origination at that time, and that individual promotion was discouraged. I suspect now that the lack of overt competition among the premier firms was a contributing cause. It was downright ungentlemanly to solicit business from another firm's good clients, and client relations were solid for decades. Business solicitations, if any, were confined to genteel exchanges at a very senior level, and young partners were not expected to bring in clients. I was once told that "Any clients a young guy like you could attract would probably not be substantial enough to be worth our time."

Nevertheless, a few of my father's business friends were substantial enough to be worthwhile clients, and some of them were good enough to call me and request that the firm provide some specialized service that their customary counsel could not handle.

I learned the hard way, however, there is a big problem if you affirmatively try to exploit an acquaintance that dates back to childhood. One day, I was talking to a mentor, Ed Barton, about some problem, and he seemed distracted and worried about something else. He said that he had a meeting shortly on another matter with a longtime client, which had a very outspoken and domineering CEO. I asked who he was, and Ed gave me the name.

"Oh, I've known him all my life," I said. "He's a golfing and shooting friend of my father, and just likes to act like a cowboy. He came from an affluent family, graduated from Princeton, and is really a nice guy." Ed jumped on this: "That's great," he said. "Why don't you come with me to the meeting?" And so I did.

When I walked into the room, my father's buddy took one look at me and roared: "My Gawd!. It's little Tommy Leary! What are you doing here?"

I never tried to be a big shot again.

I'll introduce the unpleasant part with another story. "Gus" Busch, the most colorful beer baron of the time and a client of the firm, summed up my general attitude with a remark that was widely quoted. A young reporter had asked him to estimate how much he was worth. Busch reportedly said: "Young man, after a certain point, it really doesn't make any difference. After all, you can only drink about twenty bottles of beer in a day."

Of course, I was fortunately satisfied with a great deal less money than Gus Busch could have been talking about. The unfortunate fact, however, is that I did not take his specific example metaphorically.

I do not propose to give a detailed account of my crack-up. Far too many stories of that kind have been written already and I am just one of a big bunch. All that needs to be said is that I worked hard and played hard for twenty years, but that by early 1970 I had suffered a complete physical, mental and spiritual collapse. The recovery process included a stay of several weeks at an in-patient facility and, as far as I am concerned, is a lifelong project. Books have been written about that process, too. I will just say that I have not taken an alcoholic drink since November 1970 - over 40 years ago.

Since this memoir focuses on my professional life, I also will not attempt to describe what was happening at home. However, something has to be said, because it is a burden I still carry. Stephanie, then my wife of sixteen years must have felt that she had committed her life to a madman. Our three children - Tom (age 12), David (age 10) and Alison (age 6) were too young to understand the reasons, but must have wondered why their father had become so vague and detached. Over the years I have tried to make amends to all of them for the sorrow I caused, and time helps to heal. But, I have not forgotten.

The effect on my law partners was less immediate and delayed. I know now, however, that some of them were puzzled by the evident decline in my productivity well before anything was said about it. When the reasons became obvious, the reactions were mixed. Some felt I had "let down the side;" others were concerned that the stress of a Wall Street practice would put me in continuing peril. There was a consensus, however, that I should be asked to think about other opportunities - no rush, but I had really lost the confidence of a solid majority for the long term.

As the months went by, I explored some other opportunities in a desultory way, but really was focused on squaring away my personal life. Over time, I began to do increasing amounts of work on client matters that I had developed personally, and began to get my confidence back. With continued evidence that my personal crisis had passed, I might have been able to ride it out in the firm - and some partners quietly encouraged me to do just that. Then, as always seems to happen in my life, I was made aware of a new opportunity.

Orison Marden, the senior partner who had done such an amazing job on his examination of Walt Disney, had recently served a term as President of the American Bar Association. A fellow member of that small group was a man named Ross Malone, the General Counsel of General Motors Corporation. One day, Ross Malone told Orson Marden that he was looking for an experienced antitrust lawyer to take charge of the Corporation's cadre of in-house antitrust lawyers. A newly-appointed incumbent had just died unexpectedly. Marden said he might just have a candidate.

Then, he told me about the conversation and asked if I would be interested. Indeed, I would. GM was then the most successful company in the country, and - partly because of its success - it was the world's biggest antitrust target. Orison then asked two questions. First, would you be available to go and talk to Ross Malone in GM's New York office sometime in the next few days and, second, can I tell him something about your history - the highs and the lows? I said: "of course."

So, once more by accident, I took the initial steps that led to a new challenge.

GM had a magnificent suite of New York offices in what was then called the General Motors Building, directly across the street from the Plaza Hotel. (I don't know what the building is called today, but it was sold to Japanese interests many years ago.) Ross Malone, the General Counsel, was a famous lawyer, not just because he had served a term as President of the ABA, but also because he hailed from Roswell, New Mexico - a town better known for cattle and space aliens than high-powered lawyers. When people took note of his unusual background, Ross used to say: "Don't be too impressed. My rancher friends call me 'counselor', and all my lawyer friends call me 'cowboy.'"

He was an engaging man, obviously highly intelligent but without a trace of self importance. We hit it off immediately. He said that the then persistent speculation about an antitrust action to break up GM was the biggest threat that the company faced, and that the senior in-house lawyer who had helped to steer GM through the minefield was approaching retirement age. Because of the recent untimely death of the chosen successor, they were looking for another younger man to provide similar guidance for the far future. I had the kind of "big case" experience that they were looking for, and was about the right age (40).

I was immediately intrigued because this was a more responsible job than I had ever held before, and GM then had a sterling reputation as a well-managed company. The principal downside was that it would require a move to Detroit. I didn't mind at all, but I was concerned about Stephanie and the kids.

Ross and I agreed to meet again the following week. He needed to get clearance from the Chairman of the company, and I wanted to discuss it at home. Stephanie was, frankly, not at all enthusiastic about a move because we had a number of warm friends in Chatham, and she would bear the principal burden of integrating the family into a new community. I think, however, that she was as uncomfortable as I was with the limbo state that we were living in. She agreed to the change.

GM's Chairman apparently approved as well. So, Ross and I shook hands on the deal the following week. Stephanie and I promptly flew to Detroit, with a "budget" of three days to buy a house. We spent the first day looking at houses; made a decision, and arranged for financing on day two; and closed the deal on day three. I've always admired her willingness to move fast on these things. We also met, and were entertained at dinner by Robert Nitschke and his wife. Bob Nitschke, the man I was slated to replace ultimately had an immense influence on my later life, and on the way I think about antitrust law today. In fact, he really should be recognized as one of the godfathers of the "New Economic Learning" that transformed this area of law. I was soon to find out why.

My new employer wanted me to come on board as soon as possible, so Stephanie and I agreed that I would travel to Detroit first by myself, and stay in a hotel while she took care of the move from our house in New Jersey. That was no small thing because we had accumulated the usual paraphernalia needed to maintain a good-sized suburban house, with three children and a Cocker Spaniel.

The windup at White & Case was also hurried, but cordial on all sides. I was given a sendoff dinner, the customary gold watch, and a generous check that more than compensated for the relatively small capital contributions that I had made. There was some mutual sadness, coupled with a recognition I would benefit from a fresh start. The firm still carries me on their roster of alumni; I later would often visit old friends there when I was in New York; and I have attended reunion events over the years.

In retrospect, even though the precipitating cause of my departure was a personal disaster, I'm not sure that I would have been a very good Wall Street lawyer anyhow. New York is the financial capitol of the world, and the representation of financial institutions seems to have become increasingly significant. Essential though it may be, the financial business is not something that has ever interested me. This is particularly true today, since financial institutions seem less focused on providing capital for productive activity than on the zero-sum game of swapping ever more complex pieces of paper.

MY YEARS AT GENERAL MOTORS

The hiring process had gone smoothly, and Stephanie seemed to have the family move well under control. Nevertheless, my anxiety level was high. I was used to new environments: College, Navy, Law School and Law Firm. On each of the previous moves, however, I was entering as an acknowledged apprentice, in company with other neophytes. This time, I was entering alone, and expected quickly to take charge of an important activity.

At times like this, the inner three-year old can emerge. I remember the first morning that I reported for work, when I looked out the window of my hotel room at that immense GM headquarters building directly across the street, powerfully aware of the fact that I had met only two people who work in the place but would somehow have to quickly earn the confidence of the top executives there.

Bob Nitschke was an immense help in the launching process. He had secured a place for me in the executive dining room where I would not only be able to eat a fine lunch with my clients every day, but also qualify for a brand new company car every three months and a place in the executive garage right across the street. (GM was a very profitable company then.) Apart from the obvious financial advantages and added convenience, these outward indicia of status helped to give me some instant credibility. It would then be up to me to retain it.

The process, somewhat like a fraternity hazing, had some amusing moments. One table in the dining room that I found particularly lively was informally "chaired" by an irreverent guy named Bill Harvey, who was in charge of the activity that selected, trained and (if necessary) financed new dealers. When he learned that I was a lawyer, he opined that lawyers were a pretty useless bunch and "almost as weird as psychiatrists."

I normally have no talent for fast comebacks, but the gods were on my side this time. I replied that "I assume that conclusion is based on your extensive contacts with both." Bill looked stunned for a moment, then broke into hearty laughter. "You're alright," he said, "we're going to get along just fine."

On a more substantive plane, I did have a wide experience with many legal issues of the kind that I would encounter as a member of the GM legal staff. But, I soon learned that the approach had to be somewhat different. An "outside" advocate, which I had been at White & Case, typically is consulted only after some kind of dispute has arisen. The script has already been written, facts are what they are, and your job is to package and argue them as best you can.

An "inside lawyer" by contrast, is more likely to become involved "at the beginning of the movie" and to have an initial opportunity to shape the facts. This may look like an easier job, but it sometimes can be even more challenging. We are all generally more likely to welcome the "doctor's" advice when we are sick and battling to get well than we are when we are still well and feeling cocky.

Bob Nitschke made me aware of another big difference. GM had some special problems of a scope and kind that I had never encountered before.

Multi-Level Threats

The 1960s are remembered today as a period of disillusionment, youthful rebellion and cries for radical change, but the movement really peaked early in the 1970s - when I was beginning my years at General Motors. As the largest and most conspicuously profitable industrial company in the world, General Motors was under attack on several levels.

Particular sales and marketing strategies were closely scrutinized by the Federal Trade Commission and the Antitrust Division of the Justice Department, which had a special "GM Section" that focused on the company. At an intermediate level, there seemed to be a broad consensus in the economics profession that "concentrated" industries with few sellers were inherently anticompetitive; the automobile industry was often cited as the most conspicuous example; and General Motors had by far the largest market share. At the highest level of threat, there were some vocal critics who questioned the efficiency and the fairness of a free-market capitalistic system. "Corporate power" had to be tamed, in order to promote desirable environmental and social goals. Again, General Motors was likely to be singled out for conspicuous criticism.

Bob Nitschke had been astute enough to recognize that the Corporation had to be defended at both the tactical and the strategic levels (although he did not use those words). The lowest tactical level, which involved day-to-day counseling on business strategies, would be entirely my responsibility once I became familiar enough with GM's operations. Top management had decreed that GM should always err on the side of caution - be "above suspicion like Caesar's wife," as one former CEO had expressed it. Antitrust issues were deemed to be so important for the survival of the Corporation that a special section on these matters was always included in the monthly report to the Board of Directors.

The plan was that I would phase into the strategy level somewhat more slowly, at first in tandem with Bob. Despite my extensive antitrust experience, I was initially unaware of some new economic ideas that were germinating in the academic community. As indicated in the previous chapter, I had observed that traditional antitrust sometimes seemed quixotic but did not have the economic tools for a reasoned critique. Bob Nitschke, with the expert guidance of a superb GM economist named, Brent Upson had become familiar with these new economic theories. Moreover, he persuaded top management of the Corporation to provide research funds to support their development.

All of the prominent academic economists and knowledgeable lawyers associated with these theories - people like Harold Demsetz, John McGee, Yale Brozen , Fred Westen, Henry Manne and Robert Bork - were encouraged and supported with research funds by General Motors. I was fortunate enough to work with each of them at various times. In addition, I was privileged to meet two legendary and long-lived men who had themselves inspired this group: Aaron Director, who died in 2005, just short of 103, and Nobel Prize winner Ronald Coase, to my knowledge still alive at 100.

GM's support for fundamental economic research is illustrated by the fact that it was a major contributor to the now-famous Airlie House Conference held in 1974. This Conference, led by Columbia University, featured three days of open debate between those academics who still supported traditional "populist" competition policies, and economists like those here mentioned who advocated what came to be known as the "New Learning."

It took a major effort, in which I participated with Bob Nitschke and Brent Upson, to persuade GM's top management that this conference would be worth a substantial financial commitment. As one executive said to me: "Why should we give money to provide a platform for some of our bitterest critics?" In reply, I said something to the effect that "The academics that support our side of the debate are still in a minority, but will get equal time - something they never have had before." Then I went on to say that "If their ideas are as sound as we think they are, we should come out well in the debate."

I later heard Seymour Lipset, a well-known political scientist, express a similar idea more persuasively at a business conference:

"Business should always support independent research and open debate. If the ultimate conclusions tend to support the policies that you favor, they will be much more persuasive than the conclusions of people who are always on your side. If the ultimate conclusions do not support your favored policies, you want to be among the first to know - so, you won't waste time and resources on arguments that cannot stand up to close scrutiny."

As it turned out, most commentators concluded that the advocates of "New Learning" - later identified with the so-called "Chicago School" - came out ahead in the Airlie House debate. Their view that antitrust should focus on "consumer" welfare rather than "competitive" welfare, that corporate size and industrial concentration are not necessarily harmful, that "competitive advantage" and "efficiency" are worthwhile goals, and that many seemingly suspect restraints are pro-competitive ultimately had a profound effect on antitrust policy.

Many commentators, cite the Supreme Court's 1977 decision in *Sylvania*[10] as the turning point. It should be noted that the economic rationale for the decision was not based on the Briefs of the parties, but rather on an Amicus Brief submitted by the Automobile Manufacturer's Association. This Brief was signed by Don Turner, formerly the head of the DOJ Antitrust Division during the Administration of President Lyndon Johnson, but GM lawyers and economists played a major role in its preparation.

GM's role is now well known. What is not well known is the fact that there was one strong difference of opinion between Don Turner and the GM people who had selected him as spokesman for the industry in *Sylvania*. Turner insisted that the AMA Brief include a caveat to the effect that non-price "vertical" restraints at issue in *Sylvania* were qualitatively different than resale price restraints, which should continue to be *per se* illegal. The GM group argued that the effects of vertical price and non-price restraints were indeed sometimes different, but the competitive effects did not uniformly tilt in the same direction. For example, a price restraint affects only one, albeit an important, method of dealer competition, whereas a territorial restriction can eliminate dealer competition entirely in a particular area.

Don Turner was adamant, however, and we clients concluded that his reputation for independence was more valuable for the cause. This caveat, after all, did not address the case presently before the Court. The caveat about vertical price restraints, however, was picked up and featured in the *Sylvania* opinion,[11] and it has had an impact for 20 years - until the recent decision in *Leegin*.[12]

We will never know, of course, what would have happened if the clients who paid for the Brief had refused to accept the caveat, and Don Turner had refused to sign it. I believe, however, that the decision to compromise was the correct one. High policy decisions like *Sylvania* have a strong "political" component, and arguments for incremental change are much more likely to prevail in that arena.

General Motors also provided generous support for Professor Henry Manne's "Economics Institutes for Federal Judges," a three-week summer program designed to teach basic economics to these influential people. I once audited a portion of one of these programs to see how the subject was taught. The visiting professors who taught it, including some of those identified above, were very careful to avoid advocacy of policy positions that may be outside their area of competence.

For example, they might explain why, other things being equal, price controls would tend to create shortages, minimum wage laws would tend to create over-supply (unemployment), and cost/price regulation would tend to chill internal incentives for cost-containment. But, they were always careful to point out that these policies might also be driven by non-economic value judgments.

The program attracted favorable comments from both "liberal" and "conservative" judges who had taken the course, but was often unfairly criticized as right-wing propaganda by media critics, who did not know what they were talking about. If these basic principles are thought to be something that conservatives have just dreamed up, the public policy debate is debased.

I have always thought that GM's support for Henry Manne's program was one of the best investments that the Corporation made in its efforts to influence the policy debates. I did not always agree with all of Henry Manne's causes – particularly, his all-out support for leveraged buyouts – but, I was pleased to serve for a number of years on his Advisory Board after I had moved to Washington and he was Dean at George Mason Law School.

Tactics

On the tactical side, day-to-day antitrust advice is obviously in the front line of defense. I once told the then head of the Antitrust Division that I dealt with more potential antitrust issues before breakfast every day that he saw in a week. This was a wild exaggeration, of course, but I mention the comment to illustrate a serious point. Antitrust counsel who provide ongoing advice *before* potentially controversial steps have been taken are the first and foremost enforcers of the antitrust laws in this country. This is why it is particularly important for the antitrust Agencies to publicize their current enforcement intentions in Guidelines and speeches, however controversial they may be.

It is also the reason why an antitrust counselor has to develop the ability to provide guidance quickly. I had not acquired this skill at White & Case because my practice there focused on "Big Case" litigation, and time and resources were available to research issues matters in depth. This was not true when I was on a corporate legal staff and, actually, it was no longer true when I returned to private practice in 1983 at what is now the HoganLovells firm. Clients today are demanding faster answers.

The best description of the process that I have ever heard was given to me by someone whose name I cannot remember. Many years ago, I asked him about his guiding strategies in counseling. He said: "I use the Miss Marple method!" It's right on, actually. For those who are not familiar with the Agatha Christie fictional murder mysteries, Miss Marple is an elderly maiden lady, who lives in a small English town, and always solves the perplexing mystery at the end. She will typically introduce her solution with a comment like: "These events remind me of something that happened many years ago, when …"

In my experience, that is the best approach to an antitrust problem when a quick answer is needed. The problem is not presented with a legal label attached; the client is proposing to take some action and wants an assessment of the antitrust risks, if any. If the counselor can remember previous advice on exactly the same issue, or there is a recent decision on the question, that's fine. It is more likely, however, that the proposal will raise an issue that is merely reminiscent of one that has arisen before. And, the Miss Marple methodology comes in handy.

Before I go any further, it is necessary to emphasize that these stories about the things that I did cannot begin to capture the sheer volume of antitrust issues that came up in a vast enterprise like General Motors. I had a lot of help from other experienced antitrust lawyers, who were able to provide this kind of practical advice with minimal input from me.

Bob Weinbaum, for example, was a DOJ veteran, who took full responsibility for the affairs of GM's overseas subsidiaries. Bob, of course, later served as Chair of the ABA's Antitrust Law Section. Bob and his wife May also became, and remain close personal friends. Bill Slowey, another DOJ veteran, took full responsibility for a number of private antitrust cases. Among other talents, he seemed able to remember every antitrust decision in the books - a talent I never had. I have felt free to ask him about a precedent long after I left GM.

People like this must have their own good stories to tell, and someday I hope that they will. Bill Slowey, for example, once defended a lawsuit brought by a crazy guy, who not only had a fabricated antitrust claim but also claimed that GM had tried to rub him out. It seems that he had recently been almost run down on the streets of New York by someone in a Buick - and this was proof enough!

There may be a need to communicate advice to many more people than you can talk to individually. When I became more knowledgeable about GM's legal affairs, I was surprised to learn that, notwithstanding the high priority that the Corporation gave to antitrust matters, there was no written compliance policy. This was not an inadvertent omission; it was a considered decision by a previous General Counsel that was based, oddly enough, on the recent experience of the General Electric Company in the *Electrical Cases,* which I have written about at length earlier.

General Electric had a strict written policy which went beyond the boundaries of the antitrust laws and prescribed conduct that could be benign. It also outlined severe sanctions for violations of the policy. The experience in the *Electrical* litigation - with which I was more than a little familiar - was that it was very difficult to explain to a finder of fact that an employee who had been disciplined for violation of the policy might not have violated the antitrust laws.

GE's well publicized experience spooked the former General Counsel of GM, and very eminent outside counsel who decided that a written policy was too dangerous. After some serious soul-searching, I concluded that such a highly-visible company simply had to have a written policy. (It is now, of course, a prerequisite under U.S. Sentencing Guidelines if a company seeks mitigation of punishment for its compliance efforts.) It was the first, but by no means the last time I had to stick out my neck at GM. I persuaded Bob Nitschke and Ross Malone, our mutual boss, that it had to be done, and was given the task of writing it.

I still have a copy of the initial policy, written almost 40 years ago, but it has of course been revised over the years. The initial questions for any company, however, continue to be what subjects need to be covered, who should get a copy, what sanctions should be imposed for violations, what additional training should be given to selected individuals, and who is available to answer questions.

I have since written additional policies and some articles on these issues and some of them are too company-specific to discuss here. One fact, however, may demonstrate the scale of GM's problem. We decided to limit distribution to those employees who could potentially cause the Corporation to violate the antitrust laws. We looked at the organization charts of the multiple divisions and of the home office, and identified the vulnerable job descriptions. Obviously, we would go deeper in the ranks for, say, a marketing group than a group of vehicle designers. At the end of this process, we decided we should print 40,000 (!) copies.

We also debated the question of mandatory punishments for violations. We were motivated in part by GE's litigation experience, but I believe there was an even more compelling reason. Some unrepentant rascals have been mentioned in this memoir, but they are not necessarily typical. The commands of the antitrust laws are not intuitively obvious to a normal moral person. In legal jargon, a crime like murder is described as "malum in se" (Latin, for *in itself,* with no further explanation required); an antitrust offense is "malum prohibitum" (Latin, for illegal because there is a law that makes it so). Many moral people, for example, believe it is somehow unethical to solicit business from another company's good customers, and that it is sensible to mutually agree on the subject. We lawyers should not be too sanctimonious about this because this was part of the "gentlemanly" code that prevailed on Wall Street when I first started to practice there in 1958.

Since many valuable employees may be generally confused about the boundaries of the antitrust laws, we wanted them to "self-report" when they think there is a possibility that they have crossed a line. And, employees will hardly be encouraged to self-report if punishment is mandatory.

As the years went by, I increasingly would get calls from employees across the country, whom I had never met. The calls would go something like this: "My name is John Doe from the ABCD division, and I think I may have done something I shouldn't have done." Most of the time, the actions were benign, or insignificant enough to be resolved on the phone. In very rare cases, the problem was potentially serious, and required further action. (This is inevitable in any large organization, with thousands of employees who might do something questionable.) In extreme cases, I would go to the plant site myself, or send one of the younger lawyers in my group, to investigate the extent of the problem and take steps to prevent a recurrence.

On these blind calls, I had to make it clear that I represented the Corporation, not an individual, but I could promise that I would do the best I could to protect my sources. If I was satisfied that the situation had been corrected and was unlikely to recur, I would simply inform the appropriate top executive in the home office with a terse statement like: "I learned about a potential antitrust problem in the ABCD division; it's been taken care of; and you don't need to know anything more about it."

As I look back on my professional life, there is nothing that gives me more satisfaction than the fact that - despite close scrutiny by the antitrust agencies and the large number of potential offenders in the Corporation - there was not one single antitrust prosecution by the DOJ for conduct that occurred on my watch from 1971 through 1982. There was, I believe, one FTC case, which we won. I don't know how this would have been possible were it not for the encouragement of self-reporting.

There is another counseling issue which is illuminated by two incidents that occurred at different stages of my time at General Motors.

When I came to GM, I was primarily an antitrust litigator, and in litigation outside counsel are usually in command of the ship. (*The Electrical Cases* were an exception, because strategy had to be coordinated in multiple jurisdictions.) In counseling, the situation is more complex. In some situations, the lawyers are responsible for ultimate decisions; in other situations, top executives are responsible. At GM the Legal Staff clearly was in command if there was a serious threat of criminal liability. The General Counsel could even go over the Chairman's head and lay the matters before the Board of Directors if there was an impasse - something that was never necessary when I was there. But, what if there was only a serious threat of civil consequences?

Ross Malone, who had hired me and with whom I had developed a close rapport, tragically was diagnosed with terminal cancer about a year after I had arrived. The new General Counsel was a man named Frazer Hilder, whom I really did not know well. Frazer actually had an antitrust background, and had worked at the Federal Trade Commission early in his career. He had, however, concentrated on other areas in his time at GM, and our paths seldom crossed. In addition, Frazer was a quiet man, who did not back away from ultimate decisions but did not "think aloud" in extensive preliminary discussions, as so many lawyers do.

Early in GM years, I had advised a senior GM executive about the civil litigation risks of some proposed initiative, and suggested a less dangerous approach. He chose to do it his way.

I was upset and went to see Frazer about it. In fact, I was so upset that I couldn't sit down, and paced around his office as I vented my frustrations. Frazer heard me out in silence, wreathed in his usual cloud of cigar smoke with a slight smile on his face.

When I finally wound down, Frazer simply said: "Well, I don't see what you're so excited about. You gave the management your best advice, and presented it well. They didn't choose to accept it. [Bleep] 'em. It's not your problem anymore." (As it happened, my fears turned out to be unfounded, after all.)

This, of course, is similar to the general life advice I had gotten from my grandmother and the litigation advice I had gotten from Tom Kiernan at White & Case many years before. It still took me some time, however, to refine my understanding of the boundary between what I could do something about and what I could not.

The second incident occurred toward the end of my years at General Motors, when I had a better idea about the appropriate boundaries. One day, I was given a message that the President of the Corporation wanted to see me as soon as possible. I had no idea of what it was all about.

The top executive offices at that time were located on the East side of the 14th floor in the GM building; the Legal Staff was housed somewhat less elegantly in the West side. So, it was a short walk. Jim McDonald, the

President at that time, had an immense office. He was normally an amiable guy, and usually would come out from behind his desk to greet any visitors. This time, he just sat there looking like a thundercloud.

"I have been told," he said, "that you have advised the Corporation cannot do [whatever it was that he wanted to do]. Is that correct?" These words, I still remember exactly. In reply, I said something like the following. "No, that's not quite right. When I was asked for advice about this proposed strategy, I said that it presented a substantial antitrust risk; that there was a high likelihood that GM would be sued by someone and lose; and that the damages would be large." I added, however that there was no criminal risk, "so, you can do it if you want to. The decision is yours."

He cooled down immediately; it was like a balloon collapsing. He said: "Maybe, you'd better tell me a little more."

The basic principle here is that, absent a threat of criminal liability, the decision to assume antitrust risk is one for top management, not for lawyers. We lawyers are paid to assess and quantify risks, as best we can, but not to make these decisions. In my experience, a red flag should go up whenever the lawyer and the client start to argue. The likely cause is either that the client is trying to second-guess the lawyer's opinion, which he is not qualified to do, or the lawyer is trying to make a decision that is not his to make. I think the reason Jim McDonald was initially mad at me was because he thought that was what I had done.

There is a very good reason for these boundaries. If lawyers have the ultimate authority to approve or to veto proposed strategies, the clients will be motivated - consciously or unconsciously - to accentuate the positives and eliminate the negatives when they submit the proposals for approval. The relationship may become almost adversarial. Lawyers cannot give good advice if clients are not motivated to be candid.

I have found that a simple analogy can help clients to understand the appropriate boundaries. We all have looked at the weather reports on television or on a computer. We reason we do it because the people who prepare the reports know a lot more about the weather than we do. We always realize, however, that these predictions could be wrong. And, we also understand that we have to decide ourselves whether or not to carry a raincoat.

Lawyers are the people who provide weather reports. Top managers are normally the people who have to decide the precautions they may want to take. They may, of course, try to delegate some of this authority to their lawyers, because they are not comfortable with the responsibility. "What would you do in my place," is a question that I sometimes was asked. I was willing to give an opinion, if I had one, but was always careful to emphasize that I was not speaking as a lawyer.

Prepared policy statements, speeches and draft Board and Committee minutes were always submitted for legal review. During most of my years at GM, the Corporation was popularly believed to have market power approaching the power of a monopoly. Modes of expression can become important because the issue of "intent" can arise in monopolization cases, and antitrust lawyers know what words are dangerous.

There is an amusing incident that illustrates what I mean. One day I was asked to come out to the Corporation's large research facility to hear a presentation about an innovative proposal for the design of car radios. The Corporation's engineers had figured out a way to combine most of the vehicle's electronics in a package that could be stowed in the trunk, and the tuning unit for the radio in the dashboard would be no larger than a deck of cards. (Remember, this was almost 35 years ago, long before current miracles of miniaturization were available.) The reduced bulk would facilitate attractive new dashboard designs.

The small space available in the dashboard would, of course, also eliminate competition from Japanese radios, which a growing number of customers were installing instead of ordering the Corporation's own product. (In fact, there had been private litigation when GM offered radios as standard equipment in one of its models.) This was the advantage that the research people thought would be particularly attractive to management. When I arrived at the meeting, the conference room was plastered with slogans like "Remember Pearl Harbor" and even more bellicose statements.

When the proposal was described to me, I advised that the Corporation could indeed go ahead with this innovative proposal. Even a monopolist can legally improve its project. Smiles all around. Then, I went on to say that the posters should come down, that this supposed competitive advantage should not be part of the ultimate management decision, and that written proposals should not refer to it. Banish it from your thoughts. Frowns this time. The proposal was ultimately shut down purely for business reasons, but I'm not sure that its advocates ever forgave me for depriving them of what they thought would be the most compelling argument in its favor.

Over time, the Legal Staff developed a glossary of acceptable and unacceptable language, not only for use in various company documents but as a guide for the way people should *think* about GM's objectives. Attitude of mind is an important element in antitrust compliance, particularly when monopolization may be an issue. If you discipline yourself to "think" about issues in a certain acceptable way, you are less likely to speak or write in a dangerous way. I have summed up the concept then and thereafter in these words: "Business strategies of an arguably dominant company should be justified by what they will do *for* customers rather than by what they will do *to* competitors."

We also had to provide guidance on fundamental "attitudes" that should govern supplier and dealer relations. To the extent that these relationships are governed by formal contracts, it is usual to provide for legal review of the standard forms. As discussed earlier, nuances of communication can be important, and there may be far too many oral or written communications for lawyers to monitor. Nevertheless, there are some general principles that are easy to remember.

The relationship between the Corporation and its independent dealers are not always happy marriages. Dealers are not successful for a wide variety of reasons. Contrary to expectations, the dealers may just not be very good at the job. The GM sales people responsible for a particular region may not be very good at what they do. Sometimes, even with the best intentions and expectations, demographic changes or unpredictable customer reactions will cause a dealership to fail.

A particularly tragic example was the failure of some initial efforts by the Corporation to practice a form of "affirmative action" and expand the number of black-owned dealerships. Management decided, not unreasonably, that black-owned dealerships would have a better opportunity in those areas with a large minority population. Wrong. The minority population - conditioned by a lifetime of slights - tended to think that they were being patronized, and many chose to buy from white-owned dealers outside the area. I assume that this suspicion has faded over time.

In any event, it is always a distressing event when a dealership fails. The dealer is angry and embarrassed, and so are the Corporation employees who have been responsible for dealer relations in the dealer's territory. If the termination, or failure to renew, is undertaken in a vindictive spirit, however, there is a significant risk that the dealer will attempt to recover the losses in litigation. And, regardless of the technical requirements for proof of an antitrust action or violation of federal or state franchise laws [13], the real issue in dealer litigation is likely to be whether a jury perceives that the dealer has been treated "unfairly". To top it off, the jury pool may consist of people from the dealer's hometown, and GM may be perceived as a distant and an impersonal bully.

Actions by terminated suppliers are relatively rare, but some of the same considerations may be present. The principal objective in both situations should be an amiable divorce without litigation. With top management support, the Legal Staff mandated certain preventative strategies. (Today, of course, these matters are largely governed by near-universal state laws that regulate dealer relations, but general instructions of this kind still can make sense.)

Terminations or failures to renew a dealer required Legal Staff approval. Before approval, we would review written records of correspondence with or about the dealer; including memoranda of conversations. If the written record included recent complaints by rival dealers about the competitive tactics of the dealer in question - a particularly sensitive issue - we would put an automatic hold on the termination for a "cooling off" period, in order to avoid any inference that there was a connection between the complaints and the Corporation's actions.

There was, in addition, a standing instruction that competitive complaints of this kind should be politely acknowledged, but with a caveat that they would not have any effect. I suggested language like: "You should understand that our relations with one dealer are not in any way influenced by the opinions of other dealers. We assume you would not want us to discuss your business with other rival dealers, or take into account their opinions when we evaluate your performance."

If the divorce is inevitable, try to provide a "soft landing". Help the dealer (or the supplier) to minimize the financial damage. A conspicuous example was the decision late in my tenure at GM to centralize the purchase of component parts and suppliers from outside sources. Traditionally, these items had been bought separately by individual divisions from local suppliers. The perceived advantage of close relations came to be outweighed by massive inefficiencies. Since there was no coordination among divisions, one division may have had a warehouse full of parts that another division was buying in the spot market at premium prices. If GM was only one of several customers for a terminated local supplier, there was little litigation risk. In other cases, the supplier might go out of business.

With management's approval, I put in place a policy that each one of the problem cases would be subject to legal review, so we could provide for a "soft landing." GM did so, and a massive reshuffle of the supplier base was implemented with no litigation.

There was, however, one supplier issue that at first seemed intractable. When I found an acceptable solution, the implementation took me to South Africa twice and required me to draft a significant contract for the first and only time in my life.

In the 1970s, automotive design was shaped by increasingly rigorous regulation of emissions, fuel economy and passenger safety. Engineering feasibility was not taken into account when the standards were set, and the goals were sometimes mutually inconsistent. For example, heavier cars are inherently safer than lighter ones but less fuel efficient. Emission control devices also degrade fuel economy.

These engineering challenges did not generally raise antitrust issues, and were therefore none of my business. There was one serious antitrust issue, however. The most feasible way to reduce unwanted emissions was to pass the exhaust gases through a "catalytic converter". Essential components of catalytic converters are small quantities of platinum and palladium, so-called "noble metals". Only two countries in the world had sufficient quantities of these metals to meet the needs of the automotive industry: South Africa and the Soviet Union. The apartheid policies of the South African government had strained relations with the U.S., and the Soviet Union and the U.S. were still engaged in a Cold War.

We approached potential suppliers in South Africa first. They were willing to enter into a long-term supply relationship, but they all insisted on an iron-clad assurance that GM would not resell any surplus amounts on the open market. At that particular time, resale prohibitions of this kind had been held to be *per se* illegal in the U.S. [14] We had speculated that mineral companies in South Africa might have some longstanding price agreements that would be illegal in the U.S., which we could do nothing about, but it was another matter for GM to enter into an illegal agreement itself - even if it were forced to by business necessity.

Matters were temporarily at an impasse, and GM decided to explore an alternative arrangement with the Soviets. Since antitrust issues might arise again, I was invited to join a team that was meeting in New York with the Soviet official in charge of whatever limited trade relations his country had with ours. He was an amiable individual, who offered us vodka at 10 in the morning as a prelude to discussions. We all politely declined, and I was spared from potential embarrassment. It soon became evident that we wouldn't be able to make a deal anyway, because the Soviets were unwilling to enter into any long term arrangements, and GM couldn't run the risk of massive shutdowns if testy relations between the two countries caused supplies to be shut off.

I didn't get the impression that the Soviet gentleman cared much about noble metals one way or the other; what he really wanted to talk about was a good deal on a big Buick. I was vastly amused by the fact that this avowed communist representative of the proletariat was interested in a luxury car.

Once it was obvious that the Soviet alternative would not work, I thought of a way that we might be able to resolve the antitrust issue with a South African supplier. We couldn't legally agree not to resell, but I thought we could agree to provide our supplier with an annual report on any outside sales. The supplier could then, at its option, reduce its minimum supply obligations in an equal amount the following year. This would create a powerful disincentive for any resales by GM. Our South African source was agreeable.

I cannot remember now whether I got a quiet nod from U.S. antitrust authorities on this arrangement, but I concluded it was highly unlikely that one arm of the federal government would interfere with a deal that was needed to implement a policy of a different arm. There never was an antitrust inquiry about it, and in the later *Sylvania* case the Supreme Court overruled previous authority [15] and held that a non-price resale restriction could be legal if it was "reasonable" - which this one certainly was.

Since I had become familiar with the whole subject, I was asked to accompany a small team of GM executives on a trip to Johannesburg, South Africa, late in 1972, to negotiate a supply arrangement with the Impala Platinum company. It was a memorable trip, purely as a travel experience. When the negotiations had been successfully concluded, the Impala people hosted an expedition to Victoria Falls, one of the greatest sights in the world. On a subsequent trip three years later, when changed conditions required some changes in contract terms, Stephanie came with me, and we had the opportunity to go 3,000 feet underground and see the mining operation close up. It was a fascinating, but not very pleasant, experience. In fact, the work in deep and low tunnels was so hard that native South Africans refused to do it. Labor was recruited from neighboring countries on a contract basis, and it was not easy to create an integrated work force out of tribesmen who spoke different languages and sometimes had been traditional enemies.

This time the celebratory trip took us to Mala Mala, which is often mentioned as the finest game park anywhere. We still enjoy the home movies of that experience, but our most memorable moments at Mala Mala occurred very late at night and were not captured on film.

Let me digress for a moment and describe the experience (which has nothing to do with practice of law). One evening, a dead zebra was staked out in a lighted clearing to attract the lions. We were seated close by in a dugout that resembled those on baseball fields at home, with much better beverage service. We could hear the lions rustling and sometimes roaring nearby in the dark, but something must have spooked them because they never approached their feast. Disappointed, we boarded the open Land Rovers, which were used at Mala Mala, and headed back to the lodge. As we were passing through tall grass on either side of a narrow roadway, a lioness suddenly appeared out of cover and started to run alongside Stephanie, who was in the right rear seat of the open car - in easy petting range. When Stephanie called out "a lion's right here," the guide up front in the "shotgun" seat grabbed his ever-present weapon (a high-powered rifle) and the driver called out "hands inside."

The lioness ran alongside for a while, then peeled off into the grass. She appeared again shortly thereafter, in company with a nearly full-grown cub. Same instructions from up front, and the same outcome. The incident doesn't seem all that exciting in retrospect, but there is something indescribably moving about an up-close and uncaged encounter with these magnificent animals in their own wild environment. The guides referred to them collectively in words that sound like "the Line" and Stephanie enjoyed her brief local celebrity as a premier "Line" magnet.

There was also what I thought was an important legal lesson that I learned on these two African trips. In the years since, I have tried to persuade others of its importance - with little success.

At the end of the negotiations on the first trip, the business people on both sides wanted to sign a binding ten-year supply contract. I had no experience whatever in drafting contracts and Robert ("Bob") Clare, counsel for Impala, did not have much more. Bob was a senior partner at Sherman & Sterling and later head of the firm, but he had a litigation background as well.

The issues were somewhat complicated because GM did not have a firm idea of the amounts of the "noble" metals that would be required each year. Auto sales were always unpredictable, and the amount of metal required for each catalytic converter was continuously changing with the evolution of technology and ever more stringent government standards. There were uncertainties on Impala's side as well. In order to supply GM's needs, which were vastly in excess of any amount they had ever delivered to a customer, Impala had to sink a new mine shaft and operate at a deeper level than they ever had before. So, its costs were purely an estimate. To complicate matters further, relations between the two countries were strained because of South Africa's racial policies. Neither side had much confidence in the legal system of the other.

As it turned out, this last complication turned out to be a real advantage. There was also another big advantage: both GM and Impala were in effect laying the future of their respective companies on the line. Impala's up-front investment in a new mine was big enough to bankrupt the company if GM later pulled out. GM's up-front investment was relatively smaller, but the Corporation would be seriously damaged if a supply interruption made it impossible to manufacture vehicles that met government emission standards.

With mutual recognition of these realities, and without any fixed ideas about how contracts should be drafted, Bob Clare and I produced a contract in a day. It was about 15 pages long, with double spaced type. That agreement for delivery of metals worth over a billion 1972 dollars had to be tweaked from time to time to account for changed conditions. Essentially, however, it was still running when I left GM a decade later. I shudder to think how long the agreement would have been, and how long the negotiations would have been, if experienced corporate lawyers had drafted it.

The reason we did not use a lot of customary verbiage is because we both recognized that we could not predict the future and that litigation was simply not an option. What the parties needed, first, was a succinct statement of who would do what and when. Then, we made an educated guess about immediate quantities and prices. Finally, we established some guiding fundamental principles, and a process for making appropriate changes down the road. We called it a "constitution".

I wondered then and still wonder why so many present-day business contracts take so much trouble to spell out the consequences if one party or the other doesn't live up to its promises. These things may be appropriate if the relationship is expected to be of short duration and alternative scenarios can be foreseen. But, I have questioned whether it is sensible to include this stuff when the parties are embarking on a long-term "marriage". It doesn't exactly foster an atmosphere of mutual trust.

Picture a ceremony where a bride and groom publicly enter into a marriage contract. After the promises have been exchanged in front of the congregation, the celebrant proceeds to read out the Separation Agreement which will become effective if something goes wrong. That's what GM's franchised dealer agreements looked like to me at the time. Page after page of what happens if the dealer defaults - which judges often ignored anyway because the dealer had to "adhere" to a standard form. A hell of a way to start off a business marriage.

It wasn't really any of my business, but I voiced these opinions after I returned from the first trip to Africa. I have a distinct recollection that the next round of dealer agreements had less of this offensive language but it probably has since crept back in, and I have an impression that corporate agreements today are generally more ponderous than they ever were.

My views on all this could be dead wrong. Arguably, the GM/Impala "constitution" worked because the business people on both sides were unusually decent people, who had become personal friends on the side expeditions, and had a genuine interest in the welfare of the guy on the other side. This may not be typical, because a lot of corporate lawyers, better informed than I am, make their living drafting ponderous agreements. In fact the activity seems to be essential for the survival of large legal institutions today. I'm just grateful that I don't have to write them and seldom have had to read them.

There is an irrelevant story that will close my memories of the South African experience. Our hosts at Impala had treated us to so many exotic adventures that it was hard to reciprocate when they made return visits. There just aren't any places in the environs of Detroit that can compete with Victoria Falls or Mala Mala.

I decided that one thing I could do was send a gift. In the midst of some teasing about my craving for chocolate toppings, one of our hosts mentioned that he really liked butterscotch sauce but, for some reason, it was not available in South Africa. When I returned to the U.S., I went to our local supermarket and asked for the manager. I told him that I wanted to buy some butterscotch sauce - not just the few bottles on the shelf, but all that he had available in the store. When he asked why, I simply said I wanted "to send it to Africa." A large case was brought out from storage, and I duly shipped it off.

This, of course, depleted their reserve supply of butterscotch. About a week later, Stephanie was in the same store, looking to buy some for our oldest son who was also particularly fond of it. There was none on the shelves, and she made an inquiry to the same manager. She later reported to me that he said: "Lady, you won't believe this. Last week, some nut was in here and bought all that we had. Said he wanted to ship it to Africa!" She simply replied: "Nooo! People certainly do crazy things."

While I was serving as inside antitrust counsel for GM, I found that it was useful to maintain contacts with antitrust counsel of other large companies that were competitors or had other commercial relations with the Corporation.

There were continuous discussions with my counterparts at Ford, Chrysler and American Motors, because we had to talk about the activities of what was then called the Automobile Manufacturers' Association. We also had to cooperate in the defense of some industry-wide litigation. Finally, I sometimes wanted to inform them when I was made aware of some potentially troublesome competitor contracts by people in one of the GM divisions.

More than a professional courtesy was involved. There was always a possibility that my informant - who, as described above, was often a volunteer - had not been completely candid, and competitor discussions had been much more extensive that I had been led to believe. My counterparts might be able to add useful information once they made their own inquiries. I do not remember that they ever had anything significant to add, or that they ever had something new to impart to me. But, we all felt that it was helpful to keep the lines of communication open.

It was also occasionally necessary to consult with antitrust counsel for significant suppliers. The best example that I can remember involved the introduction of the so-called "GM Tire."

In the 1970s, after years of research, our management decided that its customers would be better served if the Corporation were to change the current specifications for tires supplied by independent manufacturers. Customers were on average driving more, and GM decided that it would be feasible and desirable to pay for an improved product that would extend the current warranted life of 15,000-20,000 to 40,000 miles.

In addition, currently specified tires provided insufficient traction in winter-driving conditions, and people in the Northern parts of the country often replaced tires on the two rear wheels in the winter with so-called "snow tires." Recent research had demonstrated that if the two rear-wheel tires did not have "cornering" resistance comparable to the front two, there was a serious risk of conditions known as "understeer" (sluggish response) or "oversteer" (unexpected sharp response and risk of spinout). All in all, it would be a lot easier on the customers if the Corporation provided tires with sufficient year-round traction.

The technical problem was that improved traction required a more "chunky" tread design, which inherently reduced durability because there was a smaller tread surface that met the road. The Corporation's dual objectives were fundamentally inconsistent. However, newly-developed steel-belted radial tires would do the job.

GM wanted the tire companies to change their traditional manufacturing process and build steel-belted radial tires. This did not create a significant antitrust problem because the Corporation could consult with the suppliers individually and arrive at a spec that they all could meet. The principal legal problem arose from the fact that GM wanted a 40,000 mile warranty, but tire warranties traditionally ran from the tire company directly to the customer. So, we wanted these tire suppliers to simultaneously change a critical term of their contractual obligations to vehicle owners.

The solution to this legal problem involved the active cooperation of antitrust counsel for the various tire companies. I contacted each one of them individually to explain how we would like to proceed. We decided it would be desirable to explain the new program during a single meeting at a GM conference room in Detroit. We wanted all the supplier companies to hear the identical message, and would answer questions. But, we would caution against any expressions of supplier opinion, or any side discussions outside the group meeting. We encouraged tire company counsel to attend, and almost all did, and we also urged them to provide appropriate advice on antitrust risks. I also asked them to provide individual company opinions separately if they wished later on.

Beyond that, I informed my usual contact at the so-called "GM Section" of the DOJ's Antitrust Division about what we were going to do. He did not offer any objections, but we later had a major investigation of the GM Tire Program. After a full production of documents and interviews, the Program was cleared. The lesson here is that collective action can sometimes result in significant consumer benefits, and in cases like this there usually is a legal way to accomplish the beneficial result. This is what is meant by the term "creative counseling."

There were other noteworthy results of the fundamental research that led to the GM Tire and the extended warranties that persist to this day. Customers no longer find it necessary to buy snow tires. Extended warranties are commonplace and tire failure, which we experienced many times in past years, are virtually nonexistent today. I don't remember when or how I changed my last one. Individual tire cornering characteristics are measured and published, so individual replacement tires can be selected to match those that remain.

As an experiment, GM engineers tested surviving examples of the Corvair to see whether the newly discovered consequences of mismatched tires were the cause of the sporadic oversteer problems that had made the car notorious - and led to its ultimate demise. The engineers concluded that this, indeed, had caused the problems. We provided this information to Senator Ribicoff, the Chair of the Congressional Committee that had widely publicized the Corvair's problems some years before - and in doing so, also introduced Ralph Nader to a wide audience.

Senator Ribicoff, a conscientious man, conducted a follow-up investigation, and his House Committee issued a report that disclosed the real reason for the Corvair's safety issues. It was not just a matter of historic interest, but also provided guidance for those stubbornly loyal customers who still drove this model that they had bought so many years before.

Ralph Nader issued a statement that excoriated Senator Ribicoff, the man who helped make him famous, for surrendering to the auto industry.

There is one other story about the design and maintenance of automobiles that does not involve me personally, but has had a profound effect on my approach to my profession and life generally. Automobiles have thousands of parts and none of them will last forever. It is obvious, however, that the expected "lifetimes," of failure rates of different parts will vary significantly.

In any auto company, there is an ongoing effort to identify the anticipated lifetimes of the myriad parts (usually expressed in vehicle miles). The information can help to focus research efforts: for example, priority may be given to parts with the shortest anticipated life, or those whose failure carries the most serious consequences. The information can also shape design decisions: for example, those that normally will wear out the fastest, should be most readily accessible. Finally, the information can affect the terms of warranty guarantees or maintenance recommendations.

A common way to determine the "lifetime" or failure rates of various parts is to subject them to actual or simulated driving experiences over an extended period of time, and observe when they fail. This process is known as "testing to failure."

It has occurred to me that the concept of testing to failure is a useful metaphor for what life is all about. We never really know the limits of our capabilities if we haven't sometimes failed. Put another way, *all of us who have tried to live a full life will taste failure from time to time.* That is true, even if an individual has been spectacularly successful in the eyes of the world. I'll warrant that every President of the United States, or conspicuous business leader, knows what it is like to experience some bitter failures in public, professional or personal life.

Thomas Edison is said to have tested some 70 metals when he was attempting to create the first incandescent lamp, and none of them worked. A friend asked whether he was discouraged by the seeming waste of effort. Edison is said to have replied: "I haven't wasted my time; I've learned that these 70 won't work." And, then he tried tungsten.

I have identified a number of my own failures in these pages. Be assured that there are many more in my past, and there will be more in whatever time remains. Sometimes, my failures have taught me how to do better; sometimes they have simply made me aware of my limitations. The process of "education" never stops.

Before I conclude this summary of specific counseling experience at GM, I would like to spike a persistent myth. In GM's glory days, commentators sometimes said that the Corporation's antitrust lawyers would not allow it to capture more than a certain share - like 50% - of the U.S. auto market. This is simply not true; we saw no reason to do so, and an overall limit would be impossible to administer anyway.

In those days, GM had five separate auto divisions and each sold a large number of different models with varied competitive strengths in each sector. The GM divisions competed with each other, which complicated things. Consumer loyalty also varied across sectors. At the beginning of each model year, the Corporation's market share was not anything resembling 50%; it was essentially zero. Even if the lawyers had asked, there is no way that the Corporation's managers could orchestrate its competitive responses in each sector to yield some targeted overall market share.

Strategy

In the 1970s GM management was not only concerned about potential antitrust claims, but also with what appeared to be growing public cynicism about business generally. A huge and conspicuously profitable company like General Motors was particularly vulnerable to attack. My old law school classmate Ralph Nader was a leading business critic, and the mutual animus between Nader and GM was well known.

On any given day, pickets were parading up and down in front of GM's headquarters building in Detroit, calling for GM to display greater "Corporate Social Responsibility". The Corporation's shortcomings were variously defined as a failure to offer the products that customers "really want" and/or to take account of larger goals. In a short comment that I wrote at the time, I summed up the criticism as follows: [15]

> "What is really bothering these people? I do not believe they are mainly prompted by populist resentments, although populists are useful political allies. I suspect that basically they are hostile to the capitalist system itself and large companies serve as proxies vulnerable to attack ... They are repelled by a society that is shaped by mass-consumer choices, which they consider wasteful and tasteless, and they particularly blame those companies which have been most successful in accommodating, and to a degree encouraging these choices.

> ... By government regulation, or by interposition of special-interest directors, they would make corporations less responsive to market forces. It is politically prudent to claim corporate

managers are 'non-responsive' to the public, but the real complaint is that they are too responsive."

I was personally convinced - as were some of the leading economists who were advising us - that the "corporate responsibility" movement was just as great a potential threat as an antitrust "breakup" action. GM management had also recognized the threat as early as 1971, when I arrived in Detroit, and I was made a member of an internal study group assigned to make recommendations on how to deal with this animus. I never thought of this as a purely "legal" assignment, because the group was interdisciplinary As time passed, however, it seemed like there was a lot more "studying" than "doing".

GM lawyers and government relations people had traditionally advised inside and outside management to avoid public debate, on the theory that the less you say the less the risk of controversy. Corporate executives tended to be remote and noncommital. Public relations people wanted the company to say more, but tended to come up with slogans that sounded good but were actually dangerous.

For example, early attempts to respond suggested that GM's size and profitability actually enhanced its ability to be socially responsible: "We have to do well, in order to do good." This was a potential disaster, because it really sounded apologetic, and the public wasn't buying it. I commented openly at the time: "The implication was that the whole enterprise is rather a sordid preliminary but you, the public, should be willing to entrust surplus revenues to us so we can go out and help society with them." It's ridiculous.

There were other examples of wrong headed attempts to curry favor with corporate critics, which I tried to change - with only mixed success. For example when the Corporation elected its first minority director, and later its first female, the PR people proudly announced that they would "represent" black people and women on the Board. This, of course, is not true; every director is supposed to act for the benefit of all shareholders. It is not just a legal requirement, it is a matter of common sense. People with a special "life experience" - as members of a minority group or women in what was then a man's world - can be selected for that reason, in order to provide a new perspective. GM had named a Nobel Prize winner to the Board for the same reason, but no one would say that he was there to "represent" Nobel Prize winners.

There were lighter moments as well, in the midst of the "social responsibility" debate. Stewart Mott, a somewhat eccentric GM critic, attracted considerable attention because his nonagenarian father, Charles S. Mott, was a GM Director and reputed to be the largest individual shareholder in the Corporation. I remember one shareholders' meeting where Stewart Mott loudly berated GM management for its general neglect of social issues and its failure to actively oppose the war in Vietnam. There was a stunned silence, because of who he was and who his father was. Then Wilma Soss, a well-known and vocal advocate of shareholder rights, stood up and shouted: "Young man, why aren't you in the Army?" Wilma Soss had herself criticized GM management many times for what she perceived were bad business decisions, but she had no use for this social stuff. She was greeted with loud laughter and applause, and it was young Mott who stood stupefied.

In fairness, I should mention a successful sally from the other side, which was voiced at another shareholder meeting. Samuel McLaughlin, founder of the company that became GM Canada, lived to be 100 and served as a GM Director almost to the end of his life. When he finally retired, a spokesman announced with a straight face that, in deference to the youth movement, the Corporation now had only one director over the age of 90 (Mott). Whereupon a young man in the audience, dressed in the disreputable attire that was becoming fashionable, stood up, pumped his fist and shouted "Right On!" Again, loud laughter and applause.

Pardon the diversion, but we can't all be serious all the time.

Thomas A. Murphy, who was elected Chairman in 1977, was eager to engage in the public debate. He was anxious to become knowledgeable about public policy issues, and willing to take advice from lawyers and economists. His greatest asset was an engaging and self-deprecatory manner.

For example, the normal protocol in GM, as in other large organizations, was for juniors to come to the offices of seniors, but Tom Murphy used to wander over to the Legal Staff offices on short notice for informal meetings. This could lead to some amusing encounters.

One day, he asked for a brief meeting with those of us who advised on antitrust and marketing issues. A small group filed into a conference room, and one of our number happened to be wearing a really godawful suit with a checked pattern. Murphy stared a minute, and said: "Jim, I can see that you're anxious to get to the track. Don't worry, I won't be long." We never saw the suit again.

Because of my antitrust responsibilities, I began to get more and more requests for help in drafting policy statements for him, or op-ed pieces for newspapers and magazines. (Again, I never thought of this as a purely legal assignment.) I have a collection of statements I ghosted, which I will not try to summarize. There is, however, one fundamental theme that Mr. Murphy repeatedly wanted to emphasize; namely, the importance of consumer sovereignty. In 1975 he signed a lengthy letter in response to an article published by the historian Arthur Schlesinger, Jr. in the Wall Street Journal.

The article opens with a concession:

> "No one questions the need for government intervention in situations where one person's unrestricted freedom can seriously inhibit the rights of others. Some standards in areas like safety and environmental protection, for example, are necessary. The issues in these areas involve the levels of particular standards - the question of whether the cost to society exceeds their benefit."

The letter articulates a fundamental distinction between business "planning" and government "planning" that some influential people then (and now) were advocating in larger doses:

> "Unlike a business, a government may not only plan - it may also command … General Motors, for example, can and must plan for the future production of cars but, contrary to popular myth, cannot compel anyone to buy them. Moreover, we try to plan production on the basis of what we anticipate people will want, not according to our idea of what they ought to buy. Every rational business man knows that responding to consumer demand is more profitable than trying to change it."

Mr. Murphy's letter, then, expands on the virtues of consumer sovereignty:

> "Comprehensive national planning must ultimately involve the coercive powers of vast federal agencies which we must expect will be as remote from the influence of ordinary citizens as those which exist today.
>
> That remoteness, although our friends on the other side will never admit it, actually is the whole point of a planning scheme. If national planners merely ratified those allocations of resources which citizens themselves would choose, there would be no excuse for the planners' existence …
>
> The free-market system is the most responsive and finely tuned instrument of popular sovereignty that has ever been devised. Government is inherently clumsier - and less flexible. In the political system - citizens must delegate this sovereignty first to elected officials and these officials in turn delegate it to the actual administrators or "planners". A citizen can express his displeasure with their decisions, from which he is at least twice removed, only periodically in elections and then his particular disagreement

may be observed in a host of other issues embodied in the broad platforms on which candidates run.

In the market, however, the citizen participates directly in a continuing referendum, on every single item in a finely detailed platform. Moreover, unlike the political system, 'voters' with different ideas can each win ..."

(A critic will point out that consumer "votes" are not all equal because some have much larger resources than others. But, because people with different ideas can each "win", the market usually does provide high and low-priced alternatives. Moreover, it is has become increasingly obvious that "votes" are not really equal either. In the political arena, the voice of people with moderate views across the board tends to get drowned out by the voice of people who care passionately about selected issues.)

I cannot take credit for the origination of the ideas in this message. They are the fruits of lengthy discussions with a whole generation of public relations experts, economists and economically knowledgeable lawyers, whose names have been already mentioned. The remarkable thing is that one of the most prominent business leaders in the country at that time was willing to abandon GM's traditional reticence and engage in the public debate, over and over again.

My service as one of the prompters behind the curtain had its amusing moments, too. One day, GM's VP for Public Relations, and Tom Murphy's close confidant, sent me a memo that said something like "TM wants to make the following points in a speech; do you think these are good ideas?" I was rushed that day, and simply wrote my immediate and pungent reactions in the margin - including comments like "no, this is really stupid because..."

I assumed my good buddy on the PR Staff would sanitize my comments appropriately, but he must have been rushed that day, too, because he apparently just passed the annotated memo along. A few days later, Tom Murphy strolled into my office, completely unexpectedly, and said with a big smile:

"Tom, do you think I've done anything stupid today?" I couldn't figure out what he was talking about until after he had waved and walked out.

Later on, in the middle of a discussion about something else, Tom Murphy said: "Do you have any ideas on how I could do a better job?" I wasn't sure whether he was serious or not. And, besides, I thought it would be presumptuous for me, a relative neophyte in the industry, to offer advice to someone several ranks above me, with a lifetime of experience. (He wasn't asking for legal advice, an area in which I could claim some special knowledge.) I was really uncomfortable and said something like: "Are you serious?" He assured me that he was serious, and welcomed the thoughts of someone with a fresh eye.

This really put me on the spot. In fact, I did have some ideas, gleaned from discussions with some younger executives with serious worries about a number of growing threats. Increasingly stringent regulation of fuel economy and emissions did confer an advantage on foreign manufacturers which, because of the high price of gasoline in their markets, had far more experience in the manufacture of the smaller and lighter vehicles that the regulations would require. And, this was only part of the problem.

GM's costs were spiraling out of control, because both labor and management ranks were bloated and inefficient. The United Auto Workers had been able to negotiate wages, benefits and work rules that enabled assembly-line workers to live the middle-class dream - something that was regarded as enlightened industrial policy at the time but an increasing handicap in the face of intense foreign competition. And managers, regardless of competence, were really assured of lifetime employment with a company that we privately referred to as "Generous Motors", or simply as "Mother."

All U.S. manufacturers had similar cost-containment problems, but GM's problems were the most serious because the corporation was more "backward integrated" than any of its competitors. For many years it was thought that GM had a competitive advantage because it manufactured more of its components internally and indeed was able to supply these component parts to its competitors. (When I was there, for example, GM sold engines for Ford trucks and transmissions to Chrysler.)

Alfred Sloan, the management genius who guided GM in earlier years of the 20th century, used to say: "I like to make money on parts even when Mr. Ford sells his Lincolns." His general business philosophy was still studied with care in the Corporation.

Whatever competitive advantage the policy may have created in Mr. Sloan's time had eroded by the 1970s. It meant that GM's component parts - built by expensive UAW labor under benign management who worked for "Generous Motors" - were relatively far more costly than those that its competitors could obtain from lean and mean independent suppliers. Ultimately, it meant that GM, which sold more vehicles than any other manufacturer in the world, nevertheless had the highest per-unit costs. Anomalous, to say the least.

Tom Murphy had to have been aware of these looming problems, which I heard openly discussed at middle management levels, but I think that the pervasive GM culture shielded him from a full appreciation of how serious they were. GM encouraged its leaders to take pride in the Corporation's historic success, to continue policies that had worked so well in the past, and to avoid defeatist sentiments. People with a "can do" attitude seemed to climb the ladder, and communications with very top management seemed to become progressively more optimistic as they were edited on the way up.

(This is a common problem in many large organizations, private and public. Anyone who has read retrospective critiques of, say, The Bay of Pigs disaster in the early 1960s, or the very recent collapse of some financial institutions on Wall Street, is familiar with the tendency to dismiss the doubts of those who rain on the parade. They just aren't "team players.")

These are the kind of thoughts that were racing through my mind, when I became aware that the GM Chairman really was asking for my candid opinion. In retrospect, I think I took a cowardly way out - not that I delude myself today with the notion that anything I said off the cuff would really make a difference. Tom Murphy was always willing to take advice on legal matters or on public policy issues, but I had neither the experience nor the command of detail to converse specifically about the automobile business with the Chairman.

I decided to tell a story - a habit that has obviously persisted. I mentioned that when I was waiting for the attendants to fetch my own car in the executive garage, I would frequently see the Chairman's own driver loading two fat briefcases full of detailed reports into his car, for evening reading. I knew he read this material, too, because I sometimes had seen his meticulous edits. "Why don't you let someone else attend to those details," I said, "and spend your evenings reading stuff that might not have anything to do with our industry. Maybe, even a novel. It will clear your head."

He took it well, and said something like "That might be a good idea. I should try it." But he just couldn't change the habits of a lifetime. Shortly thereafter, I saw him in the garage again, with the two large briefcases in tow. I just assumed a sad expression and shook my head, and he smiled and threw up his hands, as if to say "I can't help myself."

I've waffled on so much about Tom Murphy because I admired him immensely and I've never had a better client. (He also was indirectly responsible for some interesting experiences that I had later in life.) He was one of the most respected business leaders of his time. Yet, his reputation has suffered in recent years because GM began its slow and painful decline so soon after he retired. Some of the Corporation's troubles have been attributed to events that no one in the industry could control. It has to be said, however, that for a time the quality of GM's products declined relative to that of its competitors, and it has been very difficult to recover from the resulting loss of public confidence. In the end, GM was done in less by government than by the free exercise of that customer sovereignty which Tom Murphy had so staunchly defended.

Murphy's immediate successor, Roger Smith, did have some of the visionary qualities that Murphy was unable to supply. He was a brilliant and far-seeing man, who did recognize the need for radical change in the Corporation's way of doing business. However, he had none of Tom Murphy's charm or charisma. In fact, he had a difficult personality. I will not provide specific examples out of respect for the charitable admonition: "De mortuis nil nisi bonum." It is enough to say that Roger's undeniable assets and liabilities sometimes resembled those of President Richard Nixon and, like Nixon, his term at the top was marred by controversies that could have been easily avoided.

I never had the same rapport with Roger Smith that I had with Tom Murphy. There was nothing personal about this because he kept all his lawyers at a distance. We were treated more as obstacles to be overcome than as oracles who can provide timely warnings of future consequences. This air of suspicion tended to affect the attitude of other managers down the line.

During Roger Smith's tenure as Chairman of General Motors, I gradually came to the conclusion that it would be best if I moved on. Personal pique probably played a part, but there were a number of independent reasons.

Final Days at GM

There were some rewarding experiences during my final years at General Motors. In 1977, I was promoted to Assistant General Counsel, and given oversight responsibility not only for antitrust matters but also for so-called Trade Regulation (Consumer Protection) issues, and Commercial Contracts (principally purchasing agreements). I had a team of outstanding experts in charge of each activity: Bob Weinbaum and Bill Slowey have already been mentioned. Bob succeeded me as the Attorney in Charge of Antitrust, and Bill took over the Commercial Contracts section. Frank Dunne, who had long experience dealing with the FTC, took charge of the consumer protection matters. I had full confidence that they all knew what they were doing.

Many of us in this group played together on the Legal Staff's softball team, and I still have a handsome plaque that they gave me for some now-forgotten accomplishment on the field. Softball was a big recreational activity at General Motors in those days, and we thought up imaginative names. (One girls' team called itself the "Chevy Pickups.") The comradery was still great, even though the business was terrible.

Books have been written about the decline of the domestic auto industry, so I'll just sum it up with a story. The Corporation enjoyed a brief recovery after the trauma of Arab oil boycotts in the early 1970s. In fact, during that brief recovery period, the Federal Trade Commission launched a massive investigation of the industry on the theory that domestic companies had a "shared monopoly" and enjoyed the excess profits that went with it. It looked like the long-feared breakup suit might soon be unleashed.

Tom Murphy, who was then still Chairman, asked me to provide an assessment of possible outcomes and likely costs of the battle. I had thought a lot about outcomes, but really had no ideas about possible costs. It occurred to me that I might get some help from people at IBM, which was still embroiled in its own monopolization case. I knew that they would be willing to share some information because GM bought a lot of data processing equipment from IBM, and we had actually provided helpful customer testimony in their battle.

One day I traveled to IBM's headquarters in Armonk, New York, and met with their legal staff people. They gave me a lot of useful information about their defense preparations, including the most sophisticated methods for keeping track of millions of documents. (With IBM equipment, of course.) They couldn't provide a precise figure on actual litigation costs, because of a broad court order on confidential information. But, they did give me an idea of outside legal fees, and said that 2000 (!) employees were assigned full time to the case. Some of these employees were very senior, indeed. I particularly remember the comment: "Suppose you have a guy who is on a career path that will probably lead to command of a major segment of the business. We are asking him to devote perhaps a decade to work on the defense of IBM's basic existence, knowing that a decade's absence will likely permanently affect his future progression. How much do you think we have to pay to make someone willing to do that?"

I reported all this to Tom Murphy on my return. On the elusive litigation cost estimate, I suggested "Why don't you just tell the Board that it will be somewhere in the nine-figure range." So, the adrenalin was up, just as it was in the Tonkin Gulf when war appeared imminent in 1954. But, the sense of emergency didn't last long.

The Commission's initial information request was massive. Production battles over same, and oral depositions, dragged on. By the time these preliminary skirmishes were winding down, the auto industry had crashed. GM no longer had to explain and defend its profits; it was incurring immense losses, in common with the other domestic competitors.

One evening, I was seated next to Robert Pitofsky at some Bar Association dinner. Bob was then a Federal Trade Commissioner, and considered to be a moderating influence in an institution then chaired by Michael Pertschuk. (I later served with Bob when he had returned as Chairman of the agency.) During the course of the dinner, I said: "This isn't the place to discuss it, but soon I would like to come down to Washington and talk to you about how we can wind up World War I." And, he said: "Odd that you should use that analogy; I said much the same thing at a meeting last week."

I was cautiously optimistic, but didn't say anything back in Detroit. Shortly thereafter, though, he called me and said something guarded like: "Do you remember our short talk at dinner? Watch the news." I knew then that the war was over, and so informed the management.

Exhilaration over the result was tempered by the realization that the fundamental rationale for my employment at GM had disappeared. Antitrust was no longer the major legal concern of the Corporation; other issues like cost containment, shareholder relations, product liability, labor relations, safety and environmental regulation were now more important. Day-to-day counseling on antitrust and consumer advertising issues was still needed at GM, as it is in any large corporation, but the battles on larger issues were over. With domestic austerity, the demands for "corporate social responsibility" had subsided. I felt that I was no longer close to the heart of the action.

Even though it was not a decisive factor, GM had stopped granting the year-end bonuses that depended on profitability, and I began to think I was underpaid rather than overpaid. I was senior enough to get stock options, but they were immediately underwater, and seemed likely to remain so. Morale of those around me was generally low. As I remarked at the time, "When I came over here, I felt like I'd been traded to the Yankees; now I feel like I'm playing for the Cubs."

There were rewarding professional activities that allowed me to learn new things, even as the antitrust pressures on GM were slackening. I had not been active in the ABA Antitrust Law Section after my experience as an associate assistant to Ed Barton, in the mid-1960s, when he was Chair of the Section. Some ten years later, I was encouraged to become active again, because the Section leaders wanted to broaden its appeal to in-house counsel. Section Chairs like Allen Holmes, Ira Millstern, Ed Rockefeller and Richard Pogue also happened to be among the thousands of outside lawyers who could call GM a client, and they made sure I was given interesting responsibilities from the start.

I was asked to Chair a newly created "National Institute" Committee, which was responsible for programs other than those at the annual Spring and Summer meetings.

As Chair of this Committee, I produced three Programs, beginning with one in 1977 on The Trial of an Antitrust Case. To my knowledge, this was the first Section program that actually involved lawyers playing a part, as counsel and as witnesses. We did not give them scripts, just a statement of facts and identification of the roles they were supposed to play. We had a real Federal

Judge on the bench. The fact that most of the dialogue was unrehearsed and spontaneous provided a sense of reality. This simulated trial attracted an audience of over 800 people, which I believe still holds the record for attendance at a program outside regularly scheduled annual meetings.

The two that followed on Grand Jury proceedings and Preventive Antitrust also included role playing. They did not draw as many people, but still made money for the Section. After that, I was made a member of the Section's governing Council, and served there for four years. GM's executives encouraged my ABA work because it provided an opportunity to identify talented lawyers who might be able to represent the Corporation as outside-counsel in the future. In my view, direct observation is still the best way to scout likely prospects.

Beyond that, I relied on recommendations from other lawyers whom I trusted. The Legal Staff also maintained loose leaf notebooks, indexed by city and state, that contained written comments of Staff members who had worked with outside lawyers in these various places. I never bothered to read the promotional material that firms were beginning to circulate. The Corporation also had stringent rules that ordinarily did not allow its employees to accept offers of entertainment from potential outside suppliers, including lawyers, and I really did not want to listen to sales spiels in any event. This experience, along with a generous measure of stubborn pride, probably explains why I really am not comfortable with the overt sales efforts that play such a prominent role in client relations today - even though I recognize the business pressures that prompt them.

Another rewarding activity that the Corporation encouraged was active participation in the affairs of an organization called The Business Roundtable. This is an Association of Chief Executives from the largest companies in the United States, across a wide range of industries. There were approximately 200 members in the 1970s, which have narrowed down to about 150 today. It differed from other business associations like the Chamber of Commerce or the National Association of Manufacturers, in that the CEOs themselves were expected to personally support the Roundtable's positions on various issues, in Washington and elsewhere, instead of relying on Association staff.

Tom Murphy served a term as Chairman of the Roundtable late in the 1970s, and because he held that position I became the co-head of a Committee that advised the CEOs on general competition issues. The other co-head was an outside lawyer on the scene in Washington. The outside lawyer at that time was Boyden Gray, a partner on the Wilmer, Cutler firm. Boyden later had an impressive public career, which included service as counsel for the first President Bush, when he was Vice President and President, and later as Ambassador to the European Union. It was a pleasure to work with Boyden. He taught me a lot about navigation in the Washington zoo, and I taught him some things about competition law. All in a spirit of adventure and high good humor.

When I joined a Washington firm myself in 1983, Boyden was working for the Vice President, and I became the outside counsel for the Roundtable's Committee on Competition Matters. It was a seamless transition, and the Roundtable became one of my most important clients in private practice. It makes sense to talk about the Roundtable in one segment, and will do so in the next Chapter of this memoir.

Before I conclude this Chapter on my experiences at General Motors, I have to pay tribute to another remarkable man, Otis Smith.

Otis had grown up in an educated family and modest means in Tennessee. He was of mixed race - with ancestors who were Black, American Indian and Irish. At the time and place where he grew up, however, he was officially Black and endured the usual indignities associated with that identification.

Like many men of imposing stature, Otis Smith spoke with a soft voice and a modest demeanor. (Big guys probably learn at an early age that listeners will recoil if they come on too strong.) He had no patience whatever for the turf battles and self-seeking behavior that seems to be endemic in large public and private institutions. On his office wall, there was a framed motto that read:

> "There are no limits on what we can accomplish, as long as we don't care who gets the credit."

I'm sure this was not original, but I've never been able to track it down. I've never forgotten the message, however, and it expresses an ideal that I have attempted to follow in my own life.

Our society seems increasingly focused on assigning "credit" for accomplishments, or on who or what institution is "number one" or in the "top ten" on somebody's list. Bonuses and business opportunities can depend on these things, even though it really is arbitrary to credit people or rank them so precisely. It just reflects the current obsession with celebrity. The pronoun "I" appears a lot in this memoir, because I am talking about things that I witnessed or personally did. And, I have won some prizes, too. But, I know that any recognition I may have had is largely attributable to the efforts of a lot of other people - in addition to random chance or accident.

Otis Smith taught me that, by words and by example.

Otis' liberation from the burdens of racial stereotypes began in World War II, when he served with the famous Tuskegee Airmen. He went to College on the G I Bill, and later graduated from the Law School at Catholic University in Washington, D.C. He became active in Democratic politics in the State of Michigan, and eventually served on the Supreme Court of the State. He was then recruited by General Motors, officially to head the Corporation's in-house general litigation team, and unofficially to provide advice to senior management on public issues.

Otis was a very large and powerful man, with quiet dignity. He was not embarrassed by references to his racial identification, but never sought any special consideration on account of it. "In all candor," he once said to me, "it was a considerable handicap early in my life, but it has been an asset in later years." He also confided, however, that he really could not identify closely with any race - partly because of his mixed ancestry. He did not like to see black people acting out old fashioned stereotypes, but he was equally turned off by aggressive promoters of Black Pride. Otis really believed in a color-blind society, where race or ethnicity played no part in employment decisions - either positively or negatively.

Otis and I enjoyed each other's company immensely, and had many lengthy discussions on the general state of the world. Despite our different political affiliations, we agreed on almost everything that was important. When Frazer Hilder retired as General Counsel, Otis succeeded to the title. He then officially became my boss, but our relationship continued much as before. He readily admitted that he knew very little about what I was doing, and I actually wrote legal opinions and speeches for him when he was called on to address matters in my area of competence.

In his final years at GM, Otis began to suffer from a variety of ailments. I began to fill in for him on out-of-town speaking engagements when he did not feel up to the trip. On one of these substitute appearances, I had a humbling experience that I have never forgotten.

He asked me to sub for him on a speech to an intellectually oriented group in the "Comstock Club", located in Sacramento, California. We had agreed that it would be a good idea to address the inevitable disconnect between the separate pressures on politicians and on business people. I had written a speech titled "A Rational Look at Regulation" - originally for him - which concluded with a statement that:

> "[T]he most rational view of government regulation is that it will never be entirely rational. Like so many other accommodations in our pluralistic society, it will continue to be a product of uneasy compromise, rather than a rigorous logic. We can improve the process only if we are wise enough to realize that we can never perfect it."

That's pretty non-controversial, and I doubt that many people would dispute it today. Since the talk would be delivered in California, however, we also decided to make specific comments on the environmental quality issue, which was a big concern in California, then and now. So, the body of the speech refers to this specific example:

> "[T]here is universal agreement that market forces alone cannot
> deal with pollution of the environment. If an industrial plant
> throws off waste into the surrounding air and water, it can impose
> costs that are not borne by the plant itself or by its custom-
> ers; there are side effects that ordinary economic forces will not
> ameliorate."

Speakers who take the trouble to look at the people in the audience - something that I think is pretty basic - can always tell whether they are receptive or resistant. This all was going over fine, so I decided to drive the point home in a more pointed way. I ad-libbed something like: " Since neither the buyers nor the sellers want to pay for the damage, it makes no more sense to blame 'greedy' manufacturers than it would be to blame 'greedy' consumers."

This went down pretty well, too. And, the later questions were friendly, so I thought I was on a roll. At the end of the session, I was approached by a young man with a mike and another guy with one of those big video cameras on his shoulder. He complimented me on a very interesting talk, and asked whether I would answer some questions for a local TV station. Full of myself, I said "certainly".

He started off by asking: "Did I hear you right when you said that these serious environmental problems we have here in California are the fault of greedy consumers?" I was paralyzed! The first thought that ran through my mind was "I'm going to be fired the minute I get back to Detroit." As second thoughts, I started to think about where I would get another job; how the family would react to another move; the process of selling the house, etc., etc.

I don't know how long this state of stupefaction persisted, or what response I managed to babble out. Probably said something like: "You have to take the remark in full context." In any event I needn't have worried. The TV station may not have played the interview, or maybe no one employed by GM saw it or particularly cared. I never heard any more about it.

Ever since that time, however, I have had sympathy for politicians who have to worry about this sort of thing all the time. It explains why they take refuge in such bland platitudes.

Back to Otis Smith. I did not pick up any technical knowledge from Otis, but by speech and attitude he taught me what the practice of law was all about. I think the best way to sum up what I learned is to quote at length from a tribute I wrote when Otis retired, two years after I had resigned from GM. He deserves it.

> "Otis Smith has many outstanding qualities and other people will undoubtedly be able to speak of them far better than I can. There is one quality, however, which impressed me most in the years that I was privileged to know him and work with him. I have never known anyone who cared more about people as individuals and who tried harder to help people achieve their maximum potential.
>
> This concern manifested itself in many ways. As head of the Legal Staff, Otis had the largest responsibilities of all - but he knew every single employee on the Staff by name and paid more attention than anyone else to individual problems, however small they may have seemed. Whenever a decision had to be made, his first concern was always for its impact on people.
>
> This human touch is what made him a fine judge, a fine lawyer and also a fine teacher. Otis taught us that legal rules, even as applied to vast enterprises, are crafted by people and have their impact on people. He never let us forget that legislators and

judges and juries are primarily responsive to human concerns, not technical abstractions. And he reminded us again and again that we didn't really represent a huge, insensate organization, but rather that we represented over a million people who had entrusted their fortunes to its care. I believe that these appreciations, subtle as they may be, are largely responsible for that rare blend of common sense and dedication which Otis inspired in the Legal Staff."

There is one additional fond memory of Otis that I didn't put in the letter, but probably should have. We once attended a dinner where my wife Stephanie was the featured speaker. Otis later said to me: "Tom, I've heard you speak a number of times, and you're pretty good. But your wife is even better." Spot on.

Otis lived with the pain of metastesizing cancer in the last few years of his life, and secluded himself from the world. Some years after I had left GM, I was in Detroit on a business trip, and decided to venture a call to his home. He seemed cheerful on the phone and said that, even though he didn't normally see people outside his immediate family, he would make an exception for me. We scheduled a visit for the following day. But he called early the next morning and said he really felt too sick for company. With mutual regrets, we said goodbye.

Otis Smith died two weeks later. He was a great man. R.I.P.

The last major project that I worked on for General Motors was the joint production venture between GM and Toyota. In the 1970s any kind of joint venture between these two huge auto companies would have been unthinkable. In the early 1980s, however, the U.S. automobile industry was in the doldrums, and judicial interpretations of the antitrust laws had become more flexible. I thought a well designed venture could pass muster.

The venture offered advantages for both companies. GM would be able to learn some production methods from a company that had many more years of experience in the manufacture of smaller automobiles that the market was then demanding. Toyota would gain experience in the manufacture of cars in the United States before it ultimately entered the country on its own.

The key legal provisions that I suggested for the venture were a finite termination date; sale of the identical product to GM and Toyota dealerships under a pricing formula that specifically excluded sales prices for other vehicles that the two companies sold independently; and a firm firewall between venture management and the management of the owners. My job was not only to design these and other parameters but also to explain them to the Japanese partners who were naturally not particularly familiar with U.S. antitrust law.

A Toyota delegation came to Detroit, to discuss these aspects of the deal. I don't remember much about the business discussions, except that they were very formal, and time consuming. At that time the day started out with set speeches on either side, with translations in between, and stilted exchanges throughout. However, I do remember an amusing exchange at a concluding social event that Otis Smith hosted.

At the beginning, this story may read like I am making fun of a Japanese gentleman's struggles with the English language. I emphasize, however, that his facility with English was far more impressive than my facility with Japanese - which was and is, frankly, nonexistent. And, as you will see, the joke ultimately was on me.

At one point in the reception, the General Counsel of Toyota, a very short man, walked over, peered up and me and said: "Mr. Weary, you remind me so much of my revered teacher Professor Yamashita." Well, I didn't know who Professor Yamashita was, but it sounded like a compliment to me. Unwisely, I decided to milk it.

I asked: "In what way do I remind you of Professor Yamashita?" I wanted to hear something about wisdom or eloquence, and had completely forgotten that seasoned trial lawyers always caution against asking that final question when you don't know the answer. "Mr. Weary," he replied, "you wook so much like Professor Yamashita!"

I don't know how I avoided the impulse to crack up on the spot, but I later told the story with great relish to fellow members of the Staff. I guess you can imagine what happened thereafter. For the balance of my stay at GM, when I passed any of these clowns in the hall, they were apt to say something like: "Good morning, Professor Yamashita." Then, as we passed close, they would feign embarrassment and say: "Oh, sorry, Tom, you wook so much like him."

There were a lot of feelings associated with my decision to leave GM, if a good alternative became available. Even today, I miss the exhilaration of those early days when the company was on a roll, and I felt like a king of the road driving all those new models in a car-crazy town. I have maintained contact with some old friends there; I still buy GM cars, and try to get one when I need a rental car. So, I am glad to conclude this chapter of my GM years with a tale that illustrates a light side of the experience.

A WASHINGTON LAWYER

Although I was convinced by the year 1982 that GM's most critical legal problems would lie well outside my areas of special competence, and the number of lawyers in my antitrust group was shrinking, there was no immediate emergency. I could take my time exploring other opportunities. I quietly informed a number of Bar leaders whom I had come to know over the years that I was not actively "looking" for a new situation but "listening" to find out what options might be available.

As anticipated, I began to get some exploratory calls from legal headhunters. Most of them were attempting to fill General Counsel or Associate General Counsel slots in major corporations, not law firms. Thirty years ago, it was common to move from a law firm to a corporate staff, as I had done, but movement in the other direction was rare. Nothing particularly exciting had turned up - but then something unusual happened.

I got a call from a headhunter who said he was acting on behalf of a major law firm in Washington, D.C. that was looking for a senior antitrust lawyer. He was calling me because I was then a member of the governing Council of the ABA's Antitrust Law Section, and might be able to identify some likely prospects for him. (To this day, I don't know whether he really wanted my recommendations, or whether this was just a discreet way to sound me out.) He didn't identify the name of the firm, but said that was one of the largest in the City and that its most senior antitrust partner was approaching the retirement age of 70. The next most experienced partners were about 30 years younger, which left a demographic gap.

The more he described the opportunity, the more appealing it sounded to me. I traveled a lot to Washington on GM business, was familiar with the City, and liked it. So, I broke in and said "I might be interested myself." And, the mating dance began - although I still did not know the name of my prospective dance partner. All I knew at first was that I was about the right age (51).

I don't remember how many exploratory discussions we had, sharing information, before he said he was acting on behalf of the Hogan & Hartson firm. I first met with Lee Loevinger - then the most senior antitrust partner - as he was passing through the airport in Detroit on a business trip. I then met with Marty Michaelson, a younger antitrust partner, in a D.C. hotel when I was in town on a business trip of my own. I later was interviewed individually by members of the firm's Executive Committee, then with other young antitrust partners, had a dinner with some of the firm's most senior partners outside the antitrust field, and finally met all the partners at a special reception.

I kept Otis Smith, my boss in Detroit, generally informed while all this was going on. There was some mutual sadness, but he understood my reasons and also agreed not to say anything to GM's top management until the process was concluded, one way or another. Finally, the deal was struck and it was agreed that I would resign from GM as of December 31, 1982, and become a Hogan & Hartson partner as of January 1, 1983.

As I look back almost thirty years on this decision, I am convinced that it was the right thing to do. My departure from GM opened running room for some of my valued colleagues there, including particularly Bob Weinbaum who assumed many of my responsibilities. The move to Washington opened new professional vistas for me, and has enriched my life ever since.

The personal aspects of the move were far more untidy. For complicated reasons that have nothing to do with my education as a lawyer, Stephanie and I had grown apart and I moved to Washington alone. In an odd way, our experiences when living separate lives ultimately brought us closer together, and made it possible for us to remarry in 1991. "Our divorce just didn't work out," is the way that Stephanie now explains our unusual marital history - and I can't do any better than that.

So, late in the year 1982, at the age of 51, I drove down to Washington alone to begin a new life with just about everything I owned stowed in my car. In retrospect, I think part of me was just like every other middle-aged man who wanted to recapture his youth - but, with a much more interesting job than most young people can aspire to and, of course, a larger disposable income. Pretty childish, actually.

Introduction to the Hogan Firm

There were about 150 lawyers in Hogan & Hartson when I joined the firm, which was roughly the same size as White & Case when I left in 1971 and the GM Legal Staff. Early on, I was given a loose-leaf notebook with a picture and brief bio of every lawyer in the firm. I studied the notebook assiduously in my spare time and after a few weeks, I was able to recognize all of the partners and most of the associates when I passed them in the hall.

The overall atmosphere was friendly and informal, and the governance loose by present standards. There was a "Managing Partner", Bob Odle, who also served as a business manager. Bob was very careful to defer to the judgment of an elected five-person Executive Committee, who served for a limited term and were also subject to term limits. For example, he did not chair meetings of the partners; Executive Committee members did on a rotating basis. (Bob actually had more influence than he appeared to have, because he was the one with the most comprehensive institutional memory - but he tried not to show it.)

There was somewhat more intra-partner "competition" than I experienced in a Wall Street firm in the late 1960s, but far less than the level that prevails today in almost every firm in the country. I am really not able to say whether the ramped up financial pressure results in better client service, but I doubt that major law firms could do anything about it even if a majority of the partners would prefer a somewhat less stressful life. It's a more competitive world all way round, not only because of ever increasing international competition but also because we white males are no longer the only competitors.

My new partners went out of their way to make me welcome; many invited me to dinner in their homes. I still have vivid memories of one such evening. The conversation was lively; the main course was excellent; and I eagerly awaited the dessert course to satisfy my sugar craving. The dessert was a fruit plate! Fine, as a first course, but no substitute for chocolate at the end of a meal. I was beginning to think of a polite way to leave early and pick up some ice cream on the way home.

While I was pondering this weighty problem, I excused myself to go to the lavatory. There was a small dish on the sink that held a group of small round brown balls. "Odd place to keep the chocolates," I thought, "but thank God I found them." Desperate people do not always think clearly. I promptly popped one into my mouth. It was a piece of soap, of course, and the taste was pretty bad. So I quickly drank a glass of water which naturally set me to foaming at the mouth! A great way to make a good impression on my new colleagues.

Fortunately, a few fast rinses seemed to alleviate the problems, and I returned to the table - hoping that my hosts and fellow guests would overlook the occasional stray bubble. And, as it turned out, the final, final course was a platter of chocolate candies, so my panic was unwarranted.

Over the years, I have tried to come up with a life lesson that justifies my fondness for this little story. One could conclude that patience is sometimes rewarded or, more specifically, that hosts are unlikely to set out bonbons in the guest lavatory. A useful piece of information.

The Business Roundtable

While I was at GM I had spent a considerable amount of time on work for this group of CEOs from the largest companies in America. The Roundtable also became my very first client at Hogan & Hartson. In fact, I was asked to work on a Roundtable project on the day that I joined the firm. In a relatively short period of time, I became the lead "outside" advisor on competition law matters, succeeding Boyden Gray with whom I had worked when I was the chief "inside" advisor. (Boyden had, in the meantime, entered public service as counsel for then Vice President George H.W. Bush.) My involvement in Roundtable matters continued until I entered public service myself almost 17 years later, and I never had a more rewarding client.

The Roundtable had a business model that differed from that of other large associations in Washington. The CEO members not only played an active part in policy decisions but were also expected to meet with lawmakers personally, instead of relying on the organization's permanent staff. The theory was that the chief officer of a large employer in any state or congressional district will at least get a respectful reception from elected representatives. This does not mean that the elected officials will necessarily agree, but they will be willing to listen. I was frequently asked to accompany the CEO, on these calls, in order to provide whatever legal advice or arguments might be needed.

The Roundtable was also highly selective in choosing issues that it would lobby, and did not focus on the parochial interests of a particular company or industry. It did not expend effort on causes that were futile from the outset, and framed its arguments in ways that would appeal to large segments of the public.

Notice that I did not use the term "public interest" here, because I really believe that it is a meaningless term. The first so-called "public interest" advocates were identified with the left, but there are now advocates on the right who also claim to represent the "public interest." The population is an aggregation of people with a variety of often-conflicting private interests and the challenge is to find solutions that will increase, or at least maintain, some overall level of satisfaction – even though no one group is likely to get exactly what it wants.

My job as outside counsel for the Roundtable in competition matters was, first, to decide whether we could mount respectable arguments on this higher level and, second, to write briefing materials for the business people who would actually carry the message. This job was very similar to my service as a sometime ghostwriter for Tom Murphy or Otis Smith at General Motors. In fact, some aspects of the job reminded me of my Navy days when I was supposed to act as "the enemy's representative on the Commander's Staff" - which is another way of saying that I had to take a larger view.

I believe that The Business Roundtable had an enhanced measure of credibility in Washington because of this internal discipline and because of the celebrity of some of its CEO members. Let me tell a story that illustrates the point. The incident actually occurred while I was still at GM, but my work for the Roundtable did not change all that much when I moved to Washington.

Late in the Administration of President Jimmy Carter (1977-1981), a prominent Democratic Congressman introduced legislation that would create antitrust liability for *any* merger or acquisition by a company with annual sales above a certain size. Anticompetitive consequences were conclusively presumed. Roundtable advocacy had to focus on Democrats because the party controlled the Administration and both houses of Congress. In the Carter years, however, there was an odd division of authority in the Democratic party, because the "White House" staff sometimes took positions at variance with those advocated by leading Democrats elsewhere in the Administration and on the Hill.

The Roundtable needed to solicit the views of Stuart Eizenstat, the President's Chief Advisor on Domestic Policy. The chosen messenger was Irving Shapiro, the CEO of the DuPont Company and a prominent supporter of Democratic causes. I was asked to brief Mr. Shapiro on the antitrust principles involved and to accompany him as an advisor at a meeting with Stuart Eizenstat in the West Wing.

My unaided memory after over 30 years is that Eizenstat came to the meeting alone. After introductions and a few polite exchanges, Irving Shapiro began his presentation, roughly as follows:

"Young man, you are not old enough to remember the Second World War, but I am sure you know that the massive productive capacity of the United States is what turned the tide in that War. Almost every one of the major companies that made those weapons of war was put together by a series of large acquisitions, and none of them would have had these critical capabilities if misguided legislation like this had been the law at the time." I then joined the conversation, and outlined the details of the proposed law.

I cannot imagine that any lobbyist or trade association official would have the self confidence and the gravitas to talk that way to the Chief Domestic Advisor of the President of the United States. Shortly after this meeting, we learned that the "White House" would not support the broad anti-merger legislation, and it quietly died.

This experience taught me a valuable lesson that I have applied in the service of other clients in other settings. An articulate and respected CEO can be a very persuasive advocate. For example, if a merger proposal is pending before one of the antitrust agencies, I have often brought the client's CEO in for an early meeting with staff. It conveys the message that this transaction is important for the company, and also conveys the message that staff members are themselves important. (I would not recommend, however, that any CEO today emulate Mr. Shapiro's avuncular and almost patronizing approach. He obviously had a special relationship with White House Staff.)

Experience with The Business Roundtable further reinforced my strong preference for cooperation and compromise rather than combat. The members of the Roundtable are the CEOs of the largest businesses in the country. Big business obviously cannot accomplish anything in the political arena by naked appeals to self interest; it needs allies. And, this means that big business advocates cannot maintain consistent ideological purity, and have to recognize that it is often better to accept a half a loaf today rather than battle for a full loaf tomorrow. A few examples will illustrate the principle.

The Reagan landslide in 1980 gave the Republican party a Senate majority after years of Democratic control. This meant that Senators Thurmond and Hatch had the helm on antitrust policy rather than Senators Kennedy and Metzenbaum, and the Roundtable had a window of opportunity to play offense after years on the defense. Senator Thurmond let it be known that he was willing to be helpful, but cautioned that he was not interested in a drawn-out battle over antitrust issues at the beginning of the term. Those of us who acted as Roundtable advisors were asked to come up with something that would be relatively non-controversial.

We unanimously concluded that the best strategy would be all-out support for the so-called "Bayh Bill." Senator Birch Bayh of Indiana (father of Governor, and later Senator Evan Bayh) was a moderate Democrat who had introduced a bill to soften the impact of joint and several liability on antitrust defendants. The principle of joint and several liability in tort law, familiar to any lawyer, means that a single wrongdoer can be liable for the full damages caused by a group. This principle, applied in the context of a civil damage complaint against the participants in a price-fixing conspiracy, means that the plaintiff can recover full treble damages from a single member of the group, irrespective of that member's contribution to the overall harm. It is not necessary to recover from, or even sue, them all.

This principle, when applied to the increasingly popular class actions, can confer an immense bargaining advantage on counsel for the plaintiff class. Consider the simplified example of a claim for $100 million against five sellers in an industry, where each has a 20% share of sales. Plaintiff counsel can offer a relatively generous settlement to those who are willing to accept early. If three of the five settle for, say $10 million apiece rather than an equal $20 million "share", the remaining two defendants are now potentially liable for $70 million, rather than $40 million. Holdouts face ever-increasing pressures. There were well-publicized examples of relatively small companies that claimed they had not done anything wrong but were nevertheless forced to pay larger total damages than larger and arguably more culpable companies who had settled early.

The Bayh Bill, or an even simpler "claim reduction" alternative, would each assure that the final liability of individual companies was commensurate with their market shares. There was some bipartisan support - Senator Bayh was, after all, a Democrat. It looked like Senator Thurmond could get the early bloodless victory that he wanted.

Than, in the last lap, opposition came from an unexpected quarter. The Bayh Bill, as usual, would only apply to future lawsuits; it would not apply to actions already brought. This meant it would do nothing for those companies whose visible exposure to potentially crushing damages had given impetus to the Bill in the first place. Counsel for these companies informed the Roundtable, and other business groups who had joined the initiative that they would actively oppose the Bill unless it were made retroactive.

Retroactive legislation is a very hard sell. For one thing, it can open up the prospect of lengthy Constitutional battles in court. The most experienced lobbyists in our number warned this retroactivity would be a "killer" amendment. I can remember lengthy and acrimonious arguments in which the larger group pleaded with representatives of the objecting companies to back off; if the objectors persisted, the whole initiative would crash and they wouldn't get what they wanted anyhow. Furthermore, we would embarrass potential allies, like Senator Thurmond, who had been assured of an early victory.

In the end, the objectors wouldn't back off; the initiative failed; and Senator Thurmond inevitably became more wary of business initiatives.

An almost identical scenario played out again a few years later. The Racketeer Influenced And Corrupt Organizations Act C ("Rico") [16], as the name suggests, was passed to make it easier to prosecute the concerted activities of organized crime. The language of the law, however, is broad enough to apply to legitimate businesses that are accused of criminal conspiracies, like antitrust offenses. Again, the Roundtable and other business groups were able to muster strong support for an amendment that would limit RICO to its intended use as a weapon against organized crime. Again, we were very close to victory. Again, a number of firms who had already been sued for RICO offenses threatened to oppose current legislation unless it were made retroactive. Again, our experienced lobbyists advised that retroactive legislation would never pass. The same bitter internal arguments ensued; opponents would not back down; and predictably, RICO reform died.

I do not remember other examples of battles lost over the retroactivity issue, but I do remember a number of occasions when defeat was snatched from the jaws of victory because some holdouts insisted that the consensus remedy was not strong enough and that, with a little more effort, it could be improved. (Federal tort reform is one example that comes to mind.)

Those who want to continue the fight will frequently claim that, even if the pursuit of a more difficult objective may take longer, "we'll always have the issue next year." The problem with this rationale, of course, is that the issue is not necessarily live next year. Congress may have moved on to other things that seem more pressing at the time. The business community missed the boat on joint liability and RICO reform, and the opportunity never arose again.

A cynic might say that the preference of some lobbyists (and litigating lawyers) for longer battles is purely economic: the longer the fight, the larger the income flow. I don't think this is a primary reason, however. The best lobbyists and litigators always have enough work to do. In our society, however, the drive for perfection is considered to be an admirable thing. From earliest childhood, we are led to believe life is a struggle between heroes and villains, and those who settle for half-way measures are not heroes.

Sir Winston Churchill - a great, if not the greatest hero of the last century - once famously said: "Never give in, never give in, never, never, never, never … " Since the quoted speech was given in October 1941, people naturally admire his defiant stance in the darkest days of World War II. The appropriate stance in a battle against someone like Adolf Hitler or similarly uncompromising and untrustworthy tyrants, however, is not necessarily appropriate in political disputes with our own countrymen. Even Churchill's repeated "nevers" were bounded. The quoted passage itself ends with a qualification: "Never give in except to convictions of honor *and good sense.*" (Emphasis supplied.)

A dose of "good sense" sometimes suggests that the best strategy is to avoid a battle altogether. The Roundtable tried very hard to maintain good relations across the political spectrum. One way to do that is to ignore issues that are not of immediate concern to the business community. The so-called "social issues" are highly divisive, even among the Roundtable members themselves. I do not remember that the organization ever addressed these matters. We might, for example, quietly support a nominee who was thought to be reasonable on economic issues, albeit highly controversial in other areas. Some people probably have no idea that they got this kind of help, and that's a good thing. (When I later got a federal appointment myself, the identity of some supporters was obvious - but I really did not want to know about all of them.)

Representation of any client is a learning experience. Clients have paid me for advice; I "teach" them some things. It is a two way process, however. In the process of consultation, clients necessarily "teach" me about their business. In my years as an antitrust lawyer, I have had to become immersed in everyday businesses like ice cream or fast-food and exotic businesses like micro-surgical instruments or space rockets. The Business Roundtable is an organization that analyzes public policy questions of interest to its members, solicits their views and then collectively supports helpful legislation and, equally important, opposes legislation that the members consider harmful. The members and their hired outside consultants "lobby" - an activity that is today popularly considered disreputable but is, in fact, essential. This is an activity that was entirely new to me; I had to learn the rules of the game.

Because I so frequently accompanied Business Roundtable members and/ or their internal government representatives on visits to various Senators and Representatives, I had to register as a lobbyist myself and file quarterly reports for many years. Nevertheless, I never pretended to be part of the experienced "Washington" crowd; most of these legislators probably wouldn't have any reason to remember who I was, even if I did a lot of the talking. I was not at all interested in the Washington social scene - the endless series of receptions where legislators and the real lobbyists go simply to meet and greet, or be seen by, the same people that they saw and greeted at another reception yesterday or earlier on the same day.

The actual visits on the Hill did, however, cause me to temper some of my previous cynicism about the legislative process. Most of the legislators come across as highly dedicated and intelligent people, with views that are far more subtle and nuanced than you might gather from their public statements. They are expected to take positions on an incredibly broad spectrum of issues because the federal government, for better or worse, is omnipresent in our society. They depend on outside sources of information on issues, and lobbyists are an invaluable source of information. Any elected official who says that he/she will never have any communication with lobbyists is either a liar or a fool.

The public impression, fostered by lurid tales of excess, seems to be one that legislator-lobbyist interactions are simple exchanges of money for the promise of a vote. That impression is simply wrong. The typical "meeting" is more like a seminar, with intelligent questions and explanations. Problems and differences are openly aired, but in a mutually respectful way. It is understood that the discussions are generally "off the record" - not because sinister things are buried - but because people may make tentative admissions of doubt or concessions that they may later have to retract. It is sometimes rather like a settlement discussion in litigation.

In the 1980s and early 1990s, when I was most actively involved in legislative matters, I was also struck by the way legislators relied on their peers for leadership on various issues. Senator A would candidly admit that Senator B (who was not always a member of the same party) followed competition issues a lot more closely, and advise us that we might count on two votes if we could persuade Senator B.

There were also a lot of personal friendships that crossed party lines. Perhaps the best known example was the close bond between Senators Kennedy and Hatch - commonly believed to occupy opposite edges of the political spectrum. Lobbyists had to be acutely aware of these ties, not because the two friends would necessarily vote together all that often, but because you had to be careful to talk about principles rather than personalities.

I am not sure that cross-party ties are generally as close as they used to be. People who are still familiar with the legislative process (I'm not) tell me that Congress is a lot more polarized today, and that's one reason why the government so often seems paralyzed.

Beginning during my tenure at General Motors and continuing when I moved to Hogan & Hartson, my close association with The Business Roundtable lasted for a quarter century.

Sam Maury and Pat Engman, successive executive Directors in Washington, were the face of the "client" and people to whom I was directly responsible. I also worked closely with some CEOs, like Tom Murphy at GM and later George Stinson, CEO of National Steel and John Ong, CEO of B.F. Goodrich. Some inside counsel for member companies, like my old GM colleague Bob Weinbaum and John Heider of Goodrich were particularly active. Fellow outside consultants like my predecessor Boyden Gray and veteran lobbyists Emory Sneeden and Charles Bangert taught me a lot about the ways of Washington. Many of these people became personal friends, and we often had lunches and dinner - sometimes with spouses - just for the fun of it.

Strong impressions remain. The U.S. Capitol office buildings have an aura all their own. The young Congressional aides are unfailingly enthusiastic, polite and helpful regardless of political affiliation. Before we met with the boss, they were apt to draw us aside and tell us that their Senator or Congressman was particularly concerned about some particular aspects of an issue, and advise on how best to handle the meeting.

One particularly helpful aide to a Senator who had served with distinction for a long time - in fact, much too long a time - would sometimes call in advance and say: "The Senator is a bit detached today; perhaps we should postpone." Later on, the Senator might be "present" again.

Congressional Hearings were always an event; I accompanied witnesses to a lot of them, and sometimes testified myself on those rare occasions when the competition issue was particularly abstruse. The word "testify" can be misleading. Legislators sometimes are actually in search of information but often they simply want to make speeches for the benefit of the folks back home, or berate a particular witness who represents a company or a cause that the legislator publicly opposes. (The same legislator may have been perfectly polite in private.) The witness' primary challenge may be to simply maintain his cool and his courage.

John Ong, the CEO of Goodrich, was better at this than anyone I have ever seen. Whatever the pyrotechnic display, he would sit with a benign expression on his face, as much at ease as he would be in his own living room. When his turn to reply came, John would simply ignore any irrelevant invective, and say something like: "Senator, I understand your point of view, but this time I just can't agree with you." Then, would follow a succinct summary of his reasons. All, in a pleasant tone of voice. Even the most hostile questioner can't make much headway against a guy so affable and unflappable.

Overall, the representation of the Roundtable was a rewarding experience. We won more than we lost, but the count may be misleading because we tended to avoid battle or to propose a compromise on issues that we knew we would otherwise lose. Actually one of the battles that we lost was one that turned out well, after all. In retrospect I think our position was wrong. The matter will be discussed in a later subsection.

Roundtable representation was a high visibility assignment in the business community generally, and I am sure it enhanced the prestige of the firm. Unlike work on a massive case, however, it was not all that lucrative. For the most part, the client was paying for the services of a single individual, and there wasn't much for younger assistants to do. As we moved into the 1990s I was able to introduce the client to Janet McDavid, a younger partner who could fill in whenever I was unavailable. She did a fine job for the Roundtable - as she has done for so many other clients in her magnificent career - and assumed full responsibility for Roundtable matters when I entered government service in 1999. In my view, older lawyers should always provide for an orderly succession, because none of us knows what the future holds.

I also cannot identify any clients who were attracted to me personally, or to the firm at large, because of the high visibility representation, although I am sure there are some. I had to be careful to avoid the impression that I was trolling for clients in the large business community with which I was closely involved. I think part of my credibility with inside counsel for Roundtable members was based on a sense that I understood their challenges as someone who had been " one of them" in the recent past. And, outside counsel for Roundtable companies would be less likely to accept me as a chair of the Lawyers' Advisory Committee if I were perceived to be in open competition with them.

The Roundtable always paid our bills promptly, without fuss. Since I probably acquired as much learning from this client as I dispensed, however, it probably would have been a pretty good deal even if I had worked for free.

Rail Merger Cases

In the mid-1980s, I became deeply involved in a series of railroad mergers cases before the now-defunct Interstate Commerce Commission ("ICC"), which are memorable for a number of reasons. One reason is purely historical; I had an opportunity to participate actively in the low-key, almost stately proceedings of what was then the oldest independent regulatory agency in the country. (The ICC was created in 1887. The Federal Trade Commission, which dates from 1915, is now the oldest.) It was a pleasure to work with, and to oppose, some old ICC hands who taught me the rules of the game.

Second, our client was one of the richest men in the world, and it was fascinating to get an up-close glimpse of entrepreneurial talent. And, finally, some limitations of economic theory were illustrated in a more vivid way than I had ever experienced before.

The client was Rio Grande Industries, parent company of the Denver and Rio Grande Railroad, which then provided passenger and freight service in the states of Colorado, New Mexico and Utah. It was owned by a reclusive billionaire, Phillip Anschutz. The Hogan firm became involved in the affairs of the Rio Grande because the General Counsel of that company was a man named Sam Freeman, who had worked on another matter with Barrett Prettyman some years before. Barrett delegated to me major responsibility for the Rio Grande matters.

At the time there were four major railroads that operated in the Western part of the United States: Burlington Northern ("BN") and Union Pacific ("UP") in the North, and Southern Pacific ("SP") and Santa Fe ("SF") in the south. The SP and the SF proposed a merger; the Rio Grande, a relatively small competitor in the West, was one of the railroads that was opposed.

The detailed arguments pro and con are discussed briefly below; they are not really important anymore. What I remember best was the archaic process. The parties all retained outside economists to help in the presentation of familiar arguments to demonstrate why the combination was or was not anti-competitive. This was not alien territory for me. However, the necessary filings also had to include such things as detailed "traffic studies" to demonstrate in detail how traffic flows would be affected by the proposed transaction, further detailed "environmental studies" to predict how the traffic diversions would affect congestion and noise levels on myriad communities along the way, predicted financial results, and "shipper statements", pro and con, from literally hundreds of companies.

I hadn't the slightest idea how to do any of these things (and neither did Barrett). Fortunately, a group of younger partners - Sandy Mayo, Peter Rousselot and Eric Von Salzen - did know what they were doing. There was no need for large associate assistance on these projects, but Mary Anne Mason, currently a Hogan partner, and Susan DeSanti, currently head of Policy Planning at the FTC, filled in as needed. We were able to submit the requisite bound volumes on time. So far as I can determine, most of this stuff was never referred to again. I don't know whether the ultimate decision-makers ever read it.

The hearings proceeded in a stately way. The hearing room was a magnificent chamber, packed with lawyers for the various contending parties. Most of these guys had been doing this sort of thing for many years, sometimes on the same side and sometimes in opposition to one another. As a result, there was a great feeling of comradery and good humor about the whole thing. I remember particularly an incident when the Rio Grande's last live witness testified.

Chuck Brainard, an experienced veteran of the business, was as good a witness as I ever saw. He was our "cleanup" guy. During preparation he was given a list of mistakes that earlier witnesses had made and opposing testimony that had not yet been answered. His job was to make sure that the necessary corrections or responses got into the record somehow, preferably in response to the questions of opposing counsel because testimony is always more compelling if it comes in that way. He had a matchless ability to segue smoothly from an answer to a question on one subject into a discussion of something entirely different.

This time, a lawyer for the SP was getting pretty badly beaten up. Every ball that he hit over the net was slammed back into his teeth, sometimes with a tricky spin. Finally, in total frustration he turned around to the crowd in the hearing room and said: "I should have known better. I've cross-examined this guy before, and he does it to me every time." He then joined in the laughter around him, saluted the witness, and said "no more questions, sir."

At the conclusion of the hearing, counsel for all parties had a big celebratory dinner, with humorous speeches and friendly insults traded back and forth. As it turned out, the opposition of our client and others was successful; in 1986 the ICC voted to disapprove the proposed Southern Pacific/Santa Fe merger. Just two years later, the same agency approved the acquisition of the Southern Pacific by our client Rio Grande. The minnow had swallowed the whale, and Phil Anschutz became the owner of one of the largest railroads in the United States. We and the formerly opposing counsel for the SP were this time working together for a common objective. In 1996, the SP was acquired by the UP, and new alliances among counsel were formed.

The pleasant and clubby ambiance enjoyed by seasoned ICC practitioners was fostered not only by shifting alliances but also by a regulatory regime that once had been all persuasive and a fertile source of legal business. At one time, for example, the railroads had to submit all their proposed rates to the agency for approval, and those potentially affected were able to comment. Shippers, of course, would typically object that the proposed tariffs were too high and competitive railroads would predictably complain that they were too low and threatened competition. These objections, with standard form language, were routinely filed whenever a new rate was proposed. In fact, they got so routine that no one bothered to read them.

Sometime around 1980, a perhaps apocryphal story was widely publicized. It seems that some railroad, as a joke, submitted a proposed tariff for the shipment of "yak fat" between two actual cities. There followed the usual blizzard of objections, which referred to common knowledge that yak fat was a very expensive commodity to transport, and that the proposal to ship below cost was obviously destructive of healthy competition, etc., etc.

This absurd yarn just highlighted the fact that the whole system was incredibly inefficient. It was on its way out when I had a taste of it in the mid-1980s. The ICC was gradually stripped of authority; and abolished altogether in 1985. The remaining duties were assumed by the Surface Transportation Board, an arm of the Department of Transportation (commonly referred to as the "Surfboard"), and the Antitrust Division of the Justice Department. But, for a lawyer, the last rides were a lot of fun.

The opportunity to work on antitrust matters for Philip Anschutz was also a worthwhile experience in itself. Mr. Anschutz is a private man who does not like publicity, and I obviously will respect that preference. All I want to do is disclose what I learned about some things that differentiate great entrepreneurs from those of us who advise them. (They are not all megalomaniacs, although some surely are.) Phil Anschutz does not try to bully or dominate a meeting and is willing to follow the expert advice he pays for - even though it may not be what he would prefer to hear. It's amazing how many other prominent people surround themselves with sycophants.

Phil Anschutz also has a high tolerance for risk. He wants to build things - not just to gamble, but to develop large enterprises. And, he seemed comfortable even when the pressure was most intense.

This willingness to take on new challenges has made Phil Auschutz one of the most eclectic investors in history. He made his fortune initially in the oil business, but then moved on to other fields like railroads, real estate, telecommunications, sports franchises, journalism and entertainment generally.

Sometimes he won big and sometimes he lost big. In his early 70s now, he's still at it.

Those of us who are more comfortable as advocates and advisors, with the responsibilities of "staff" rather than "line," simply do not have the same personal willingness to take risks. In my opinion, that's the principal reason why they are rewarded more richly than we are, and I'm alright with it.

I once read a thoughtful article which offered a possible explanation for the fact that so many journalists and academics seem to have a residual hostility to capitalism. These people are generally articulate and comfortable in the world of ideas. They excelled as students; many won the prizes and the admiration of their teachers. In short, they were made to feel superior.

Then, in later life, they discover that a capitalist society does not distribute rewards the same way. People who may have run in the middle of the pack at school, who did not enjoy or excel in intellectual jousts, had the power and were earning the big money. Expanded government control of the economy would at least reduce the income disparities and give intellectuals greater opportunities to command.

I suspect that many people in the private practice of law occupy a middle ground. I know I did. I actually enjoyed debates in the world of ideas, and I still like to speak and to write. I recognize that some government oversight of the economy is necessary. But I also believe that government oversight inevitably is imperfect, and that overall a private enterprise system is preferable to the alternatives. My association with people like Philip Anschutz makes me realize they have talents that I simply do not possess. I am not at all attracted to the "politics of envy." I have no reason to envy people who have been able to acquire things that I never wanted in the first place.

One final word about the most significant substantive issue in the rail merger cases. Unlike most merger cases, the controversy largely involved the competitive effects of so-called "vertical" foreclosure. No single railroad serves every location in the country; they all depend on myriad interconnections to handle their customers' traffic. Different combinations may be selected, depending on the characteristics of the traffic. Some routes are more circuitous than others, but that disadvantage may be offset by other advantages like milder gradients or less congestion. Suppose, however, that railroads A and B compete for service from city X to city Y, and rely on other roads to move their traffic beyond city Y to city Z. What will happen if railroad A acquires one of the roads that runs from Y to Z?

According to classic economic theory, the mere change in ownership should not affect traffic flows at all. The efficient and mutually satisfactory arrangements that existed before the acquisition would persist. But, in the real world, that is not what happens. Post-merger, it is commonplace for railroad A to favor the new wholly owned affiliate on traffic from Y to Z, and to downgrade or discontinue the connecting service that the new affiliate provided to railroad B. These changes could reduce efficiency or possibly lead to local monopoly, with adverse effects or shippers.

These inefficient outcomes may be attributable to what is called the "agency" problem. A salesman for A who is compensated on a percentage of sales will earn more money if he sells a customer on the "long haul" from X to Z over wholly-owned tracks, rather than a possibly more efficient routing via A's competitor on the Y to Z segments. Alternatively, the inefficiency may be attributable to imperfect "information." If a salesman cannot readily determine which route would be preferable for a given shipment, there will be an inevitable tendency to favor the home team.

The "agency" problem and the "knowledge" problem were familiar. There is, however, an even more fundamental issue that has only recently been widely discussed. The emerging field of "Behavioral Economist" relies on experimental evidence to show that individuals and organizations are not always the rational profit-maximizers that theorists assume.

I was aware of possible distortions caused by individual emotions and goals while I was at General Motors, and some reference has been made to them in the previous chapter. I had never seen the phenomenon on this scale before, however, and it was the first time I became fully aware of possible shortcomings in the simple and elegant - indeed, mathematical - predictions that were based on the new economic learning I had so fully embraced. I have since seen many other examples, which will be mentioned later in this memoir.

Mergers Generally and General Dynamics in Particular

In an earlier sub-chapter on representation of the Business Roundtable, I mentioned that the Roundtable had opposed the passage of the Hart-Scott-Rodino Act [17] which required companies to pre-notify proposed mergers that exceeded certain size thresholds to both the FTC and the DOJ. Our fundamental concern was that these antitrust agencies would take advantage of the burdens of process to chill mergers that they might not be able to block on the merits. There was some basis for this concern because in the mid-1970s the agencies seemed to be less receptive to new economic learning than the courts were.

After the Act was passed in 1976, however, the opposite happened - simply put, our fears were misplaced. Since the majority of the mergers that had to be notified were benign by any standard, staff members in the agencies began to take a more benign view themselves. When they embarked on the review mandated by the Act, they were no longer in a prosecutorial mode with a perceived obligation to find fault. Instead, they simply wanted to be educated about the competitive pros and cons.

This shift had become obvious to me by the time I was settled in at Hogan & Hartson early in the 1980s, and others in the firm were receptive. We believed that the traditional defense lawyers' adversarial response to government investigations was counter-productive in this context. Instead of resisting the disclosure of information and our defense theories to the extent possible, we adopted a strategy of open disclosure as soon as possible. The object was to educate agency staff about our affirmative case, and to address any weaknesses up front. If we could persuade staff early on, they would become powerful internal advocates for our position. This point of view was articulated in speeches and articles [18] over a period of years.

One simple example will illustrate the distinction between our approach and the traditional one. In 1990, the Hardee's fast food chain notified the proposed acquisition of the Roy Rogers chain. Since there are myriad eating establishments, the big issue was whether an antitrust agency - in this case, the FTC - would be able to argue for some narrow market definition. During the 1980s and early '90s, the agencies focused more on "concentration" than they did later on. (They were, however, more receptive to "entry" arguments than their successors.)

The problem was that the parties internal memos tended to identify the "competition" as roughly comparable fast food establishments like McDonald's, Big Boy, and Wendy's, and they kept "market share" statistics that measured performance against this limited group. If the group of fast-food outlets were considered the relevant "market", there would be troublesome overlaps in both Baltimore and Washington, D.C.

It was obvious to us, that this definition would be unreasonably narrow for antitrust purposes, despite the language of our client's internal documents. Both cities had substantial downtown business districts. The office buildings had an indeterminate number of cafeterias that offered fast food service for people who worked there. There were also a substantial and growing number of "deli" sections in supermarkets, where people could take home a fully-prepared meal. (In fact, people in Washington, D.C. were relatively less likely to prepare food at home than those in any other city - a fact that was obviously related to the unusually high ratio of working women.) If these outlets were included, however, there were no precise statistics available to measure the size of the "universe" from which to calculate post-merger concentration. Our consulting economists, were able to come up with ingenious "proxy" measures to demonstrate that these alternatives served a very large number of customers.

We, as counsel for Roy Rogers decided to volunteer an affirmative demonstration that essentially said: "We cannot provide precise statistics, but common sense suggests that the 'market' statistics in our own internal documents are not satisfactory for antitrust purposes."

Counsel for the acquiring company, in this case Hardees, normally take the lead in defense, and they were affiliated with a proud and eminent New York law firm. They thought our proposal would be a terrible mistake. We shouldn't admit that we cannot define a market, but rather should limit ourselves to a rigorous critique if the FTC staff argues for a narrow market. But we weren't interested in picking a fight with staff; *we wanted to get them on our side,* and the sooner the better.

So, we respectfully refused to follow the strategy advocated by Hardee's counsel; and we presented our affirmative case. Staff readily agreed, and said they would recommend that the merger be cleared by the agency, without a further request for information. And, so it was.

I don't know whether our record of success with a non-confrontational approach had come to the attention of a potential new client but, for whatever reason, Nicholas (Nick") Chabraja, the incoming General Counsel of General Dynamics, came to see me early in 1992. Nick had been a longtime partner in the Chicago firm of Jenner & Block. He explained that his former firm would continue to maintain close ties with General Dynamics ("GD") and members of the Crown family, the largest shareholders.

He then went on to say that GD was about to embark on a large program to divest some businesses and acquire others, in order to reposition the company. He had come to the conclusion that a Washington firm like Hogan & Hartson would be best able to provide strategic and tactical antitrust advice going forward. Once I had determined that there were no conflicts, I told Nick that we would be happy to take on the assignment. Thus began a mutually rewarding relationship that consumed a substantial amount of my time until I joined the FTC late in 1999 - a relationship that continues to this day, under the leadership of Janet McDavid and, most recently, Joe Krauss.

The man whose vision would initiate the transformation of General Dynamics was William Anders, who served as Chairman from 1991 to 1994. Bill Anders was once an astronaut, a member of the famous crew that first orbited the moon in December, 1968, and marked the event by reading those moving passages from the Book of Genesis. He is also the man who took that striking picture of the blue earth rising in a black sky over a desolate moonscape - an image that still inspires the environmental movement throughout the world.

Despite his military background, Bill Anders was able to take a detached and hard-nosed view of future prospects for a defense-industry supplier like General Dynamics. The Cold War which had dominated U.S. foreign policy for over 40 years wound down in 1989-90. And the first Gulf War began and ended quickly in 1991. In the euphoria of the moment - overly optimistic, as it turned out - it seemed likely that the country's defense expenditures would be cut back for an extended period of time. And, when defense dollars are reduced, inevitably weapon procurement budgets take the hardest hit.

Bill Anders used to say that executives with companies in the defense industry are likely to have a military background, just as he did, and they are understandably interested in weapons of war. Because they are so fascinated by the products they make and sell, they are reluctant to let go of the business even when it has become unprofitable. (The tendency of people to fall in love with their occupation helps to explain why so many service station owners or real estate agents will work so hard for so little.) Anders was willing to sell off relatively unprofitable pieces of General Dynamics, even if it hurt, and then invest in companies that complemented the pared-down operation.

In order to get the necessary antitrust clearances for this far-reaching program of sales and acquisitions, we lawyers carried our preferred strategy of voluntary affirmative disclosures beyond anything we had ever done before. Merger advocacy in the defense industry has some special requirements.

In the first place, the Department of Defense has a keen interest in the structure of its supplier base. There were people in various service commands, located in the Pentagon and elsewhere, with strong and sometimes conflicting views about proposed transactions. The degree of central coordination in the Department has varied from time to time, but, however expressed, these opinions can be decisive. The Defense Department is, after all, not only the agency with responsibility for defense of the nation, but also the sole customer for weapons systems.

The antitrust agencies were initially slow to recognize the unique preferences of this customer. They believed that the Defense Department was wedded to a cost-plus procurement policy that chilled incentives to cut costs, just as a similar policy was reputed to do in regulated public utilities. It took some initial effort to convince the antitrust agencies that reduced costs were not necessarily the primary objective of a military organization, and the customary economic measures were not necessarily appropriate. For example, effectiveness in battle was the paramount consideration, followed closely by concern for the lives of our warriors. (This could lead to expensive, and sometimes frustrating, changes in specifications over the life of a contract.)

In addition, the Defense Department was always concerned about maintenance of healthy domestic suppliers. In most situations, the antitrust agencies - with a focus on consumer welfare and a strong belief in free trade - are not concerned about the survival of a domestic industry. The Defense Department, mindful of the interruptions on commerce imposed by a global war, cannot be so cavalier. The Department might also want to preserve more than one supplier, a plant location, or a particular weapons system, as a hedge against war damage. This means there might be some tolerance for alliances and allocations that would normally be objectionable from an antitrust standpoint.

As lawyers, we not only had to become familiar with the special requirements of our clients' customers, we also had to explain to antitrust agency staff how those special requirements could be accommodated under traditional antitrust principles. Agency staff could and did talk to Defense Department people directly, of course, but I believe we had an important intermediary role in talking to each group in ways they would understand.

We would meet with agency staff in advance of notification, or promptly thereafter, and provide them with a "fact book" about the weapons systems involved in the transactions, identification of present or likely future competition, and other relevant information. The fact book was not argumentative, as a lawyer's brief would be, but obviously we hoped that the facts presented would support the conclusion we hoped for.

We also believed that an early presentation by a knowledgeable executive could sometimes be critical. A traditional litigator might be horrified by the notion that a senior guy would be offered up for what could turn out to be an open-ended deposition, but we believed that this very openness conveyed our confidence and added to our credibility. A couple of examples.

In 1993 General Dynamics agreed to sell its fighter plane business to Lockheed. A superficial view of the industry would suggest that this acquisition would reduce the number of potential suppliers, from three to two, since McDonnell Douglas was the only other company that currently produced fighter planes. A prolonged antitrust review seemed inevitable.

For obvious reasons, this was a fascinating assignment for me. I vividly remember a visit to the GD plant in Fort Worth, Texas. The final assembly building was actually a mile long, and plant personnel traveled around the place on little carts. I also was particularly impressed by Gordon England, the man in charge of the whole operation. He was not a showboat, but exuded a quiet competence and confidence. He had a good answer for every tough question that I could think of. (Gordon later served as a Secretary of the Navy under the second President Bush.)

Gordon explained that military aircraft currently have a much longer life cycle than they did, say, in World War II when new models seemed to appear almost annually. In addition to General Dynamics' F-16, introduced in 1976, the McDonnell Douglas contemporaneous F-15 for the Air Force, and its new 1983 F-18 for the Navy, would be in service for a long time, and no new competitions were expected for many years. (In fact, these aircraft are still in service today.) Furthermore, the development of a new fighter plane was such an expensive undertaking that it is unrealistic to suppose there will be a large number of competitors in any event. Standard antitrust analysis that focuses so much on the number of competitors simply does not make sense.

I decided then and there that I wanted to bring Gordon into a meeting with the reviewing agency as soon as I knew which one it would be. The trouble was that it took an inordinate time for the FTC and the DOJ to agree among themselves on this question. They share responsibility for reviews of pending merger transactions. In most cases, the choice is routine, based on past experience with a particular industry. Most defense industry deals are reviewed by the DOJ, by joint consensus. On this one, however, the FTC had a plausible claim, and finally prevailed after a turf battle that lasted for 21 days.

A three-week delay may not seem like all that much time, but the trouble is that the reviewing agency has only 30 days after the initial merger notification to serve a so-called "Second Request" for additional information when it does not feel it knows enough to make a decision. The 30- day deadline is imposed by the governing statute, and cannot be waived by agreement of the parties.

It looked like it would be impossible to avoid the Second Request, and I so informed the client. We nevertheless brought Gordon in to meet with the FTC staff immediately, with the understanding that he would answer every question that he could. I think the meeting lasted for about three hours, with free discussion back and forth. Gordon did a superb job.

Before the 30-day deadline had expired, we were informed that the proposed sale to Lockheed had been cleared, and we were free to proceed.

The roughly contemporaneous sales of GD's Tactical Weapons business to Hughes, and its Space Systems business to Martin Marietta were equally memorable, for different reasons. Both businesses were located in San Diego. The most famous tactical weapon was the "stinger missile," which was supplied in large numbers to the rebels who successfully battled the Soviets in Afghanistan late in the 1990s. The Space Systems business produced the Atlas missiles that had powered the early ventures into earth orbit.

A launch vehicle is not just a big firecracker; it is an incredibly intricate and frighteningly fragile piece of machinery. In order to conserve weight the skin of the vehicle is thinner than the metal in a beer can. Before it is filled with rocket fuel, it is not strong enough to stand on its own. In fact, you can easily make a temporary dimple with the touch of a finger. The fuel payload is what makes the vehicle rigid and, as it burns on ascent, it is necessary to fill the vacated space with compressed air at a rate that will precisely compensate for the decreasing support provided by the burning fuel. All of the necessary precision machinery has to work perfectly under conditions of extreme acceleration and temperature variations.

The engineering skill required to design and build these things is awe inspiring. The fact that human beings are willing to ride into space on top of them boggles the mind.

On the Tactical Weapons transaction, we did get a massive Second Request from the DOJ for documents. Normally, we preferred to avoid a full response to these burdensome requests. With the agreement of agency staff, we would just set the Request aside - without prejudice to their right to insist on full production and our right to object. In the meantime, we would undertake an informal "rolling" production of documents they specifically requested, at a pace that they could digest. At this particular period of time, our experience was that agency staff invariably indicated they had seen enough and called a halt before full compliance. A big saving of time and effort for everyone.

In this particular situation however, an executive in the client organization had already collected a mass of responsive documents on his own authority, and it would actually be more efficient to produce what he had collected in bulk. Accordingly, I went to San Diego, with a team of younger lawyers that included partners Phil Larson and Janet McDavid, to provide the necessary legal review of the material the client would turn over.

They did all the hard work, and I mostly enjoyed myself. I met with executives who explained the fascinating business, and I toured the facilities. I savored the warm chocolate chip cookies that were brought to the visiting lawyers all day long. And, most of all, it was a joy just to be in San Diego again. Stephanie and I had recently remarried, and I was overwhelmed by the sweet memories associated with this place where we had first met, courted and married.

Since the overall rationale for the transaction was not adequately disclosed in the written documents, I decided that the best spokesman for the company would be the CEO, Bill Anders himself. This required some extensive preparation back at GD's headquarters in Virginia because, like many decisive individuals accustomed to command, he could be a bit impatient with inquiries that seemed stupid,. That was fine since this time we had the time, and I would rather that he took it out on me than on some guy in the DOJ.

The presence of the legendary astronaut in the DOJ headquarters was obviously a big deal. A large conference room was filled with curious staff members. The then-acting head of the Antitrust Division, Charles James, made an unexpected appearance, and the questions were friendly and intelligent. Bill Anders performed magnificently; in fact he seemed to be really enjoying himself.

I sensed that we had made the sale, and was notified shortly thereafter that indeed we had.

These were the most prominent client divestitures that I remember. General Dynamics has also made a large number of acquisitions, particularly under the leadership of Nick Chabraja, the man who had originally hired our firm. Nick served as CEO from 1997-2009, and was widely recognized as a leader in the industry. A substantial number of these acquisitions involved command and control systems for the most advanced weapons, which has transformed GD from a company principally known as a supplier of "hardware" - like submarines, ships and tanks - into one that is also a leading "high-tech" enterprise. I was once told that the electronic equipment in the GD M1 battle tank is more costly than the massive hardware.

It is the hardware that I remember best, however, simply because it is easier to visualize. It is hard to forget experiences like a tour inside a nuclear submarine in GD's Electric Boat facility in Connecticut, a destroyer in the Bath Iron Works purchased in 1995, or a massive cargo vessel under construction at the San Diego Shipyard of the National Steel and Iron Works ("NASSCO") purchased in 1998. I particularly enjoyed the work on the NASSCO deal because it took me back once more to my favorite place in the world.

One of the great joys of an antitrust practice is the opportunity to learn about the competitive dynamics of so many industries, and to note for future reference the similarities and differences among them. That Miss Marple thing that I mentioned before.

I was also proud of the firm's overall record of success in merger matters. It is second to none. When I later served in the government, I learned that the firm's reasoned approach enhanced its credibility, which has to be a major contributing cause. The approach also benefitted the clients in another way: our reluctance to argue about trivia meant that we could staff lean. Sometimes, when a matter had been concluded, I asked the client's General Counsel if he/she could find out how our bills compared with those submitted by counsel for the other party. I didn't want to know the number, just the comparison. Our bills were uniformly much lower - and this, of course, was information that our client was free to share. Indeed, I hoped that it would happen.

Antitrust and Athletic Competition

In the early 1990's, the Antitrust Division of the DOJ, then under the leadership of James Rill, a longtime friend, brought an antitrust action against the so-called "Ivy League" schools, and a handful of other similarly prestigious institutions. The claim was that these schools had violated the antitrust laws by agreeing on the terms of financial assistance offered to incoming students. The Ivy League schools, also had a common policy of "need blind admissions need-only assistance," which was particularly designed to prohibit athletic scholarships. Cornell University had a longtime relationship with David Tatel, then one of our specialists in educational issues and today a much respected judge on the D.C. Court of Appeals. I was able to lead the team for Cornell because, apart from the aging Lee Loevinger, I was the most experienced antitrust lawyer in the firm, and well acquainted with members of the prosecuting team of the DOJ. I was joined by Marty Michaelson, one of the first Hogan people who had interviewed me while I was still at General Motors, and someone who had since added education law to his antitrust credentials.

The matter has been memorable, not so much for the battle which was actually ended rather quickly and amicably, but for the terms of the settlement. The universities did have a plausible claim that agreements on financial assistance should not be deemed per se illegal like the usual price conspiracies, because they also fostered an important social objective. It was desirable for applicants to choose a university that would best serve their particular educational objectives rather than the one that would offer the most assistance. A defense of this kind would be drawn out and expensive, however, and most of the universities - including our client Cornell - opted for a relatively innocuous settlement.

The noteworthy part of the settlement is not what would be *prohibited*, but what was *excluded*. The universities were permitted to maintain agreements that would prohibit the grant of athletic scholarships.

Athletic competition has special characteristics. In the normal commercial world, close competition can create incentives for better products and services at lower prices. But, it is the resultant *improved values* that will enhance consumer welfare, not the competition that is the *precipitating cause*. The public may care if Hertz or Avis is number one, but it is not interested in how close the race may be. Athletic competition is different. Close competition *for its own sake*, actually improves the experience for most consumers - it adds value or, in antitrust jargon, increases the "output".

The Ivy League's desire to even the playing field for intra-League contests explains why the DOJ did not want to interfere with the concerted ban on athletic scholarships. (For general policy reasons, the DOJ did not choose to interfere with the broader principles of need-blind admissions and of aid solely based on financial need. What the DOJ wanted to prevent was any discussion of the appropriate assistance for identified individuals.) I was probably the most outspoken advocate of this reasoned compromise among defense counsel, and I don't regret it.

It should be noted in passing that the objectives of the Ivy League are in some ways similar to those of other organizations. The special characteristics of athletic competition - and associated dispensations - explains why professional sports leagues are able to enforce various "handicapping" rules like player drafts structured so the last shall be first, and a "tax" on total player compensation above certain levels.

The Ivy League experience also helps to illustrate an even more general principle. The rule against athletic scholarships is obviously not ironclad. Gifted high-school athletes who weigh 300 pounds or stand close to 7 feet are rather rare, and the number in that subset who can satisfy the Ivies' scholastic standards for admission are rarer still. Obviously, the rules are sometimes bent a bit.

Some theoretical economists maintain that cheating will invariably doom the viability of any conspiracy. My practical experience has convinced me that illegal price agreements, as well as perfectly legal ones like the Ivies' ban on athletic scholarships, can survive some cheating so long as it is kept within reasonable limits. Competitor conspiracies are not all-or-nothing affairs; they can continue to have effects even if they are imperfect. If you doubt it, just look at the Ivies' overall performance outside their own League in big ticket sports like football or men's basketball.

The opportunity to become familiar with the special characteristics of athletic competition served me well when I was first asked to advise on a proposal to rationalize post season Bowl contests between the top teams in college football. The system now known as the Bowl Championship Series, or "BCS", had its origins in an agreement among the premier Bowls, not the College Conferences.

Historically, the system for determining the matchups in post-season play was flawed in various respects. First, it was almost impossible to schedule a game between the teams that ranked one and two in respected nationwide polls, like that published by the Associated Press. There were two reasons. Some Bowls had long pre-existing relationships that committed them to host the champion of a particular Conference. The Rose Bowl's commitment to a match between the Big Ten and the Pac 10 is probably the best known. There were others like the Cotton Bowl's agreement with the old Southwest Conference, the Orange Bowl's agreement with the old Big Eight, and the Sugar Bowl's agreement with the old Southwestern Conference. The Fiesta Bowl had two open slots to fill.

It might appear that the available open slots would materially improve the chances for a National Championship game, but it didn't work out that way. Because of the keen competition for the open slots, the Bowls tended to get commitments after about 3/4 of the season, and it was not unusual for the selected teams to have losing streaks at the end of the season and sink in the poll rankings. This not only reduced the likelihood of a National

Championship game, but also increased the likelihood of a mismatch. This was unfortunate because, as we have seen in another context, the potential for a close contest increases the fan appeal.

In 1992, four of the leading post-season venues - the Cotton, Fiesta, Orange and Sugar Bowls - decided to do something about it. They formed a Coalition that proposed to attack the problem in two ways. First, the selection of teams for the open slots would be deferred until the end of the season and the Bowl that had a contractual relationship with the conference of the higher ranked team would get the first pick. If the two teams ranked #1 and #2 were not committed by contract with a particular Bowl, they would play in the Fiesta Bowl which had two open slots.

Counsel for these Bowls recognized that there were potential antitrust questions. One of them contacted a young partner at Hogan & Hartson, whom he had known when they both clerked for a Supreme Court Justice. The Supreme Court Justice was William Rehnquist, later the Chief, and the young Hogan partner was John Roberts, who became the Chief Justice himself in 2005. John Roberts, although an experienced appellate advocate - later recognized as one of the best, if not the best of his time - was not an antitrust specialist. Therefore, I was asked to advise on the legality of the proposal.

Because a cooperative arrangement of this kind was novel in college football (although cooperative determination of post-season matchups existed in professional football and other sports) and because I realized that counsel for the colleges would also need reassurance, I wrote an unusually long opinion letter of 50 to 60 pages - replete with citations of precedent and arguments by analogy. The ultimate conclusion was that the Bowl Coalition's arrangement would not violate the antitrust laws because, even though it was not perfect, it was a significant improvement on what had existed before.

The Coalition lived up to its promise. A post-season game between the two top-ranked teams had previously been a rare event. Under the Coalition, it happened twice in the first three years, and there were closer matchups in the other contests.

The cooperative arrangement of the Bowl Coalition expired after three years, according to its terms. This time it was the college football conferences that wanted to try something new. We obtained the necessary waivers from our original Bowl clients, and began to advise this new coalition of the Conferences. Their arrangement, first known as the Bowl Alliance and then as the BCS since 1998, has been a client of the firm ever since. I continued to lead the team until I left for government service late in 1999, and the representation has since been in the more-than-capable hands of a younger partner, William "Tripp" Monts. Tripp is not only a fine antitrust lawyer, but also an avid college football fan with an encyclopedic knowledge (which I have never had) of which teams beat which other teams, and when.

The BCS has evolved over the years. The original Bowl Coalition members were not automatically invited to host the teams who ranked high in the BCS standing; they have had to bid for it. Longstanding arrangements between the successors of the original Conferences and particular Bowls have been continued to the extent possible, but modified as necessary under the BCS to improve the likelihood of a championship match between the teams ranked #1 and #2. For example, the Bowl selected to host this match rotates from year to year. The Rose Bowl, which is now included in the arrangement, continues to host the champion of the Big Ten and the Pac 10 every year unless it is the Rose Bowl's turn to host the #1 and #2 match, and the usual teams are not so ranked.

The BCS has consistently delivered a National Championship game between the two top-ranked teams - something that was historically rare. Precise comparisons are not possible because the BCS has a somewhat more sophisticated ranking system than a single poll. If you just look at the Associated Press ranking, however, you will get an idea of the change. Before the BCS, the two top-ranked teams on the AP poll met in a single bowl game only 11 times in 62 seasons. Contrast this with the BCS record. The top two AP teams have met 10 years in the last 13 under the BCS system and, of course, the matchup is 13 out of 13 under the BCS' more sophisticated ranking system.

The BCS arrangement has also been modified to tighten the standards for automatic inclusion of Notre Dame - which nevertheless continues to be a popular choice if it qualifies for an optional "at large" slot. (Notre Dame has immense appeal because so many football fans either love or hate the team - it's rather like the New York Yankees that way.) Even more significant, perhaps, is the fact that the BCS has progressively opened access for teams from Conferences outside those that put the BCS together. Before the BCS, these teams played in a top-tier bowl only 6 times in 54 years. Since the BCS, they have done so 7 times in the last 7 years - including an appearance in the Rose Bowl, probably still the most prestigious of them all.

Despite this record of improved access, some of these non-BCS Conferences continue to complain that the BCS is an illegal antitrust conspiracy. These complaints have stimulated a series of Congressional Hearings, and at least two unsuccessful appeals to the DOJ that we know of. We were informed that yet another DOJ investigation was begun in 2011.

This is not the place to make a comprehensive case for the BCS. It is enough to say that any arrangements for post-season championship play - including a playoff - will require the concerted action of independent college conferences, so the present one cannot be illegal on its face. The recognized test for the legality of any joint venture is whenever it is more or less anticompetitive than what would prevail in the "but for" world without it. The BCS is by any measure more successful and open than the situation that existed before. It is also more successful and open than the situation that would prevail if it were dissolved tomorrow, because neither the college Conferences nor the top-tier Bowls are interested in a playoff with eight or more teams.

Finally, a venture which is an improvement or a likely alternative is not illegal just because a number of commentators would prefer an extended playoff. (The Conferences and BCS Bowls have valid reasons for their opposition. A playoff would diminish the significance of the regular season and traditional intra-Conference rivalries.) The BCS is also not illegal just because the evident benefits in non-BCS Conferences are not as great as those conferred on the Conferences that put together the venture.

Defense of the BCS is now in the hands of Tripp Monts. I am, however, proud of the contribution that helped to make the BCS possible. If the services of a moldering old warhorse are ever required again, I will be pleased to respond.

Day-to-Day Counseling and Sentencing Guidelines

Apart from major projects like those described, a lot of my work at Hogan consisted of quick, informal opinions on various business strategies. Collective action in trade associations would give rise to a lot of inquiries, as did attempts to influence the resale policies of dealers. Some of these inquiries came to me directly from the clients, but in many cases they were referred by my fellow partners. Phil Larson, for example, was the primary contact for many clients, and was an experienced antitrust counselor himself. But he sometimes wanted to run his preliminary views by a second pair of eyes.

I really enjoyed the challenge of this off-the-cuff advice. It was not particularly lucrative, because the time charges were relatively modest, and sometimes it wasn't possible to charge at all. That was fine with me because I have always been more interested in the accumulation of experiences than the accumulation of billable hours and the associated monetary rewards. (That "mental furniture" thing that my mother used to emphasize.)

I did have some longterm clients of my own, who sought everyday advice. One particular client, no longer represented by the firm, had particularly challenging issues. The client had a very large market share in one product line, but was a small and struggling new entrant in others.

The client's in-house lawyers were very much aware of antitrust concerns, and often asked me to lecture on antitrust issues at sales meetings in very pleasant resorts. One of the side benefits of an antitrust practice is that the clients are so often sales executives, and salesmen - like lawyers - are sensible enough to convene in very nice places.

Another rewarding longterm client was the Auto-Steel Partnership, a research joint venture whose members included not only the so-called "Big Three" U.S. auto companies but also the major steel companies in the U.S. and Canada. The focus of the joint research was the interface between the two industries. A steel plate or forging enters one side of a plant and emerges as an auto part on the other side. The Partnership's research sought ways to improve the technology involved in the transition. The whole subject was particularly interesting for me because of my own extensive exposure to both industries.

A lot of the antitrust issues were similar to those that you would encounter in any joint research venture. This one was unusual, however, because it included representatives of steel suppliers and their auto customers. The presence of two levels in one group sometimes inhibited free discussion, but it automatically reduced the likelihood of an antitrust problem. Industry members are unlikely to illegally conspire in the presence of their suppliers or customers.

A second thing that I learned because of my close association with this group was that valuable research is not confined to experiments in a laboratory. New technology may actually be employed in some factories overseas, which can be visited. Even more may be described in technical literature, which is available if you know where to look. So, the first job in a particular joint project may be to look for knowledge that is already available elsewhere.

Viewed that way, it became obvious to me that there are a lot more research joint ventures than we realize. For example: the Antitrust Section of the ABA is, among other things, a giant joint research venture. It collects information on antitrust developments throughout the world, and makes it available to members in publications or programs. It does not set "standards" but particularly knowledgeable lawyers do recommend "best practices" for their fellow practitioners. When this analogy occurred to me, it helped to dissipate the mystery and suspicion that initially had clouded my views on joint research. For one thing, the "market share" of the participants in the venture is not necessarily important.

Over the years, I have written ten briefs that were filed with the Supreme Court of the United States, and about half that number that were filed with various Courts of Appeal. All of them were so-called *Amicus Curiae* (Latin for "friend" of the court) briefs, rather than submissions on behalf of a party. The majority were written on behalf of The Business Roundtable or individual Roundtable members who had an interest in the outcome of a particular case.

Most of the cases like *Cargill, ARC America, American Stores, Brown & Williamson, Khan,* and *Leegin* [19] are familiar to antitrust lawyers. Sometimes the side that we supported won, and sometimes it lost, and I have no idea what effect, if any, my briefs had on the Court. The reason I mention these projects at all is because they ultimately made an important contribution to my legal education.

An *Amicus* brief that simply parrots the arguments of a party is useless. The objective is to inform the Court about significant policy issues that may not be of immediate concern to the party we support. The court's decision may have a profound effect on companies and industries that are not directly represented. These projects, therefore, forced me to take a more detached view than I might if I represented a client directly involved in the litigation. In that sense, they helped to prepare me for what I had to do when I served on the Federal Trade Commission, and have had an impact on the ways that I approach antitrust issues today.

One other project did not last very long, but taught me a lot. The Sentencing Reform Act of 1984 [20] is designed to increase penalties for federal "white collar" crimes across the board, and to reduce regional variations in criminal sentences imposed by federal courts. In accordance with the Act, specific Guidelines were published by a newly-created U.S. Sentencing Commission, after an extended period of public comment and deliberations.

On behalf of The Business Roundtable (a client discussed at length above), I commented on various proposed drafts and testified at the Commission's open hearings. In the course of this representation, I obviously acquired some marketable expertise about the Guidelines. Of particular interest for the corporate world was a provision that allowed for reduced fines if a defendant company had a law compliance program with certain mandated features.

Among the mandated features were written instructions, a system that would enable employees to report possible violations without fear of retaliation, supplemental training as needed, and top executive supervision of the compliance process. As discussed in the Chapter on my General Motors experience, there were already familiar concepts. But, the devil was in the details. For example, how do you decide which subjects require instruction beyond written policies?

When the Guidelines were fresh, I spoke at a two-day program on employer education in New Orleans. As it happened, my segment on Antitrust Law came at the end of the program, which had already considered other areas like financial regulations, foreign corrupt practices, environmental and employment offenses, safety regulations, etc., etc. The attendees, who were largely corporate general counsel with broad responsibility for all these matters, became progressively more gloomy. I stood up to address a group in a near-cataleptic condition.

I led off with something like this:

"Ladies and Gentlemen, I realize that you have already sat here for almost two days, and listened to lawyers tell you about the myriad criminal offenses that your companies can commit, the serious consequences of violation, and the need for extensive employee education. My subject is antitrust, and I propose to say similar things. But I want you to know that if you scrupulously followed my advice, and the advice you have already heard, your company's employees would not have time to do anything but attend lawyers' seminars."

The immediate result was a standing ovation - the first of only three that I have ever enjoyed at the beginning of a talk. There is, however, a serious point here that a lot of corporate critics tend to ignore.

Any large company is subject to criminal prosecution, and associated civil consequences, for literally thousands of offenses - as set out in Statutes and voluminous Federal Regulations. It is not possible to adequately educate employees about them all. Counsel are forced to engage in a triage process and focus their efforts on the offenses that are most likely to occur and/or do the most damage. The process is necessarily imperfect, but it is not fair to castigate a company as a "criminal" enterprise or a "recidivist" if it has been vicariously liable for employee misconduct, any more than it would be fair to condemn the U.S. Government as "criminal" just because some federal employees violate the law - which they assuredly do.

The magnitude of the problem was brought home to me when I was asked to advise a major corporation on modifications of its already-existing compliance procedures, in order to meet the mandates of the new Guidelines. I knew virtually nothing, of course, about federal laws other than competition and consumer protection, and would have to rely on the client's in-house experts. What I could do was craft a "compliance program for compliance programs."

As a first step, I requested a meeting with the company lawyers responsible for each of the major subject areas - there were about a dozen of them. Then, I asked them individually to collect a copy of each internal instruction in their area that was already in circulation. We adjourned for about a month. When we reconvened, a large conference room was bursting with written materials, covering every available horizontal surface and piled on the floor. They varied from high level policy directives to meticulous instructions on plant level operations, collected in loose-leaf notebooks that had not been updated for years.

The company lawyers' reaction was almost as astonished as my own, and the mere collection effort had a salutary effect. These lawyers did not have to be told that a major ongoing effort was necessary to keep this material current, and to focus educational efforts on the most serious directives. Together we agreed on an overall compliance procedure that would require these periodic reviews - recognizing that the process could never be perfect. This is where high-level executive direction becomes important.

The chapter on General Motors gives some reasons why it is a mistake for lawyers to be responsible for decisions that operating managers should make. But, an exercise like the one just described highlights another reason. The lawyers can best identify more potential offenses which are most serious, and recommend the most training, but managers should be asked to approve the educational effort recommended, and ensure that it happens. If they give the imprimatur to a certain level of effort, they have endorsed a standard of due care, and personally risk the consequences if the standard is not met. In my experience, this creates a powerful incentive.

It is up to the lawyers to use the available training time effectively. A dry recitation of statutes and decisions will put the audience to sleep. You need to use vivid examples and allow significant time for questions.

For example, I remember a presentation to sales executives for a company with a near-monopoly "share" in some localities, if the relevant geographic "market" were defined narrowly. During the question period, one man identified himself as the "sales manager for the Seattle market." I interrupted him and said there was no such thing as the "Seattle market." He was startled and offended until I explained that I was not trying to put him down but rather to emphasize the risks associated with the use of the word "market" as a noun. It has legal overtones, like the word "agreement," of which he may be unaware. Better to say "region" or "territory," words that do not carry the same baggage.

It was always helpful as well to explain that an illegal "agreement" with competitors can be inferred without a written document, or even verbal words of assent. Mere discussions, followed by actions consistent with the discussion, are enough. The most vivid example here is a story that I have told many times before but is worthy of repetition. [21]

"I once was outside antitrust counsel for a good client, which had a number of executives who seemed to delight in skating as close as possible to the edge. It made for a lively, if nerve-racking, practice. One of these executives was fixated on the idea that he should have lunch with his opposite number in a competitive company, who had been newly appointed from outside the industry. There was no obvious reason: 'I just want to find out what kind of guy he is.' (Maybe, he had once been to the Naval Intelligence School.) I said, of course that it was a bad idea, absent a legitimate business purpose - particularly since the client was the market leader in a tight oligopoly. We went around in circles for weeks. Then, he came up with the notion that I should attend the lunch, as well, along with a designated lawyer from the other company. In a weak moment, I agreed.

The four of us had a fine lunch in a neutral city, talking about the usual things you would expect of four men who do not really know one another very well. (Sports, and sports.) I heard nothing that was remotely problematic and, when I returned to my office,

I prepared a memo for future reference and mailed a hefty bill, which included the travel time. A happy outcome? Not quite.

About three years later, visiting on another subject, my client said out of the blue: 'By the way, did I ever tell you what happened after that lunch as we were picking up our coats to leave the restaurant? When you two lawyers weren't watching, the other guy nudged me and whispered 'You lead.'

Once I recovered my bearings, the obvious question was: 'What did you say?' He replied: 'Oh, don't worry, I didn't say anything. I just nodded, like I'd heard.' You can imagine the lecture that followed, to the effect that he was very lucky that there had been no unusual price movements that had attracted anyone's attention; that, if there had been, this five-second exchange could supply evidence of a price-fixing conspiracy; that he ought to know better, etc., etc.

The point of this story is not just to confess my own lapse of judgment. The point is to illustrate once more that the antitrust laws can be violated in the most unlikely settings (almost under the nose of two chaperones) and with a moment's thoughtlessness or recklessness. The perp left the company shortly thereafter and, to this day, I do not know whether he was a naive innocent or an active collaborator. It really doesn't matter because the antitrust laws do not distinguish between the two."

Other Activities

Every active partner in a large firm necessarily has responsibilities that are not directly related to client service or client development. For me these included the recruitment of new lawyers and their subsequent evaluations. In addition, almost every client matter that I worked on provided an opportunity to help younger lawyers develop their talents.

I have been actively involved in recruitment in every legal job I ever had.
I did it at White & Case, at General Motors and at Hogan & Hartson. I
particularly enjoyed the challenges of the initial contact in a Law School setting. The students were sometimes in and out so quickly that I didn't really
have time to record my impressions in detail - just a few cryptic notes on
physical appearance, and any obvious pluses or minuses. This did not mean
that physical appearance was all that important; the quick descriptions were
simply to help me remember the interview at the end of the day when there
was time to make more detailed notes.

The demographics and the demeanor of the students varied by location and
over time. Some of my interviews in the late 1960s and the early 1970s were
amusing in retrospect.

One guy showed up with beautiful blonde hair down to his shoulders; he
rather resembled Veronica Lake, a movie star who became famous for that
look in the early 1940s and was much admired for it by at least one young
boy. He went out of his way to assure me up front that, appearances notwithstanding, he was a conservative conformist at heart; he was simply con-
forming to the customs of the campus, and would get a haircut as soon as he
graduated. I don't remember whether we made him an offer, but there were
no hard feelings in any event. He must have taken another Wall Street job,
because about a year later he came up to me on the Street and re-introduced
himself - a necessary step because he was unrecognizable with short hair and
pinstriped suit, like everyone else.

At about the same time, I had a very different reaction in another interview.
The applicant looked normal enough and had a good Law School record
except for a couple of "incompletes" in his second year. When I asked him
about them, he said he had missed the exams because "That was the week we
took the library." I said something brilliant like "Huh?" He explained that
people on campus were upset about some development in the Vietnam War,
and a group had held a prolonged sit-down strike in the library. I decided he
was wacko, and recommended that he not be invited for future interviews.

For all I know, he's a hedge-fund billionaire today, with two 20,000 square foot houses, a private airplane, and a new crusade called energy conservation.

The process was particularly difficult for minorities and women then because they were pioneers in unfamiliar territory. In my view, racial minorities are not helped by well-meaning university administrators who facilitate self segregation, and by so-called "sensitivity" training that focuses almost exclusively on explaining minority culture to the majority and neglects the equally, if not more important, need to explain the majority to the minority. People who have been excluded from the larger society can misread situations, too.

I think the full integration of women has been more successful. Early on, some of them came across as either overly submissive or overly prickly. A couple of personal experiences will illustrate the change. Around 1970, I had an interview with two women who wanted to meet together at the start, with an understanding that they would separate later. I thought this was a little odd, but assumed that they just wanted some support to deal with the opening jitters. But, they didn't act nervous at all; in fact they seemed downright aggressive. One of them explained that she had just married a classmate, who intended to practice law in another city, but she intended to stay in New York. They both seemed to be waiting for a reaction It was one of those rare occasions when I was wise enough to keep my mouth shut. After that, they both appeared to lose interest in the whole thing, and it seemed like we were wasting time.

About a month later, I read in the legal press that a civil rights action had been brought against about ten Wall Street firms, and named individual partners. The plaintiffs were the two women I had seen, and the claim was that partners had shown some sexist dismay at the notion that a woman would not follow her husband. The second woman at the interview was there to provide testimonial rather than emotional support. (One of the perps sued was a neighbor and close friend, and I liked to razz him about his obviously sexist attitude.)

Contrast that with an experience about 15 years later when I was interviewing for Hogan. This woman seemed to be genuinely enjoying herself. At one point, she mentioned that she hoped to have a baby in the next few years. Again, I said nothing. She looked at me for a minute, and burst out laughing. I had to smile myself, and asked what was so funny. She said: "You're pretty fast, but I caught you." After the standard "huh?" from me, she said: "When I mentioned a baby, you flicked your eyes at my finger to see if there was a ring." She was right, of course.

Overall, I thought someone with that sense of humor and confidence would be a fine addition to the firm, and I recommended her. She wound up somewhere else, but I still enjoy the memory. It also shows progress when people can laugh about once-sensitive things instead of brooding about them.

A day-long series of interviews can be a challenging job. Asking and answering the obvious questions is the easiest part. The hard part is to adequately convey the culture or "personality" of the firm. Earlier in this memoir, I mentioned that, even though the partners are likely to have similar resumes, each law firm has a distinct personality, which appeals to different types of people. If you do not fairly represent the attitudes that make your firm different, there is likely to be mutual disappointment later in the interview process or, worse, after a candidate has been hired.

I think I knew what the personality of the Hogan firm was when I was an active partner there in the 1980s and 1990s. I am, frankly, less certain that I know what it is today because the Hogan firm has merged with another giant firm, based in the UK. The resulting HoganLovells combination now has over 40 offices all over the world, and I obviously am not familiar with them all. In simpler times, however, I thought I could sum up the Hogan culture with a good story.

Around 1990, the firm thought it would be a good idea if those of us who did a lot of recruiting got some training at the job. About 30 gathered in a conference room for a seminar that was led by two articulate women who were professional consultants. They gave us some basic education, like the caveat that most interviewers talk too much and listen too little. They also presented us with some statistics on the characteristics of the people we typically met in our campus visits, including the valuable information that most of those who got offers from us also got offers from several other large competitors, with similar profiles, in the same city.

At one point in the seminar, they put a large chart upon the wall, with a list of about 50 summary descriptions like "good grades, self assurance, wide-ranging interests, etc., etc." We were each given a slip of paper and asked to list, in no particular order, five characteristics that we thought were most important in a candidate. We were instructed to do so individually, with no peer consultation.

When the "secret ballots" were collected, one woman left the room to tally them, while the other lectured. After a short interval, the ballot counter returned - wide eyed. She said "I have given this little test to a lot of firms with profiles similar to this one, and you collectively have given a top priority to a quality that I have never seen mentioned before."

The quality was "sense of humor." I included it in my top 5 and apparently a substantial number of my colleagues did, too. What I meant - and I know they meant - was not that we looked for someone who cracked jokes all the time. We were looking for people who took the clients' business seriously but did not take themselves too seriously. People who could laugh at themselves. A number of well-known law firms have collapsed because they were led by fundamentally humorless and self-centered egotists who always had to have their own way, in things great and small.

In addition to actual recruiting, I have always had the opportunity to serve on firm committees that monitored the progress of younger lawyers and helped to train them. At General Motors, for example, at the request of the General Counsel, I helped design a program that rationalized the annual evaluation process. (The second senior lawyer on the Staff, who served as the Executive Officer, previously had made decisions in a way that can only be described as whimsical. His idea of an event that justified a "merit" pay increase was the birth of a baby.)

The contribution of which I was most proud was the idea that the annual evaluation session should be conducted by the lawyer's direct supervisor in the presence of the evaluator's own direct supervisor. This facilitated a two-sided exchange, and helped to illuminate situations where young lawyers may have under-performed for reasons beyond their control. A system like this works when the organization has a pyramidal structure, as the GM Staff did; it cannot necessarily be implemented in an organization like a law firm with a structure that looks like a trapezoid.

In my opinion, the Hogan system for evaluating associates in their early years - and a separate process for weighing partnership potential later on - was comprehensive and impartial. Like some others, I did not particularly enjoy the job because I had come to like a lot of these young people. I didn't want to be one of the "gods" who decide on their future. It's just another reason why I would make a lousy executive. That lifelong preference for "staff" over "line" responsibilities.

Two extreme examples may illustrate why the evaluation process can some-times be rewarding. One guy, whom I will not name, consistently got wildly inconsistent evaluations. Each year, one group of partners would report that he was the most talented associate they had ever seen, and another group would report that he was by far the worst. I knew him personally, and thought he had an impressive mind, with a wide range of outside interests, but had never worked with him. It was a mystery.

The answer, of course, was really obvious once someone in our Committee thought of it. He was simply a free spirit, who worked hard on the assign-ments that captured his interest, and neglected those that he found boring. He was completely unsuited for the work in a large organization that had to provide quality service for a wide range of clients with varied problems.

He was, however, well suited for the academic world, where professors can pretty much do what they feel like doing. (That is, apart from the time spent in actually teaching students - which too many regard as a nuisance.) The academic world is where this fellow ultimately found a home, and the last time I saw him he reported that he liked it immensely.

I will identify the subject of another set of highly unusual evaluations. I did not interview Warren Gorrell, because he joined the firm in 1979, while I was still at General Motors. When I did arrive at the firm a little over three years later, I learned that he had already been identified as a potential leader of what was then the entire firm by his mentors in the Corporate Practice Group. (He is, of course, now Co-Chair of the combined HoganLovells, along with his counterpart in the UK David Harris.) When I had access to his evaluations as a member of the Committee responsible for them, the reasons were not immediately apparent. Then, and now, he comes across as relaxed and amiable, rather than intense and driven. I wouldn't know enough about Corporate practice to distinguish a brilliant lawyer from one that is merely competent, anyhow, and it is a quality that is hard to describe. I do know that Warren had far more than the usual level of energy - something that is characteristic of most top executives that I have met. (Ed Cole, a legendary President of GM, used to go hunting in the woods for half the night during the season, and still put in more than a full day at the office.) I have also been aware of Warren's ability to remember, and instantly access, a vast amount of detail about the business of the firm. That is also an ability shared by successful top executives.

Warren Gorrell's most important attribute, however, is best described by telling a story. A few years ago, when I was serving on the Federal Trade Commission, I accepted a speaking engagement at the Hotel del Coronado, just up the road from where I am writing now. The speaker who preceded me on the platform was a man named Peter Drucker, at the time considered to be the world's leading expert on corporate management - in fact, he is widely acknowledged as the founding father of his field of study.

Peter Drucker was over 90 years old. He had to sit down as he lectured, but there was nothing feeble about his mind. In the open question period after his speech on a rather technical issue, Mr. Drucker was asked to sum up his view on the most essential attributes of a good manager. The following is the gist of his response, as I best recall it. Actual words that stuck in my mind are set off between quotation marks.

"There is no single personality trait. I have known some who were martinets and some who were approachable. The one thing that they all have is the ability to assure their subordinates that they know what they are doing. These subordinates have put their personal or professional lives in the hands of their leaders and if they are confident that the leader knows what he is doing they will follow him anywhere."

He then went on to cite the example of the World War II General Patton. It was no secret that Patton sometimes acted a little crazy, and was a demanding leader. But, the German enemy believed he was their most formidable foe, and his men had immense confidence that "he knew what he was doing and would look after them."

"There also is an important correlate," he continued. "The leader has to demonstrate that he has full confidence in his subordinates' ability to carry out whatever responsibilities are assigned to them. If he does not have that confidence, he should replace them with people he does trust, and let them know that he does." If he does not have full confidence in his people, he will be continually looking over their shoulder and continued second-guessing will smother their creativity.

I have observed that Warren Gorrell has an uncanny ability to assure present or potential clients, and his colleagues in the firm, that he knows what he is doing and confident about the abilities of others who will work on any given project. That is why he is where he is. This is not purposeful flattery, by the way. I am genuinely impressed that someone who really is a member of my children's generation has organizational skills that I never did. And, I would have nothing to gain from exaggeration, anyhow. The firm has been very good to me over the years, but the river rolls on. No words I use can change the fact that this is a December song.

Jury Service

In Washington, D.C., lawyers are not automatically excused from jury service. There probably are so many of them that an automatic exclusion would seriously deplete the jury pool. Nevertheless, a lawyer is unlikely to survive the selection process because one side or the other is likely to exercise its right to make a peremptory challenge. The general assumption is that counsel for a plaintiff in a civil case or a defendant in a criminal case will challenge lawyers because they are perceived as resistant to emotional appeals. Despite these obstacles, I was lucky enough to serve on two juries during my years in Washington. I say "lucky" because the experience was not only educational, but actually inspiring.

In the first case, the plaintiff was a legless man in a wheelchair. He was petitioning for release from the St. Elizabeth Mental Hospital, where he had been involuntarily confined. In the District, a mental patient in that situation is entitled to a jury trial on the issue of sanity.

The witnesses for the district were policeman and mental health professionals, who testified about the petitioner's long history of mental problems. It seems that he did fine in the hospital when he was taking his medication, but invariably stopped taking the pills and became seriously disoriented when he was released. He had lost his legs from frostbite when he lay in an alley throughout a cold winter night, and most recently he had been wheeling his chair in the middle of a major highway. The unanimous expert opinion was that he was a menace to his own health and safety.

The sole witness for the other side was the petitioner himself, who testified in a seemingly lucid and appealing way that he had learned his lesson and was able to take care of himself. The direct testimony was very confined, which left very little room for a searching cross examination. There was no redirect, and the judge told the petitioner that he could wheel back to his place. (The relief of his assigned counsel was palpable.) The man then turned to the judge and said: "But, your honor, I really didn't get a chance to explain why I hate that hospital." His lawyer, obviously distressed, stood up and tried to object. But the judge said: "This is his case, and I'm going to let him say more if he wants to."

Anyone who has seen Humphrey Bogart's classic portrayal of Captain Queeg in The Caine Mutiny can guess what happened next. The poor fellow launched into a long monologue about the "sacred temple" of his body which is being systematically poisoned by those mind altering pills they were forcing him to take, which was "impairing his immortal soul, etc., etc." As he rambled on and on everyone in the courtroom sat in stunned silence.

It was obvious to me that this man was mentally ill, but I wondered how my fellow jurors would react. The petitioner was black, as were 9 of the 12 members of the jury. All of the policemen and experts were white. I wondered if racial tensions would play any part in the deliberations.

Because I was a lawyer, my fellow jurors wanted me to act as foreman. I thought it would be best to decline and instead suggested that we elect a dignified elderly gentleman of color. After he was elected, he asked me what I thought he should do first. I suggested that we begin by polling each juror for his/her preliminary views.

The first person he called on was an equally dignified and elderly black woman. She had no trouble, at all, and simply announced: "That boy is nuts!" There was pretty quick agreement all round, but we took time just socializing in order to avoid an appearance of undue haste. I was impressed by the common sense of my peers, but the most memorable thing came in the courtroom after we announced our verdict. The petitioner showed no discernable reaction, but then raised his hand and asked the judge whether he would be permitted to address the jury. No one objected, but no one really knew what was going to happen next. There was some tension in the air.

The man wheeled around and rolled up to the jury rail. He then smiled and said how much he appreciated our consideration of his case and that, even though he was disappointed by the verdict, he understood our reasons and had no hard feelings. I think everyone in the courtroom, including the judge, was blinking back tears. It seems the poor fellow was just grateful that people had been willing to listen respectfully.

My second jury case was equally dramatic, in a very different way. It was a criminal complaint against a policeman, a veteran of the Vice squad who had for many years supposedly extorted sexual favors from prostitutes by threatening them with arrest. The prosecution witnesses were all prostitutes themselves or internal affairs officers who believed their stories. The defense witnesses, apart from the defendant himself, were fellow officers and neighbors who vouched for his good character. There were no independent observers of his conduct. So, it was basically his word against the word of about half a dozen women who had made a career out of living outside the law.

I was very surprised to have survived all challenges and serve on this jury. In fact, I was the first one seated, and this time did serve as foreman. I speculated that one possible explanation might be that the prosecutors thought a lawyer would be trained to believe that even society's outcasts are entitled to legal protection. The defense counsel might have thought that someone with an Irish surname would be sympathetic to a cop. After the trial, when I was free to inquire, I asked each how I had survived. They both said: "By accident. I assumed my adversary would object, and didn't want to waste a challenge."

Because of the lurid nature of the charges and the occupation of so many witnesses, the trial was covered at length on the evening news and in the *Washington Post.* To avoid even a suggestion of outside communications,

I stopped watching the TV news altogether and asked Stephanie to review the morning paper first and to cut out any stories about the trial.

The trial lasted about two weeks and there were frequent recesses, so I got to know my fellow jurors pretty well. They were evenly split by sex and by race, as well as education level, and I was impressed by the seriousness with which they all approached their task and their scrupulous avoidance of any premature conversations about the trial evidence.

During the course of the trial, I became convinced that the defendant officer was a liar and corrupt to the core. I believed that the complaining prostitutes might have obscured some aspects of their personal life, but were basically telling the truth about the officer's conduct. When the trial was concluded, and I had been elected foreman, I began by asking the jurors individually to state their views. I was somewhat surprised when every one of the jurors had the same general reaction that I did. We still had a lot of work to do, however, because there were about 15 separate counts and the evidence on some was a bit murky.

In the course of a discussion on one count, where tentative views were split, one juror asked a very intelligent question. She said that she could not reconcile the judge's standard instruction to follow her individual convictions but, at the same time, be willing to take account of the opinions of her fellow jurors. She thought she was being instructed to do two wholly inconsistent things, and she wanted to know whether any of us could help her.

For better or worse, I stepped into the breach. I said that I couldn't speak for everyone, but I sometimes have to decide questions on legal strategies on which I have split feelings - they are close calls. And, I find it helpful to check out a tentative view with other people whom I respect. If they agree with me, I feel reassured; if they disagree, I may re-think my original view. The test, of course, is 'reasonable doubt' but you can legitimately question whether your doubts are 'reasonable' if a lot of people don't seem to share them, and vice versa. To bring the example closer to home, I said I was willing to change my minority vote on the count under discussion, and accept the views of the majority.

I have no idea how a legal purist would react to this rationalization, but we were able to reach unanimous agreement on the merits of all counts. We voted for the defense on about five counts and with the prosecutor on about ten. The guilty group included the most serious count of all, which was based on testimony that the cop had not only threatened one prostitute with arrest but had also shown her his gun, in order to keep her in his car and coerce the sexual favors. Under the law of the District, this is tanta-mount to kidnapping while armed and is a very serious offense, indeed.

At the last minute, a wholly unexpected snag arose. A young black woman, who had seemed to agree on the merits, said that she did not quarrel with our view of the facts, but her religion taught her that only God had the right to pronounce judgment on another human being. On reflection, she really couldn't declare that someone was "guilty". This, of course, was an impedi-ment that all the prospective jurors had been asked about in the selection phase, but it would have been futile to chastise her for her silence. She was already too depressed. I didn't know what to do; it looked like two weeks of a high visibility trial and three tough days of jury deliberations would go down the drain.

Then a young black fellow - who seemed to be a bright and amusing guy with a somewhat irreverent personality - said "let me try." He moved his chair, and sat down beside her, and began to talk in a low and soothing tone. I cannot remember exactly what he said, and I never could have done it myself, but it was about the best argument that I have ever heard. The rest of us just sat silently. After a while, she began to nod her head in understand-ing, and finally said in the midst of sobs: "OK. I can vote with all of you."

When we reported we had a verdict, and returned to the courtroom, it was my job to announce the verdict on each count - which I did in as firm a voice as I could muster, while looking at the defendant square in the eye.

However, the ordeal was not quite over. Defendant's counsel, of course, asked that the jury be polled. The young woman who had such a tough time was Juror #3. When she was individually polled there was a dead silence. It seemed to last forever - or at least long enough for me to think "Oh [bleep]!" Then I heard a soft "yes". I hoped my exhale was not too obvious.

It should be apparent that I still savour the experience. We jurors had really bonded by then, and most of us joined in an impromptu celebratory drink at a restaurant across the street. We indulged in the usual exchange of addresses, and promised to stay in touch - but of course, never followed through.

This trial, along with the earlier one involving the mental inmate, taught me some things about litigation that I never could have learned as a practicing lawyer. I have come to believe that most jurors take their responsibilities very seriously, try to do the best they can, and collectively have good judgment on issues of credibility. Whether they can do well in cases with complex business facts is something that I am not prepared to say.

There was an interesting sequel to the case of the corrupt and concupiscent cop. He was sentenced to 15 years in federal prison, which will be no picnic for someone in what had been his line of work. A few weeks later, I ran into a friend at a party who told me that she had been made the head of the sex crimes unit in the District. I didn't know that she was there, and neither of us knew before that the other had anything to do with this high visibility case. She said: "You wouldn't have heard it, but this SOB had been on our radar screen for a long time. However, we thought it would be hard to convict him, given the occupation of the complainants, and offered him an opportunity to resign quietly. He was so arrogant that he flatly turned us down - and look where he is now."

The "Fulbright Table"

For over twenty years, I joined a rather boisterous group gathered for lunch in the office cafeteria. It varies in size from day to day, depending on peoples' schedules, but most of "the regulars" have chosen to eat there if they can. The superannuated are heavily represented, presumably because we have more spare time to participate in often-frivolous conversations. The group is almost exclusively male, presumably because not many women enjoy the continuous exchange of insults that seem to bond men together. (My usual table in the GM executive dining room had the same ambiance.) Mary Anne Mason has been one of the few women who are sometimes willing to tolerate us.

The table is named after William Fulbright, the Arkansas Senator who is famous today for the fellowships that he sponsored as well as for the sometimes maverick political views that made him hard to place in the political spectrum. He practiced international law at Hogan & Hartson after he left the Senate in the 1970s, and was active there for roughly 15 years, until his health began to fail in the early 1990s. In his last years, he really enjoyed lively debates over lunch in the cafeteria. He never pulled rank or sought any deference on account of his vast experience. He believed, for example, that the separation of executive and legislative powers in the U.S. led to government paralysis, and expressed a preference for a parliamentary system like that in the UK. Often, he would ask the most junior guy at the table to debate this issue with him.

In deference to the Senator's fondness for debate on questions of no current relevance, we regulars not only named the table after him, but adopted two governing rules for discussion. First, no discussion of current business is permitted, in order to ensure a needed respite from that stuff. Second, no one is allowed to base an argument on superior knowledge, in order to encourage participation by all regardless of whether they know what they are talking about. It makes for a richer, if often irrelevant, debate. A regular like Kevin Lipson, for example, is cherished because of his amusing narratives on subjects of no interest to anyone other than himself and his keen enjoyment of the consequent brickbats.

Occasionally, however, we learn something. For example, Bob Michel, once the Republican Minority Leader in the House, is still a regular in his late 80s; and the late Paul Rogers, a longterm Democratic Congressman, was a regular until his final illness in 2008. John Porter, another former Congressman, people with high-level experience in other branches of government, and Bob Bennett, who has represented prominent politicians in both major parties, also regularly join the group. Sergey Chetverikov, a former Soviet diplomat and present consultant on business in Russia, is a regular. People like that cannot help but contribute something meaningful, in the midst of the general raillery. The table rules are sometimes waived by general consent, and all learn from it.

Let me provide one example. The rule against discussion of current business does not forbid discussion of *past* business, and most of us have good war stories to tell. One day, I particularly enjoyed an extended account of the firm's work for the reclusive billionaire Howard Hughes. A former senior partner named Seymour Mintz, who died in 2010 at 98, used to visit from time to time. He was Hughes' tax lawyer, and other Hogan lawyers represented him on different matters. They all had to adapt to some very odd work habits.

One of Hughes' minions would call the knowledgeable Hogan lawyer and ask him to travel to Los Angeles, check into a particular hotel, and wait for further instructions. The wait in Los Angeles might extend for days, even though the lawyer's meter was running. When the call finally came in, the Hogan lawyer would be instructed to rent a car and drive at midnight to the intersection of two highways out in the desert someplace. When he arrived and was waiting in the lonely dark, the mysterious client would typically appear at the wheel of some rattletrap jalopy and they would discuss their business while driving around aimlessly.

The firm also represented Hughes when his voice was heard publicly for the last time. This was the famous incident when an author named Clifford Irving claimed that Hughes had hired him to write a biography and supplied him with written diaries. On the basis of this material - vouched for by some recognized handwriting experts - Irving's regular publisher, McGraw Hill, had paid a substantial advance to him and they thought to Hughes himself. Presumably, Irving believed he would get away with this scheme because Hughes had lived in total seclusion for years.

To everyone's surprise, Hughes broke a long silence in 1972, and participated in a teleconference with a number of journalists who had known his voice well. They vouched for him, and the fraud unraveled. Irving ultimately served a brief jail term for his deception, and McGraw Hill was profoundly embarrassed.

This particular story fascinated me because I had represented McGraw Hill many years before, when I was working on some general litigation at White & Case. The Hughes fraud broke after I had left for General Motors, but earlier I had represented McGraw Hill on a different matter involving the same Clifford Irving! Ironically, but perhaps not coincidentally, Irving had written a biography of another imposter - a painter named Elmyer de Hory, who had an uncanny ability to reproduce the style of many famous artists.

The forgeries had been exposed and acknowledged, but de Hory objected to some details in Irving's book and sued for libel in the Federal District Court in New York. I was asked by McGraw Hill to defend the action. It appeared that the client had very little to worry about, at least initially, because de Hory was so preoccupied with his legal troubles in Europe that it was not likely he would be able to pursue an action in New York anytime soon. I remember that I advised on various strategies to keep the action on ice until de Hory untangled his affairs, and the lawsuit eventually died of neglect.

A story not really worth telling, except for one brief conversation with my contact at the client. I remember saying something like: "If we ever have to get to it, how are we on the merits with this thing?" And the answer was: "No need to worry about that. Clifford Irving has a reputation as one of our most reliable authors."

These ancient memories are things that we old guys like to talk about.

One final comment about the Fulbright Table. One of the regulars was a much younger guy named John Roberts, now Chief Justice of the United States. By his own estimate, we probably had lunch together a thousand times. You don't need to ask what he is "really like" because you already know. John Roberts' public face and his private face are exactly the same. He doesn't think out loud in private any more than he does in public, nor does he do what so many of us do at the Fulbright Table, namely, talk without thinking at all. I will mention John Roberts again in the following Chapter, but it is just a story about an interesting coincidence - there is nothing at all newsworthy about it.

In fact, John's record is so clean, that during his confirmation an adversarial journalist, desperate for something to criticize, made one of the more idiotic comments of our time. He said John Roberts' record was disturbing precisely because he never seems to have done anything wrong. Daniel Moynahan's famous comment that modern society was "defining deviancy down," has here been carried to newer depths. In this journalist's view, some history of deviancy now seems to be an essential qualification for high public office.

On the wall adjacent to the "Table" in the cafeteria, there are now two small metal plaques. The original one honors the memory of William Fulbright, who really was the inspiration for the group. The second one notes the fact that The Chief Justice of the United States once regularly dined there.

Personal and Professional Changes

As mentioned briefly above, Stephanie and I remarried in June of 1991, after we had lived apart for 8½ years. In the interim, we had talked on the phone about matters relating to our children, and exchanged an occasional greeting card, but we never saw each other until we met at our daughter Alison's Seattle wedding in June of 1990. The second time we met during the period of our separation was the following Spring, when we agreed to marry again

- and then did so shortly thereafter. Needless to say, the fast decision was a total surprise to a lot of people, but the interesting thing is that some people were not at all surprised. It seemed that they sensed undercurrents at Alison's wedding that we were not aware of.

Since Stephanie had professional obligations in Seattle that would take some time to unwind, we had a long-distance commuter marriage for awhile. If the gradual termination of a business relationship can be described as a "soft landing", as I have done several times here, I guess the renewal of our married life could be called a "gradual takeoff." After a short second honeymoon in a mountain resort near Seattle, we flew together to Michigan to attend the wedding of our son David. So, we had three family weddings in the space of a little more than a year, and welcomed a new son-in-law, Robert Estep, and a new daughter-in-law, the former Kelly Hutchison.

This was excitement of a pleasant kind, but beginning just six months later I had a very different kind of prolonged excitement. In December, 1991, I had the first of three cancer operations in a three year period. The third tumor turned out to be benign, but it still was plenty big and no one knew until after the fact. As a result of these operations, I am missing some body pieces, which fortunately have had no noticeable effect on my day-to-day life. The mental fallout, however, has been profound.

Someday, I may write a full account of my spiritual journey, but all that needs to be said here is that the whole experience was not nearly as scary as I expected it to be. Mother Nature is kind. And, when something similar happens again, as it likely will in the relatively near future, I am confident that I will be able to bear it. That's a profoundly liberating thought.

All of this has also changed the way I view my professional life. I have done some things that were both interesting and rewarding. But, I don't kid myself that I am irreplaceable or will leave a lasting legacy. That's liberating, too. It was easy to follow my father's advice, and begin to clear the way for younger people. When I was uncertain about my health and strength, I took advantage of a recently announced firm policy and arranged to reduce my workload and my compensation in a corresponding amount. I had fully expected my life as a lawyer to just gradually wind down. Then, out of the blue, something entirely unexpected happened. From my point of view, another accident.

In early 1998, Christine Varney asked for a private conversation right after one of the weekly meetings of the firm's antitrust group. Christine, among other things, had served as a Secretary of the Cabinet in the Clinton White House, and as Federal Trade Commissioner. She was then a Hogan partner. (She recently served as the Antitrust Attorney General in charge of the DOJ's Antitrust Division.) She said that a Republican seat on the Federal Trade Commission would be available in a few months, and the current Chairman Bob Pitofsky wondered if I would be willing to make a run for it.

I was speechless. At various times in my earlier life, I had given some thought to the possibility of government service, but assumed that the opportunity had long passed. I was, after all, closing on 67. Christine said: "Why don't you think about it, and let Bob know if you're interested."

Well, I did think about it, and talked to Stephanie about it. (She raised no objections.) So, I decided: What the hell. I might as well take a look at it - it's a long shot anyway.

Bob Pitofsky and I met for lunch the next week, and he really got me interested. We had known each other for years and there was a lot of mutual respect, even though we didn't always agree. He said he would welcome the opportunity to work with me as a colleague.

I had one big question. Although I was a lifelong Republican, and had taken an active interest in some issues that had to be resolved politically, I had never taken an interest in the process itself. I had never tried to establish a personal relationship with any active members of Congress and had never worked on, or given a substantial amount of money to, any campaign. Bob said that the President would likely appoint whomever was recommended by the Republican leadership in the Senate. "If you can get Senator Lott to recommend you, I will take care of the White House." I said that might just be doable, even though I had never met the Senator. I had some ideas that might work, and was willing to try.

We left the lunch with those mutual assurances. I began to plan the first steps in a process that eventually led to an immensely rewarding experience in my life as a lawyer.

SIX YEARS ON THE FEDERAL TRADE COMMISSION

Federal Trade Commissioners are appointed for terms of seven years. Many resign roughly halfway through the term, and another appointee serves out the balance. The reason is that most Commissioners are not career federal employees; they come from the private sector and are not willing or able to serve for an extended period of time.

I was not in that position. Our kids were adults, no longer living at home. Stephanie and I were able to live comfortably in a small city house on Capitol Hill in the District, and never had developed expensive tastes. If so appointed, I hoped to serve for a full term and I ultimately did stay until expiration - actually, a little beyond. So, why six years instead of seven?

The reason is that I was affected by an almost unprecedented chance event and the vagaries of the confirmation process. I have told this story many times with some high emotion. I'm in a more mellow mood now, because a one-year delay no longer seems like such a big thing. I will quickly review it again, however, because I think it highlights a serious flaw in the process - one which limits the pool of people who are willing to serve in government.

The Long Story

When Bob Pitofsky told me that I needed to get the recommendation of the Republican Senate leadership, the first person I talked to was Bob Michel, my frequent lunch companion and former Republican leader on the House side. I also talked to Frank Fahrenkopf, a Hogan partner who had chaired the Republican National Committee in the Reagan years. They both were cautiously optimistic, and said they would enlist help from their wide circle of influential friends.

I also talked to a handful of prominent people in the client world and in the American Bar Association. I emphasized, however, that I did not want to get into a battle with some other viable candidate, if there was one, because I had neither the stomach nor the aptitude for it. I also did not want to get feedback on progress or know the identity of other people whom they might enlist in the effort, unless it were essential. The reason was that, if the effort were successful, I did not want to feel affected, one way or the other, by the perception that I might be obligated.

The reason I say "one way or the other" is because conscientious people in public office do not necessarily favor the causes advocated by highly visible supporters. Clients or potential clients of a law firm may assume that the firm will get a particularly sympathetic reception from a former colleague or ally. This is not necessarily so. The reason is that many government officials want to avoid even the appearance of impropriety, and will bend over backwards to avoid it. On a more mundane level, they may be particularly aware of the weaknesses in some policy arguments that they once advocated themselves. I know I was.

Because of this self-imposed isolation, I gave very little thought to the FTC project for some months. I had no advance notice whatever of a call I got in early May of 1998, from someone whose name was unfamiliar to me. The caller identified herself as an aide to Senator Trent Lott, with responsibility for facilitating various federal appointments. She said the Senator had received "hundreds" of letters of recommendation about me, and would request President Clinton to appoint me to the Republican slot that would soon be vacated. She wanted to send over a copy of the draft letter, for my review.

Taken by surprise, I sputtered something like: "That's very considerate. I have never spoken to the Senator, and would be pleased to meet with him if he liked." She said "That won't be necessary. You have been recommended by people he trusts, and that's good enough." As an aside, I would add that I have never met Senator Lott and, while on the Commission, I never received a direct or indirect communication from him on the merits of any matter that came before me. A lot of public cynicism about the integrity of the federal government is really unjustified.

On May 8, 1998, Senator Lott wrote to the President on my behalf. The letter obviously had the desired effect because shortly after, I got a call from a White House aide, requesting that I come over to pick up some questionnaires that I should fill out, in order to move the process along.

I will mention her friendly opening greeting, not because I took any particular notice of it at the time, but because of a supposed public scandal that was much discussed almost ten years later. As the second term of President Bush drew to a close, the Justice Department was under close scrutiny. The adversarial Washington press made much of the fact that an applicant for a position in the Department had been asked "why she wanted to serve President Bush?" Some writers professed to be shocked, shocked that anyone would say such a scandalous thing, and the young interviewer was pilloried for days.

In 1998, my introduction to the White House was a cordial greeting: "Welcome to the Clinton team!" Well, of course, I didn't consider myself as a budding member of the Clinton team; I hoped to be appointed to an independent agency that was not supposed to be on the "team" of any President - unlike an employee in the Justice Department. And, I was clearly identified as an adherent of the opposition party.

Of course, I wasn't inclined to lecture an eager young staffer on the separation of powers. I admired her enthusiasm, and was warmed by her courtesy. (Some persnickety critics in the adversarial press need to lighten up.) I might add that all the Clinton people were unfailingly helpful to me, and gave me some useful hints on how to best deal with the process. I might further add that, while I was on the Commission, I also never received a direct or indirect communication from either President Clinton or President Bush on the merits of any matter before us.

Shortly after my initial discussions with the White House people, I was given a lengthy personal questionnaire to initiate the necessary FBI review. Later on, there were additional questions. (My personal life had sometimes been a bit complicated.) My contacts at the FBI, however, were also friendly and cooperative. The whole process seemed to be moving smoothly, so smoothly that I was already being welcomed as a new colleague by longtime acquaintances in the Commission.

I was wrong.

In September 1998, the Monica Lewinsky scandal broke wide open. The need to respond, and the subsequent impeachment trial, must have taken top priority in the Administration. There obviously was also a large staff turnover. I heard nothing whatever about my appointment until the following year, and a new set of people were involved. It was not their fault, but I had to give them a lot of information that had already been supplied months before.

There also was apparently some sentiment in the White House to "pair" my nomination with the nomination of one or more people who were expected to be highly controversial. The theory was that the linkage with an uncontroversial guy (me) would ease the confirmation process for the controversial ones. The good efforts of a number of people - including Senator John McCain, then Chair of the Senate Commerce Committee - got this mess untangled. In August, my nomination was sent over to the Senate "unencumbered" - a funny way of saying "by itself." I promptly began the customary courtesy calls on Committee members and other influential Senators and Congressmen.

Let me interrupt this sad saga with stories about a couple of meetings, which should lighten things up.

Senator John Ashcroft, later Attorney General, was the next most senior Republican on the Commerce Committee. The Commission's legislative liaison was then a woman named Lorraine Miller, an experienced hand who seemed to be on kissing terms with everyone from the guards at the Capitol entrance to the most senior members. She briefed me before every interview on the personalities that I would encounter. She told me that John Ashcroft was a conservative man, who would nevertheless sometimes surprise you, and a deeply religious one - something that I already knew.

Anyway, the interview was humming along fine, and I felt very relaxed and comfortable. So relaxed that, when he asked me a hypothetical question I couldn't answer right away, I said "damned if I know." Well! He assumed a very grave expression and said that while he was a "man of the world and accustomed to profanity," I would be well advised to avoid it until I had been confirmed.

I had no idea whether he was serious or not, and decided to play it safe. So, I said: "Senator, let me revise my comment: I'm darned if I know." He laughed and said "that's much better." We parted on very good terms, and he later presided over my confirmation Hearing in John McCain's absence, and did an outstanding job.

By the way, Ashcroft was castigated as a prude later on when, as Attorney General, he had a curtain placed in front of a couple of semi-nude statues in the Great Hall of the Justice Department. I don't think I'm a prude, but I'm on his side this time. The statues are appallingly bad examples of the bombastic public art you see all over Washington. If I were in charge, I wouldn't cover them; I'd have them cut up for scrap.

Another amusing interview was with Congressman Thomas Bliley, Chair of the House Commerce Committee. He would, of course, not vote on my confirmation, but he was an influential man whom I should know. Lorraine warned me that the Congressman was a dignified and reserved Southern gentleman and that things might drag a bit. I should be prepared to carry the conversational ball.

His first inquiry was "tell me something about yourself." So, I started with my college education, and mentioned that I went to Navy OCS in Newport right after graduation. I was prepared to drone on, but he stopped me and said: "You went to Newport OCS; well, so did I. I was in Class 7, what was yours?" I said I was in Class 7, too, but we would not have had occasion to meet there because of the alphabetical grouping of the barracks assignments. That didn't stop him; he lit up and said, "you must remember that Chief, who was such a martinet on the parade ground," and I said "of course" and volunteered a memory of my own. We were then off to the races, with Navy tales back and forth.

As the conversation rolled on - with no reference whatever to current matters - his aides kept interrupting with comments like "Congressman, we really have to wind this up" because of some other commitments. And, he kept waving them away. Lorraine Miller had a pressing need to cover her mouth, to avoid an outbreak of unseemly levity. The meeting sure didn't drag. We were doing fine.

My Committee Hearing was held on September 9 (9/9/99); it was also largely a breeze; and I was voted out unanimously a few days later. Prompt confirmation by the Senate seemed assured. In fact, some office redecoration at the FTC - approved by Stephanie and me - was already underway. It looked like the long process was finally coming to an end.

Wrong again.

We were actually visiting Stephanie's mother in Coronado - on what we thought would be a transitional holiday - when I got the news that there had been an unexpected further delay. It took a while for Loraine Miller and her aides to figure out what was going on, but the following bizarre story slowly unfolded. It appeared that Senator Olympia Snowe was upset about the fact that a protégé of hers had not been appointed to some Commission on Fisheries. In order to vent her displeasure, she put a "hold" on Senate consideration for a Treasury Post of a protégé of Senator Byron Dorgan of North Dakota. (The involvement of a Senator from that State in a Fisheries matter remained a mystery.)

In order to vent his displeasure Senator Dorgan put a "hold" on me. (The most likely explanation is that the Committee Hearing on Senator Dorgan's guy was held the same day as mine, or it's possible I was the only Republican available for retaliation.) So, my fate depended on the resolution of a quarrel between two Senators that had nothing whatever to do with me. It is doubly ironic since both had previously expressed support for my nomination. Senators can, however, singly hold up a nomination for unstated reasons for an indeterminate amount of time.

In the meantime, I really had nothing to do. I had turned over the affairs of my regular clients to younger partners in the firm, and couldn't take on any significant new projects because of the uncertainty. I was so disgusted that I decided we should look for a vacation house in Coronado - so we could wait out a long delay in a very nice place.

This resolve turned out to be impractical because we did not find a house that we liked well enough right away, and we returned to Washington. (We did, however, buy one a few months later, sight unseen, based on floor plans and photos that the broker had sent to us. This is the same house that we live in full time today.)

Weeks went by, then months. Finally, the great Fisheries matter was resolved and the holds were lifted. One day, the Commission people monitoring the situation learned that my confirmation was expected that evening in a "Unanimous Consent" process.

It is not unusual for the Senate to vote on a group of uncontroversial nominees together late at night, after regular business has been concluded. Typically, the only Senators present are the designated Chair that day, a Senator deputized to read the names on the Consent list, and one Senator from each of the two parties to formally voice the unanimous consent. Unfortunately, the Senator who was supposed to read out the names was in an overly exuberant condition after some social function and stumbled badly in this rather simple assignment. The Senator in the Chair promptly gavelled the session to a close.

This was beginning to get tiresome. We were now well into November; the two-year congressional term would expire at Thanksgiving time; and there was no word on when the Consent Calendar would be taken up again. Daily reports from the FTC's Hill watchers were negative. If something didn't happen before adjournment, we would have to start over in the following term.

The evening before Veteran's Day, I got the usual message from one of the FTC's watchers that no action was likely that night, and the next day was a federal holiday. Both the Congress and the FTC would be closed. It was not a holiday at Hogan, however, and I was in my office in a foul mood. I probably was just there to eat lunch, because I had no work to do, and no computer to play with since I didn't want my office to look too much like an office. (I was one of the last holdouts. Barrett Prettyman, another holdout, had recently weakened and agreed to accept a computer on a trial basis. After one of the firm's tekkies had taught him how to turn it on and access his e-mail, he was greeted with the announcement that he had "501 e-mail messages." Horrified - he asked them to take the damn thing away. That was enough for me.)

Anyway, I got a telephone call that morning from John Roberts, then a hard-working young partner. He said "Congratulations, Tom, I see that you got confirmed last night." I voiced some surprise and skepticism, but he said that he just seen the announcement on the Senate website. I went up to his office, and he showed it to me. My name was indeed on a list of people who had been confirmed unanimously late the night before.

Fast forward now about four years. John Roberts had been in the first group of judicial nominees announced by the new President Bush, for a place on the D.C. Circuit Court of Appeals. He, too, had advanced through the process and voted out of the Senate Judiciary Committee, which is responsible for review of judicial appointments. Some "liberal" Senators opposed him, however, and for a long time the leaders of a Senate under Democratic control refused to vote on his nomination - even though he clearly had a filibuster-proof majority in his favor. I knew how he felt.

By that time, I was past the halfway point of my Commission service. If I wasn't out somewhere, I usually went up to the top-floor cafeteria to buy a carry-out, and ate at my conference table in the immense office that the good taxpayers had provided. My advisors had a standing invitation to join me but, if I was alone, I would sometimes watch Congressional proceedings on the television.

By some wild chance one day, I happened to catch the tail-end of a joint appearance of the majority and the minority leaders on the floor of the Senate. Senator Lott, the Republican, turned to Senator Daschle, the Democrat, and said: "Do we have an agreement that there will be no more than three hours of discussion on the John Roberts confirmation this Friday, and then we will have an up-or-down vote?" Senator Daschle then said that there was such an agreement.

So, I promptly called John Roberts at his office at the Hogan firm, and told him what I had just seen. He was taken completely by surprise. Since it was obvious that he would prevail in the promised vote, I was thus able to return the favor that he had done for me. He has since, of course, moved on to our nation's version of the Imperium, after a poignant series of events that is well known.

The reason I have taken up so much space with this story is because it provides a personal illustration of the reasons why the appointment and confirmation process seems to be broken. I didn't really suffer anything other than annoyance at the long delay. I already lived in the District; Stephanie's position as an adjunct professor at a local university would not be affected; and there were no children living at home. Most important, perhaps, the Hogan firm was generous and I was not hurt financially by the fact that my work had gradually ground to a halt.

Suppose, however, I had been a considerably younger person in a city a good distance from Washington, with a spouse who also had an established job there; that there were children to consider; and an employer would not continue to pay me generously, even though I was contributing very little. The potential for a lengthy delay like mine - which is unfortunately, all too common - might be a powerful deterrent. Good people are not willing to take their chances in this meat grinder.

This callous indifference to individual and public welfare, for reasons that I can only characterize as silly, does no credit to elected officials, whom I still respect in many other ways.

In my farewell talk to the Commission in the Fall of 2005 [22] - an occasion in which Chief Justice Roberts was good enough to participate - I deviated from the written version, with some remarks that showed how my own experience still rankled. I described the view from my office window: first, a playground for the pre-school toddlers in the day-care center, five floors directly below. I noted that kids that age seemed to be wholly self-centered, playing in their own little world, alongside but indifferent to the others. I then said how fitting it was that I could raise my eyes and see the Senate side of the Capitol on the horizon. My advisors were primed to interrupt right there and warn against any future indiscreet comparisons.

The episode was intended to introduce a note of levity, but I also hoped that the people in attendance would realize what I was talking about. If there are any in doubt who have troubled to read this far, they will know now.

The Differences between the Private and Public Sectors

People sometimes inquire about "how it feels to change sides" after over 40 years as a lawyer in the private sector, sometimes in litigation with one of the antitrust agencies. The best response I can provide is that there are differences, but I really did not feel that I had changed sides. Let me explain.

What is true is the fact that you always know what "side" you are on in the private sector- it's the client's side. There may be a lot of strategic decisions to be made; in fact, the best strategy may sometimes involve a candid admission that the client did something wrong. Even in these situations, however, the admission may avoid an expensive trial and mitigate the damage of public disclosure. The client's interests, as determined by its management, are still paramount.

In the public sector, however, it is not at all clear whose interests you are protecting. You are supposed to act in the "public interest," but the public is a diffused body of people with diverse interests and multiple advocates who claim to speak for them. In antitrust matters, there is a consensus that so-called "consumer welfare" is paramount - but, consumers are a diverse group, as well, with different priorities. (Not all of them are primarily interested in the lowest price.)

Learned advocates and economic experts, who apply similar well-respected tools of analysis, will arrive at different conclusions. As a Commissioner, I really did not know what "side" I was on.

My service on the Commission did not seem all that strange for another reason. The experience there confirmed the validity of advice that I had been given a long time ago by mentors like Ed Barton. The government does not bargain like ordinary litigants in settlement discussions. There may be some haggling around the edges, but the opening position of the Commission's decision makers is likely to be very close to their bottom line position, on matters of substance. People in the private sector are well advised to do the same. At the very least, it will save a lot of time, and preserve credibility.

My own rationale for this stance as a Commissioner - a view that I know many of my colleagues shared - was that I preferred free-market solutions to those imposed by government. I did not *want* the Commission to get more relief than was justified. There was also a practical consideration, particularly in high-visibility matters. If we initially ask for a lot, and settle for less, Congressional watchdogs may want to know why.

For this reason, service on the Commission was the most challenging, as well as the most liberating job that I ever had. It was liberating because I had no "boss" and no identifiable client. I was appointed by the President and confirmed by the Congress, but neither could remove me unless my conduct was outrageous enough to warrant impeachment. A court might ultimately review Commission decisions in which I had joined, but litigation was rare and reversals were rarer still. (Although some were highly visible.)

We had no internal culture of "party discipline." The Federal Trade Commission has, in recent years, been the least politically polarized of the independent agencies. So, I was ultimately accountable only to my own conscience - for the first time in my professional life. The challenging part arose from the fact that the available tools of economic analysis are not nearly as precise as I had believed. This is a theme that will appear in various aspects again and again as this memoir draws to a close, but let me try to sum up the problem as simply as I can.

If you are dealing with a claim that certain conduct is "per se" illegal, the only issue is whether people did or did not do certain things. The answer to these questions tends to depend on witness credibility or sophisticated surveillance techniques of the FBI. At the Federal Trade Commission, we had very few "per se" cases.

The vast majority of our antitrust work involved so-called "rule of reason" inquiries, which are characterized by the need to make predictions. If you are reviewing a proposed merger, for example, it is necessary to predict what the competitive world will look like once a deal has been consummated. If you are reviewing the legality of a business strategy that was implemented in the past, it is necessary to compare what actually happened with a prediction of what would have happened if the strategy were not in place. As I will detail later on, there is no rigorous way to do this.

There are other policy makers who also make predictions, by the way. When courts have to decide issues that arise under the Constitution - a document as laconic as the antitrust laws - they will often rely heavily on predictions. A majority opinion might say that our view of the document will lead to desirable outcomes that our forefathers would favor, and the minority will say that this reading will have terrible consequences. You, as an observer, may have firm opinions - which are likely to depend on your individual value judgments - but there is no way to be really sure which view is right.

In the subchapter below, I will mention some controversial FTC matters where none of us foresaw what actually happened.

Some Examples of Mistaken Predictions

I have tried to provide a sample of the uncounted mistakes that I have made at various stages of my life. The most serious were in the personal arena, but, on reflection, it is also obvious that I have made my share of professional mistakes.

A once-famous Supreme Court advocate (whose name escapes me now) supplied a vivid example. A few days after an appearance before the Court, a journalist asked him whether he was satisfied with his argument. And the advocate said something like: "Which argument are you talking about - the argument I prepared, the argument I was actually able to give in the intervals between the Court's questions, or the really marvelous argument that has occurred to me since?"

I was taught by various mentors that it is useless to torment yourself when, in retrospect, you believe you could have done a better job. You just absorb the lesson and move on. I have forgotten most of the incidents that once troubled me.

I better remember some decisions I made while I was on the Commission that had unforeseen consequences - perhaps because they were more recent and have had a more visible effect. The examples I will cite here are or were controversial matters where I did not act alone; they were collective decisions of the Commission as a whole. I was, however, always free to do what I wanted to do, and take individual responsibility for my choices.

The first example is a case where economic predictions, based on trend data, turned out to be faulty. The second example is a case where inherently unpredictable human choices led to a surprising outcome. The third, and probably most important, example is a case where we on the Commission made some tactical mistakes as a result of over-confidence.

The combination of Time Warner and AOL was then the largest one that had ever been proposed. After extended "clearance" discussions with the Antitrust Division, Bob Pitofsky was able to secure agreement that the Federal Trade Commission would review it. It was a big job, not just because of the transaction's size (initially valued at $180 billion), but because there were potential competition issues at three levels.

The first level was "content". Time Warner then had the most extensive inventory of potential internet entertainment in the industry. AOL had its own portfolio of content, but the most significant issue was its seemingly inevitable dominance as an Internet Service Provider ("ISP"). There was concern that the combination would solidify AOL's dominance at this second level, as well as Time Warner's position in the content level. In addition to these issues, we had to consider the fact that Time Warner had a cable monopoly in a very substantial "section of the country," a third level.

The investigation and complex decree negotiations consumed a considerable amount of time and internal resources. We Commissioners each had a steady stream of people who wanted to convey their serious concerns. A number of them were well-known luminaries in the entertainment business, whom I cannot identify because outside commentators have assurances of confidentiality. All I can say is that we took their comments seriously because they knew a lot more about the business than we did. (That doesn't mean that they knew more about how the antitrust laws should be applied.)

We had multiple interim meetings of the full Commission to discuss the matter - something that is highly unusual - and many more exchanges of views in one-on-one conversations. For example, Bob Pitofsky and I agreed that we should make every effort to agree on the outcome, because it would be particularly unfortunate if there was a party line split on this one. And, our views swung back and forth as the weeks went by.

The Commission ultimately cleared the deal with an unusually complicated regulatory decree. And, in the end, almost all of us were wrong. AOL did not become the dominant internet service provider that had been expected. Time Warner paid much more than the company turned out to be worth, and the shareholders took a big hit. The fears of experienced and respected industry leaders were unfounded. And, the Commission wasted a lot of time and effort on a matter that turned out to have little competitive significance.

I don't know about the industry people, but I think we in the Commission were mistaken because we assumed that data on recent industry trends, projected into the future, would support our predictions. Things don't necessarily turn out that way. I should have known better.

I remember when I was at General Motors, so-called "CB" radios were becoming increasingly popular as an automobile accessory. People could join in the chatter of truck drivers, who habitually interchanged information about things like traffic slowdowns or police speed traps. They had colorful nicknames (their "handles") and a growing number of auto drivers thought it was amusing and "cool" to make up their own handles. The installation trend line was climbing so steeply about 30 years ago that GM seriously considered inclusion of CB equipment as standard equipment on some models.

Then, entirely unexpectedly, the fad ran out of steam. It seems that people just decided it wasn't all that much fun to make up a sexy or menacing name, and talk to truck drivers. Today, of course, cell phones are a far superior communication device, anyhow.

The entertainment industry is particularly subject to seemingly sudden changes in consumer tastes, but today there are serious controversies about the validity of predictions based on the projection of trends in many other areas. The current debate over the severity of future global warming is probably the best known example.

The uncertainty of predictions based on a projection of trend lines is just one source of possible error. Two other sources will be illustrated immediately below. There is a further question, however. What would have happened if we, and so many others had not been mistaken?

One easy answer is that we on the Commission would never have occasion to look at the matter because the deal would never have been made in the first place. But, suppose that the parties were more optimistic about AOL's future than we were, and the deal had been submitted for review? That sometimes happens. My guess is that the outcome would have been much the same: clearance with a protective decree. However, we probably wouldn't have agonized about it so much, and the process would not have taken so much time.

Still, I took the lesson to heart, and the experience contributed to a growing recognition of my own limitations, and the limitations of tools on which I had relied.

The so-called "Baby Food" merger case was the one in which I cast what was probably my most controversial vote. [23] I caught a lot of flak about it at the time from some of my more conservative friends, although I doubt that many people remember it today. What startled people is that I voted with two Democrats (Bob Pitofsky and Mozelle Thompson) to block the merger, over the opposition of a Democrat (Sheila Anthony) and my Republican colleague (Orson Swindle). In fact, I was criticized so much at various Bar Association programs, that I published a short article to explain the vote. [24]

There were three major U.S. competitors in the baby food business. Gerber was by far the industry leader, while Heinz and Beech Nut trailed badly behind. Heinz proposed to buy Beech Nut, and we in the FTC had to decide whether to clear the deal or oppose it.

There is some economic support for the idea that competition can actually be improved if two smaller companies combine forces to challenge the market leader. The problem with this argument in this particular case, however, was that Heinz was then the largest baby food supplier in the world outside the U.S., and also had an impressive array of other food products. It could hardly be described as a weak competitor.

Counsel who supported the merger were an impressive array of people who were longtime friends, and frequent allies when I was in the private sector. They pulled out all the stops. If the parties were permitted to merge, they could more efficiently utilize available productive facilities; Heinz would have the volume to justify the development of innovative products; and, finally, Heinz and Beech Nut really didn't compete anyhow because they focused their efforts in different areas of the country.

My reason for rejecting these arguments can be summed up briefly. First, there are less restrictive ways that two competitors can rationalize productive capacity - supply contracts or production joint ventures, for example. Second, the investment necessary to fund innovative products was a great deal less than what Heinz proposed to pay for Beech Nut. Finally, as I observed in my article: "It would be perverse to permit parties to merge just because they have not chosen to compete hard in the past."

Shortly after Heinz had lost its case in the D.C. Circuit Court, it chose to sell its U.S. baby food business to Del Monte. This entirely unexpected development has ever since been good-naturedly raised with me by former critics as proof that they were right all along.

I have sometimes asked myself whether I would have voted differently had I been told that, absent the merger, Heinz would exit the baby food business in the U.S. It is not unusual for companies to claim that they will exit the business altogether, and sell off or scrap their productive assets, if they cannot sell their business to a competitor that has offered to buy it. The argument is that the alternative to a facially anti-competitive sale is the loss of jobs and productive assets. The "but for" world would be worse than a post-merger world. I have successfully deployed the argument myself. I must say, however, that I have never used, or seen this argument made, on behalf of the potential acquirer. Moreover, I have never seen an analogous warning that the alternative to the proposed acquisition is not a market exit but rather the replacement of one company by an arguably less potent competitor. In addition, of course, the threat has to be credible. Absent, an unequivocal resolution at the Board level, the threat may be a pretext.

In retrospect, however, it's possible but not proven that I could have been wrong, and I cannot hide behind my peers on this one because I was the swing vote. I had to call things as I saw them at the time, and there's no instant replay.

Without question, my most important decision on the Commission was the opinion I wrote in the Schering-Plough case. It's still cited a lot today, but unfortunately, only by people who are trying to change the current state of the law. The reason is that the opinion was promptly reversed by a Circuit Court, and the Supreme Court refused to take the Commission's appeal. [25]

The facts and arguments in this case were complicated, and involved the intersection of patent law and antitrust law, with an overlay of statutes and FDA regulations. The issue, simply stated, is whether or when it is permissible for the seller of a patented drug to settle a patent challenge by a generic competitor by paying the generic to abandon the challenge and delay its entry into the market. These are called "reverse payments" because patent disputes are usually resolved by payment of royalties to patent holders. There are potentially billions of dollars at stake when generic entry is deferred in reverse-payment settlements.

I wasn't the swing vote on this one. My opinion was unanimous, and the roughly 80 closely-printed pages were vetted by the four other Commissioners who signed on. (Chairman Tim Muris, Mozelle Thompson, Sheila Anthony and Orson Swindle.) In addition, I know that all of the predecessor or successor Commissioners who have looked at the issue before or since are in basic agreement with the principles set out in the opinion. However, even though the Supreme Court has not definitively resolved the issues yet, it is fair to say that the trend of judicial authority is now in the other direction. And, even though I did not stand alone, I have to take responsibility for the way the issues were framed and the arguments presented. The *Schering* case was the biggest failure in my term of public service, and I sometimes muse about what I might have done better.

In the light of hindsight, I believe my most serious mistakes resulted from overconfidence - something that probably affected my peers, as well. After all, a number of pharmaceutical companies with agreements comparable to those at issue in *Schering,* had promptly capitulated and signed consent decrees. We also had become aware of the fact that eminent defense counsel had advised their clients to avoid reverse-payment settlements.

The following are some of the drafting choices that I made, which were probably affected by over-confidence:

(1) The Administrative Law Judge ("ALJ") who presided over the trial of the case made a number of factual findings, that were adverse to the Commission's staff and with which we Commissioners disagreed when we heard the appeal. It is well settled law that, if there is a disagreement of this kind, it is the Commission's factual findings that prevail.

When I wrote the opinion, I just assumed that any appellate court would be aware of this basic principle. Accordingly, although I set out our agreed-on findings in detail, I did not go into a lot of detail about the reasons why we believed the ALJ was wrong. I suspect I just wanted to be tactful because he was a pleasant guy, a fellow employee of the agency, who would preside over a lot of trials in the future.

The 11th Circuit, for reasons I still do not understand, ignored settled law and relied on a number of the ALJ's conclusions, that we had explicitly rejected.

(2) The ALJ's opinion, favorable to the patent holder, was also based on a faulty legal premise. When there is a patent dispute between a patent holder and a putative infringer, the infringer has a very heavy burden to prove patent invalidity, but the patent holder has to prove the fact of infringement. Both were issues in the *Schering* matter, and the ALJ's opinion was partly premised on the faulty assumption that the infringer had the burden on both issues.

Again, my opinion for the Commission noted this fundamental mistake, but did not go on at length about it. Again, I just assumed that a reviewing court would be aware of well-settled law on the subject, and again I was wrong.

(3) We were aware of, but probably underestimated, the strong judicial preference for settlements - particularly, in patent cases which tend to be complex and technical in areas with which most judges are unfamiliar. With greater experience in a broad variety of cases, we could have made a stronger argument that the reverse payment settlements often should not be considered "settlements" at all.

There have been cases since *Schering* where the payment that the would-be generic entrant received in settlement for the agreement to delay entry exceeded its own profit expectations for the period of delay. In other words, the generic got more in a so-called "settlement" than it would have gotten by an outright victory. This is a very odd compromise, indeed.

Consider the following thought experiment. Suppose there was no open dispute, no lawsuit, and no "settlement." A would-be generic competitor quietly approaches the patent holder and says "We think there are serious questions about the validity of your patent and/or the issue of infringement. But, let's not get into a fight. We're willing to delay our entry until close to the date your patent expires, if you pay us what we would expect to earn if we had entered earlier plus a bonus for being such nice fellows."

I suspect that any good antitrust lawyer would say this hypothetical states a serious problem. But, many reverse-payment "settlements" are just a round-about way of accomplishing exactly the same thing. It still puzzles me that so many lawyers I respect, and well-regarded judges, just don't see it.

If we had made these points more forcefully, it may have allayed judicial suspicions that we were undermining established judicial preferences or were hostile to the legitimate rights of patent holders. I certainly was not hostile, nor were my peers. I firmly believe that the U.S. Pharmaceutical industry is more innovative than any in the world, and that protection of intellectual property plays an essential role in that success. That does not mean, however, that every strategy is justified.

(4) It also might have been desirable to frame a rule that took greater account of the strength of the patent. We were very reluctant to bog the Commission down in the merits of this dispute and, at the same time, were frustrated by the fact that the parties' own internal assessments on the merits of this issue - clearly relevant in a settlement context - were unavailable because privilege was claimed.

I still have not been able to figure out a solution to this dilemma, but we would have been better served if the opinion recognized the need for some preliminary inquiries into the merits.

Finally, there are a couple of perhaps Machiavellian strategies that I considered, but ultimately rejected. The parties claimed that the settlement issue did not involve a "reverse payment" at all because the generic did simul-taneously sell some of its own intellectual property to the payment holder - the payment was not just for delay.

If this argument were even arguably credible, we could issue an opinion that would outline the legal tests we advocated, but ultimately dismiss the case on purely factual grounds. Parties who have been dismissed have no right to appeal, and we could have avoided judicial review altogether.

The Commission has made law this way in the past. For example, the *Pfizer* case[26] established the principle that ad claims have to be substantiated in advance; "It is not enough to collect the support only after a challenge." There was no appeal in the Pfizer case because the Commission found there arguably was enough contemporaneous evidence, and dismissed the complaint.

The fact that this strategy was under consideration should be obvious from the structure of the opinion. Most opinions state the facts first, and follow with the legal analysis. In *Schering* I set out what we thought were the applicable legal principles in the first half, and devoted the second half to an analysis of the facts.

I had three experienced legal advisors, who scoured every word of the voluminous record in the *Schering* case and consulted with their counterparts in the offices of the other Commissioners. They unanimously agreed that the record simply would not support any claim that Schering's payment was for the intellectual property it bought rather than for delayed generic competition. So I concluded that the strategy would be transparently dishonest, and gave up.

The second Machiavellian strategy that I considered was to propose that we rest our conclusions on Section 5[27] of the Federal Trade Commission Act rather than the antitrust laws. There is some authority, and historic support, for the proposition that the Commission has the ability to decide that certain practices are "[u]nfair methods of competition," even though it is not clear that they violate the antitrust laws.

This might have made it somewhat more difficult for a reviewing court to reverse us, because agencies are normally given some deference when they interpret their own governing statutes. It was an unattractive option, however, because I doubted that there even was agreement among ourselves, on the parameters of Section 5, and in our optimistic frame of mine we were not inclined to rely on the contentious alternative.

(Controversy over the meaning of Section 5 continues to this day, and I have actually participated in the debate well after I left the Commission. I won't bore you with my views on the subject; in fact, I suspect I have already bored most readers with the extended discussion of the [bleeping] *Schering* case. I just can't help it, even though I know I shouldn't clutter up my head with these things that I cannot do anything about anymore.)

Other Lively Antitrust Issues

Although the three cases discussed may be the most significant or controversial, this selection does not begin to exhaust the difficult antitrust issues that we faced. Two other matters merit a brief mention.

The Commission's focus on health care issues extended well beyond the problem of "reverse payments" in patent settlements. In my view, the fundamental dilemma in the lively and continuing debate over health care can be summed up briefly, as follows: [28]

A Brief Essay on Health Care Economic Issues

Perhaps the most serious and pervasive problem, with which readers are undoubtedly familiar, is the fact that the consumers of medical services and products normally do not pay the full incremental costs of their care. They may pay collectively and indirectly through insurance premiums and taxes, but these costs are relatively fixed. Accordingly, there is a tendency to "over-consume." The overall tendency to over-consume may be mitigated in this area - as in other areas characterized by third-party payments - by provisions for larger co-payments or deductibles.

There is sometimes strong resistance to these measures, however, when it comes to health care.

Health care providers (like doctors) have a corresponding incentive to "oversupply" to the extent that they are paid for inputs like tests and procedures. Their patient-customers have neither the incentive nor the requisite knowledge to discipline this tendency. The mutually reinforcing incentives of providers and consumers means that supply and demand cannot reach an equilibrium. Some rationing or gate keeping system is required in order to temper the inevitable upward pressures on prices.

The political will to devise an acceptable rationing system that will contain collective costs is compromised by the fact that any individually identifiable human life is popularly considered to have an almost infinite value. This immense and widespread solicitude for the individual is one of the glories of our society, but it makes it hard to apply the rational economic models with which antitrust lawyers are familiar. This solicitude is even harder to accommodate when elected officials are almost compelled to say that everyone, regardless of means, is entitled not only to medical care but the "best possible" medical care. This is, of course, literally impossible, just as it is impossible for all the children in the mythical town of Lake Wobegon to be "above average." But, we have to pretend that we believe it.

As a result, the keepers of the gates will never be popular. If they are health maintenance organizations (HMOs) or insurance companies, they are broadly excoriated in the press and on the floors of Congress. If the gatekeeper is the State, like our neighbor to the North, people not only complain, but also pour across the border to bypass the system. (In fact, we can assume that the relatively affluent or well-connected will find a way to jump the line in any seemingly objective and egalitarian rationing regime - whether we are talking about health care or education or anything else where the perceived stakes are high.)

It is important to acknowledge that the Commission has a limited role in the development of a national health care policy. It does have jurisdiction under well-established principles of antitrust law, although in this industry - as in some others like national defense - it is necessary to be sensitive to some special characteristics. The Commission also has a role as an advocate for competition values, within the larger framework established by the political arm. Government monopolies or government-sanctioned private monopolies tend to be relatively inefficient and slow in their response to changed conditions. It was our job to point this out, and argue for some competitive disciplines to the extent possible.

During my term at the Commission, we spent a substantial (perhaps inordinate) amount of time on antitrust issues involving physician practice associations. These groups of providers had grown exponentially, in response to the perceived power of payors like insurance companies or managers of employee group health plans.

The applicable legal principles may facially appear to be simple. A "unitary" organization like a corporation, or a labor union, or a partnership, can set prices or fees for the products or services that may be provided by a large number of people. If these people are not employees or members of a unitary organization, however, it is *per se* illegal for them to negotiate prices or fees collectively. It is not necessary for a prosecutor to prove competitive harm; the only issue is whether they did it or not.

The situation is not so simple, however, when you are dealing with a medical group. The docs are obviously the "sellers," but who are the "buyers" - the patients themselves or the entities that may pay most or all of the costs? For convenience, we assume that the payers are generally the representatives of these patients, but should we trust them to make all the decisions? If you were to poll patients on whether they trust their insurers more than their doctors, I suspect they would overwhelmingly vote for their doctors.

This means that antitrust principles have to be applied with some flexibility. We *wanted* the doctors to have a major role in "quality of care" decisions - collectively, if necessary - to counter the power of large payers, even though these decisions can obviously have an effect on prices. We also wanted the doctors to act collectively in order to share information and adopt the most up-to-date practices.

In order to strike a balance between these competing interests, the Commission and the Justice Department had used guidelines that set out their enforcement policies. [29] The basic idea was that, regardless of the formal legal structure, physician groups could collectively negotiate prices with payers if they were "financially integrated" (had a financial structure that shared risk and rewarded performance) or "clinically" integrated (established programs to provide better care.)

For some time, these were treated as alternate and independent tests, but a little thought should make it obvious that they really are linked. Financial integration tests alone may make it easier to draw a line between what is legal and what is not, but it really does not guarantee a benefit unless the right things are rewarded. For an analogy that lawyers might better understand, imagine a law firm that based compensation solely on business generation.

Similarly, even the best clinical integration plan on paper will not necessarily be implemented, unless there is a sufficient collective investment in the necessary computer technology and sufficient rewards and sanctions to help ensure compliance. To complicate matters still further, a physician group may understandably want some up-front assurance from the agency that it has taken the necessary steps to avoid the serious consequences of an antitrust prosecution, and the agency has to do the best it can to respond.

Moreover, the task may not be any easier if the agency has to evaluate performance after-the-fact. The usual indicia of anticompetitive consequences, such as reduced output and/or price increases, are difficult to measure or evaluate in this context. What is the "output" of a medical group anyway, and increased outlay by payers may simply be the result of improved quality. The best doctors in the world, like those at Mayo, are not cheap. And, larger expenses will inevitably be incurred if patients live longer because of their improved quality of care.

I worried a lot about these issues while I was on the Commission, and sometimes expressed my doubts in print. [30] I still do not have any easy answers. The best global advice I could give to any budding physician practice group is a variant of the legend you see on some television ads for high-performance automobiles: "Do not try this at home." Don't necessarily rely on your hometown generalist to structure your group; seek out the best antitrust advice that you can find.

The effort to achieve some "convergence" in the antitrust laws of countries was, and continues to be, a matter of great concern. When I began to counsel an international company like General Motors in the 1970s, I really did not have to worry about the differences between U.S. antitrust laws and the laws of the relatively few foreign countries that had laws of their own. I could simply assume that U.S. law was more restrictive than those anywhere else, and if a given business strategy was alright here it was alright everywhere.

Late in the decade, however, things began to change. The judicial acceptance of the "new learning" meant that in some situations U.S. law was less restrictive. For example, our new tolerance of most territorial limitations on resales by dealers did not accord with EU law that prohibited impediments to cross-border trade.

A difference like this one was relatively easy to manage. Over time, however, more and more countries passed and began to enforce their own antitrust laws, complete with requirements to pre-notify mergers or other potentially anticompetitive arrangements. I've lost track of the number of countries, but it is well over 100. The implementation of a large international merger can require consultation with multiple law firms, and the preparation and submission of multiple notification forms. This would be bad enough if the substantive standards were the same, but the burden is even heavier if substantive standards are markedly different.

This explains the priority that is given to the "convergence" effort by various Bar groups and by both the antitrust agencies in the U.S. The effort is even more intense and well organized today than it was when I was on the Commission (from 1999-2005), but it took up a lot of my time and thought when I was there. A few things stand out in my mind.

Our efforts in the international arena are compromised by the fact that we continue to have multiple antitrust enforcement authorities in the United States. The fact that we have two federal enforcement agencies, the FTC and the DOJ, is not the most serious problem because, for the most part, they apply the same standards, and they amicably divide authority and focus on different sectors of the economy.

The fact that we have 50 sovereign states, with their own antitrust laws, is facially an even more serious embarrassment when we preach the virtues of convergence in our travels abroad. It is even harder to explain the fact that the "National Association of [State] Attorneys General" (NAAG) has collectively published its own substantive standards, on things like merger review but differ from those published by federal representatives of the "United States." The European Union, which has been acting collectively for some 60 years, has actually done more to arrive at a rational division of authority between the EU antitrust agency in Brussels and the agencies in its various member countries than we have done in a federal system that we have had in place for over 220 years!

I suggest that anyone who thinks this is necessary or tolerable try to explain it to a representative of a foreign government. I certainly couldn't. As I look back on my years of public service, one big regret is that I didn't try harder to focus the attention of my colleagues on this problem. I suspect that everyone was, and still is, wary of an issue that could become intensely political. If the Commission took up the battle, it might stir up a storm of hostility from all sides of the political spectrum. Many so-called "liberals" welcome the consistent State advocacy of stricter antitrust enforcement and many so-called "conservatives" still have a residual attachment to "states rights" generally.

The voice of my grandmother, still in my head, tells me there isn't a thing I can do about this now, and I should just let it go. We're having another beautiful day in Coronado.

One area where I may have been able to make a small contribution was the general tone of the discussions with our foreign counterparts. Without naming names, I will say that I was dismayed by the way that some of our prominent Bar members - and even government officials - talked to their colleagues overseas. The general message was "We know more about these things than you do, and you should do things our way." Early in my FTC term I published a brief "Comment" on this general subject, [31] and I was told that it attracted considerable appreciative attention overseas. If that's true, I'm glad.

While I was on the Commission, I had the opportunity to practice what I had preached in extensive meetings with our counterparts in China and in Russia, and these are experiences that I still remember fondly. I don't think many people have had the opportunity to lecture before a scholarly audience in Beijing or to appear on a televised news conference in Moscow. "Public" service isn't necessarily just about sacrifice; it can also lead to high adventure.

We went to China first, in late June of 2004. The adventure began with the flight over, when we flew to Beijing non-stop from Chicago. I had flown the Pacific twice many years before, but this time I didn't see the Pacific at all. From Chicago, you fly almost due North over the wilds of Northern Canada, cut briefly across the Arctic, and then turn South over Siberia - which looks a lot like Northern Canada from the air. At that time of year, it was daylight all the way. Magnificent!

The trip had been arranged by the U.S. State Department, at the request of the Chinese government. I was co-head of the delegation with Hew Pate, then head of the DOJ's Antitrust Division, and our job was to advise our Chinese counterparts about a new competition law that was then under consideration. Hew had a number of more junior colleagues with him, but I had only one, Randy Tritell, then an Assistant Director in charge of the Commission's International Antitrust unit, who actually knew a lot more about the subject than I did.

Both Randy and I had brought our wives (at our own expense, of course) and that was the occasion for an amusing encounter when we went through Customs at Beijing's airport. Stephanie had been born in China in the mid-1930s, when her father was a destroyer officer on what was then known as the U.S. Navy's "China Station." Because it was an extended tour of duty Stephanie's pregnant mother was permitted to travel there, as well. The Customs officers had to have been stunned when this very tall, very blonde woman presented a U.S. passport with Shanghai, China, listed as the "Place of Birth". He was too polite to say anything, but the look on his face was priceless.

Because the journey was so long, and the government sessions so intense, we devoted a couple of extra days at the beginning and the end to sightseeing and general unwinding. In retrospect, I wish we had spent more time in China, because we barely touched the surface. We'd really love to go back, but I'm not sure we have the stamina for such a trip anymore.

We spent most of the first day in the Forbidden City, which was only a few blocks away from our modern and comfortable hotel. We spent most of the next day on a visit to the Great Wall at Simitai, a segment that is located well North of Beijing, but unlike the popular tourist site closer in, still standing in an unrestored condition. The overwhelming visual impressions - the sheer scale of both the City and the Wall cannot be adequately described in words, and the videos we took are not much better. Like the huge monuments in Egypt, you really have to be there.

I will only note a few oddities that I had not realized before. A large portrait of Mao Tse-Tung still hangs over the gateway of the Forbidden City, notwithstanding the fact that the palace would appear to be a symbol of everything he opposed in his life and the fact that the present Chinese leadership would appear to have repudiated all of his fundamental economic policies. It's almost as if a huge portrait of King George III were hung on Independence Hall in Philadelphia.

The most conspicuous unexpected thing about the Great Wall is the fact that it is built atop the highest mountain ridges, not in the valleys where construction would be so much easier. When we stood on the Wall at Simitai, we could see it snaking over a procession of ridges, endlessly, into the deep horizon.

In order to get there, we had to take an airy ride over some deep valleys in something that looked like a ski lift; then move up the mountain-side in an open cog-railway car; and finally climb up several hundred steep and wet steps. The younger members of the delegation forged on ahead, while Stephanie and I took it slow. About halfway up, we were met by a couple of tiny Chinese ladies who offered to help us up the rest of the way.

Actually, they were more like guides who held an elbow on the particularly slippery spots, and we were grateful for their cheerful assistance. When we got to the top, I wanted to give each one the equivalent of about $5 in Chinese currency as a tip, but they both refused - somehow communicating that tips were not allowed in China, but that we could buy some picture books from a little stand they maintained on the route down. (When we bought the books, the obvious premium in the price amounted to a generous tip.)

This strange dichotomy between appearance and actual practice seems to prevail in modern China. The blood-red flags of a Communist State flew outside our comfortable hotel, with all the services you would expect in the West. The doormen and bellmen accepted tips, too, but surreptitiously as if you were passing an illegal drug. The leaders of the State still call themselves Communists, but - as we will see - are eager to benefit from the lessons of a capitalist society.

Apart from the historic monuments, the most impressive thing was the prosperity of many people in a city like Beijing, and their adoption of Western ways. The traffic jams are worse than those in New York, and the best-selling luxury car is the GM Buick. The stores look familiar, and sell the same mix of good stuff and junk that we see here. The familiar logos of the yellow arches and "KFC" are there. All the signs are in English, as well as Chinese.

The young people who have grown up in an increasingly free-market environment, have obviously been better nourished than their elders. They are much, much larger, and dress in Western clothes. They are actually much better dressed than their U.S. counterparts because their clothes are colorful and well-pressed - unlike young people here who, for some reason, uniformly try to look like ranch-hands who have been riding the trails for a month. (I realize this is a curmudgeonly comment, but I've earned the right.)

Back to work. I would like to think that we did some good missionary work in China; the people we saw seemed genuinely interested in what we had to say about competition law. I was also aware that the country's history has made China's people hyper-sensitive about any suggestion of foreign direction - something that was also emphasized in preliminary discussions with our State Department people. The outline of my talk on "The Economic Roots of Antitrust" to an academic audience deliberately adopted a conciliatory tone. [32]

> "The United States is a young country - particularly when
> compared to China. Competition law is one of the few areas

where we have had a longer experience than most, so it is not surprising that we are proud of it and like to talk about it. We hope that other countries will benefit from a discussion of our experience, including a candid admission of some mistakes that we have made."

"With that objective in mind, I would like to provide a brief overview of how competition law principles have evolved in the United States, from early populist concerns to the present emphasis on economics."

* * * *

"This does not mean that other social or political objectives - like employment, balance of payments, health and safety, or environmental protection are unimportant. It does mean that these matters are not relevant when interpreting competition laws."

* * * *

"Competition laws focus on effects within the United States and make no distinctions based on the nationality of enterprises.

Foreign companies that do business in the U.S. are subject to the same rules as purely domestic concerns.

We do not regulate the competitive conduct of U.S. firms abroad unless there is some spillover effect in the U.S., and expect that these firms will be governed by the competition laws of the countries in which they do business."

* * * *

"The present consensus on basic economic principles in the U.S. does not mean that every case can be decided on a purely objective basis by the manipulation of statistics, or that there is no room for future evolution.

Economics is itself an enduring science and the job of competition authorities to apply 'whatever we know at any particular moment about the economics of industrial organization'."
[A well known quote from Bill Baxter].

Many, if not most, competition cases involve an effort either to predict the future or to reconstruct a past that never was. They may also require a balance between potential anticompetitive effects and potential efficiencies. Despite advances in our ability to measure and to model alternative scenarios, these decisions will contain elements of uncertainty and subjectivity."

* * * *

"…[d]ifferences of opinions between the U.S. agencies and agencies of other countries may be based on the fact that there are different effects in different areas."

The academic audience for this talk was highly educated, and they all understood English. I therefore did not have to pause with each paragraph for translation, or speak with the slower pace that is desirable when there is simultaneous translation. The English outline was also distributed to the audience, and the State Department later prepared a Chinese version that was widely distributed elsewhere. I used to keep a copy of the Chinese version - although I couldn't read any of it - but it somehow got lost on my perambulations. That's too bad because it would do much to elevate the general tone of this memoir if it were attached.

Our various hosts in China - the U.S. Embassy people stationed there, the representatives of U.S. businesses there, the academics, and the Chinese government officials were unfailingly gracious and pleasant. The Chinese officials were obviously proud of the economic advances that have been made in recent years, but also were candid about the problems that remain. One of them said to me that "Beijing and Shanghai, and some other large cities are as modern as any in the world, but if you travel deep inland you also travel back a thousand years." True economic unification is hampered by the lack of an efficient nationwide transportation system, and local protectionism that has deep historical roots.

I believe that protectionism is still a problem in China - as indeed it is in various localities in the U.S. It is hard to root out politically because the loss of existing jobs is much more visible than the increased costs and loss of potential jobs created by trade barriers. China has come a long way in this respect, but still has a long way to go. So do we.

I particularly enjoyed extensive discussions with Chang Ming, head of the most important of the competition agencies in the country. He speaks no English, and I speak no Chinese, so we always needed an interpreter. He seemed a bit reserved at first but I really believe we established a friendly rapport - and he has a good sense of humor.

When he and some of his colleagues made a return visit to Washington a year later, he spent the first part of the day at the DOJ. I went over there at midday so I could escort him over to the FTC building, a few blocks away. When we entered the building, he asked about the meaning of that statue of the man holding back the big horse.

I said that I wasn't really sure but suspected that it was probably a representation of the widely held view early in the New Deal years that aggressive competition had to be restrained. I then added that we probably should replace it today "with a statue of the man kicking the horse on the backside." He got the point immediately and almost collapsed with laughter.

Perhaps my most memorable encounter in China occurred at a meeting Hew Pate and I had in Beijing. I have already told the story in my farewell talk when I was leaving the Commission.

> "One highlight for me personally occurred about a year and a half ago when I was part of a joint DOJ/FTC delegation that traveled to China to share our views on competition law with

officials there who are working on their own law. I will never forget a meeting that Hew Pate and I had with a key legislator in an immense conference room in the immense Great Hall of the People on Tiannamen Square. This Chinese lawmaker - who still calls himself a communist, by the way - was one tough guy, and I couldn't help but wonder how he survived the murderous years of Mao. He was in a musing mood, and said through his interpreter: "I never dreamed in my youth that I would be here in this place, seeking advice on how to improve a market system from representatives of the United States of America." That sent chills up my spine.

I had a comparable experience in Moscow last year, and I cannot overemphasize how important this outreach is. The eyes of the world are on these two huge countries. If competitive market systems fail in either or both of them, there could be a chain reaction and widespread return to the top-down economic controls that impoverished so many people for so long. A lot is at stake."

Before I finish this segment on the Chinese trip, I want to say a word about the political environment in China. The suppression of dissent is intolerable by our standards. By any standard you want to apply, however, the political system is far less repressive than it was when we were at war with the country in the early 1950s, or the even worse conditions that prevailed later under Chairman Mao's "Great Leap Forward."

It has always seemed odd to me that so many well-known advocates of "human rights" never called attention to the abuses of human rights during those terrible times, when China was openly hostile to the United States. Instead, we were treated to a lot of blather about the "new Chinese man" who placed societal interests ahead of his own. In a word, crap. It is only after China began to move toward an increasingly capitalistic economic system and toward a more open relationship with the West that we began to hear so much about political repression there.

I much prefer our system to theirs, but I also recognize that it is not easy to undo years of tyranny. We continue to have policy differences with the Chinese government, but I am optimistic that they can be resolved without open war - perhaps by ignoring differences that can be ignored and concentrating on things where talk might accomplish something. I wish them well.

On our last full day in China, with all business done, Stephanie and I were on our own. We hailed two of the crazy little three wheeled cabs that scoot all around the city of Beijing and visited the Temple of Heaven, that serene round building, with multitiled roofs of tile, that is so often pictured in travel magazines. Crowded as it was, there was a strange air of calm and peace about the place that we both noted at the time. I wonder now if it had something to do with a coincidence that we only became aware of shortly thereafter.

Stephanie's mother, aged 97, had been in failing health for some time. We were concerned about the situation before we left for China, but had been assured that her death was not imminent. After we returned to the hotel to prepare for the flight back to the U.S., we got an e-mail from our daughter with the news that "Granny," as the kids called her, had died peacefully in her sleep. When we learned the exact time, we realized that she had died precisely when we were visiting the Temple of Heaven.

Stephanie has always been touched by the fact that she was visiting such a beautiful spot in China at the moment her mother died - the same country where that gallant lady had brought her into the world so many years before. RIP.

Our next major trip while I was at the Commission was a trip to Moscow in November of the same year, 2004. This time I was not a member of a U.S. delegation, but rather part of a program organized by the Organization for Economic Cooperation and Development ("OECD"), a group that evaluates the competition laws in various countries.

The Russians have approached privatization in a very different way than China. While China has retained tight political control of the process, the Russians attempted to reform both the political and the economic system overnight. I'm not sure that the Russian approach - which some will call "chaos"- has worked any better. In fact, it may be worse. The Russians are amazingly resilient and good-natured people who have endured, and to a degree still endure, anything far beyond anything we have ever experienced.

Stephanie and I had first become aware of it when we visited as tourists in the Summer of 1997. We were on a Baltic cruise, and the two days in St. Petersburg were the high point of the trip. We both agree that the river front of St. Petersburg is the most spectacularly beautiful cityscape in the world, more beautiful than the best of Paris, Rome or Venice - and that's saying a lot.

The Cold War had not been over all that long in 1997, and we were warned that the Customs officials who screened arrivals at the dock might show some lingering hostility. The shipboard experts couldn't have been more wrong! We were greeted with a brass band, and the Customs officials waved us through quickly with friendly greetings. When we left, they did something that still brings a lump in the throat after all these years. As the ship pulled away, all these people in their official, if threadbare, uniforms stood on the roof of their little shed and waved goodbye, blew us kisses, and repeatedly called out: "Thank you for coming and please come back again."

The reason, of course, was that Russia was suffering from a particularly severe depression in 1997. Apart from our cruise ship, the port was eerily empty and silent. For a few dollars street vendors were selling not only the usual colorful dolls within dolls, but also things like military uniforms, medals and other mementos of what they still call "The Great Patriotic War" - a war which took the lives of 20,000,000 people. Twenty million!

We saw another glimpse of Russian fortitude in an all-day excursion to the summer Palace built originally for Catherine the Great at Tsarkoye Selo in the countryside. Tsarkoye Selo is not anything like your idea of a summer cottage. It is bright colored and covered with gilt and elaborate ornamentation. The facade is over 1000 feet long - about as long as a side of the Pentagon. (Oddly enough, it had been restored after the War and beautifully maintained in the Soviet era, when there was very little tourist travel.)

On the trip out, one of the passengers asked our Russian guide about the poverty that was so evident on the shabby back streets of the city. The guide, a strikingly handsome and outspoken woman, answered this way:

> "Don't worry about us. The economy of this country was destroyed by seventy years of Communist rule, and it's going to take a long time for us to make our way back. But, we've experienced much worse. During the War, this city [then Leningrad] was under siege for three years, and a million people lay starved and frozen in the streets."

When we traveled to Moscow in the Fall of 2004, Russia seemed to have become a more dangerous place. Our hosts were uniformly friendly, and went out of their way to see that we had a good time. (More about that later.) But, our contact at the State Department, the staff in the hotel that catered to "Western" visitors, and our hosts themselves emphasized that Moscow can be dangerous. We were warned to avoid the Metro, particularly at night, and to conceal any valuables we might be carrying. We were warned to avoid cruising taxicabs, and rely on the cars and drivers provided by the hotel.

The wife of one of our Russian hosts - both longtime residents of the city - was attacked and her auto stolen in broad daylight while we were there. Fortunately, she was not hurt, but the thieves also made off with a large amount of cash which she had just withdrawn from a bank - which suggested that a bank employee was also part of the plot.

Unlike China, which has privatized its industries in a slow and deliberate way, Russia did it all at once, without paying much attention to who was buying what. As a result, organized crime became a more powerful force in the economy than it ever had been before, and in the economic sphere Communist terror and incompetence had been replaced by Capitalist thuggery.

I hate to say this because, like most Americans I admired Boris Yeltsin's brave leadership in the struggle to overturn Communist rule. But, once he was established in power, he lost his grip completely - perhaps as a result of his alcoholism - and hoodlums filled the void. It's easy to understand why the Russian people seem to welcome the more disciplined leadership of Vladimir Putin, even if it means some loss of political freedom.

I do not want to create the impressions that the trip was a frustrating experience; it wasn't. A lot of young people who serve in various administrative capacities are intelligent and eager to create a modern capitalist society. However, some of the crusty regional politicians that we met were a lot less receptive. I suspect they were old Reds, with a lifetime's exposure to outdated Marxist theology. I also suspect they knew nothing about competition, and didn't care to know.

(As an aside, I offer the view that Marxist theology has been such a spectacular failure because the fundamental economic premise has things upside down. Marx claimed that, in the capitalist world, the laborer provided a "surplus value" which was unfairly appropriated by the capitalist. In reality, however, the vast bulk of the "surplus value" is created by the investments of the capitalist. Before the industrial revolution, when laborers did not have access to powerful machines provided by capitalists, there was precious little surplus value for anyone.

This explains why pre-industrial societies cannot pay wages that we would deem adequate, much less support a "welfare state." This also suggests that we should provide these states with capital goods, which cannot be sequestered in Swiss accounts by corrupt officials, rather than exhortations and embargo threats if they do not improve labor conditions.)

If the younger crowd advances and acquires more influence, the situation in Russia could improve dramatically. And, the head of the new competition agency, Igor Artemeyer, is one of the finest and most likeable individuals that I have ever met. I sincerely believe we talked the same language, and formed a bond, even though we could only converse through an interpreter. It was a real honor to be asked to share a televised press conference with Igor Artemeyer during my visit.

The message I tried to convey was roughly the same as the one I had employed in China - with no pretense that we in the U.S. had all the answers. It seemed to go down well.

Stephanie and I stayed over for a couple of days, after the rest of the delegation had left. Moscow is not as beautiful as St. Petersburg, but some of the sights are impressive. Red Square (the name predated the Communist revolution) is a spectacular space; St. Basil's church, with its multicolored domes, is almost surrealistic; and it was fascinating to see that tomb of Lenin where so many grim and fat guys, in bulky coats and fur hats, used to stand on top in the cold as the parade of weaponry passed by. We passed up the opportunity to go inside and look at Lenin's corpse, which is still there although Joe Stalin has been planted elsewhere. We enjoyed a performance at the Bolshoi Theatre, as guests of the government, in the most luxurious box I have ever occupied - complete with a private retiring room and refreshments.

I also spent some time in de-briefings at the U.S. Embassy in Moscow, an immense complex with tight security and all the facilities of a small town. Employees who are nervous about life in the city itself can live, dine, shop, educate their children, and enjoy a variety of entertainment choices without leaving the secure complex. Embassy staff also introduced me to a couple of former Russian officials who served as informal advisors. I still vividly recall the candid comments of one man, who spoke excellent English and had once served as a diplomat posted in the United States.

"You Americans are well-meaning but naive in some ways. You come here and offer thoughtful suggestions for various legal reforms, because laws are very important in your country. This is because you have, for the most part, prosecutors and judges who are honest. That is not true here. You have no idea how corrupt and backward many officials still are in this country."

On re-reading this subsection, it may seem that I became more optimistic about the future of China than the future of Russia. I could be very wrong about that. We did not interact with the same broad range of people in China that we did in Russia, and the Chinese officials seem to be more reserved than the more volatile Russians - probably a cultural thing. Oddly enough, the situation in the streets was the exact opposite, at least among the young. The young Chinese were openly friendly, wanted to show off their English facility, and even wanted to have their pictures taken with the odd-looking visitors. (Stephanie was particularly popular with young girls in touring groups - perhaps because of the blonde hair.) The young people on the streets in Russia totally ignored us - which actually seemed more normal. Older people were invisible when we were young, too.

One favorable omen for Russia is the fact that, Igor Artemyev is still the head of its competition agency. I was concerned that he might not last long in office because he had been affiliated with an opposition party.

The last time I saw Igor Artemyev was a couple of years ago, after I had left the Commission. We shared a table at an ABA lunch event during the Washington Spring meeting, and had a cordial reunion. When we left, I didn't want to be publicly dramatic, so I whispered to the interpreter: "Tell Mr. Artemyev to keep the faith." When the message was passed on, this great Russian gentleman nodded his head and smiled a big smile.

Consumer Protection Matters

Meetings of the Antitrust Bar do not focus much about the Consumer Protection side of the Commission's responsibilities, possibly because the respondents in these cases often cannot afford the services of big firm lawyers who attend the meetings and possibly many consumer protection matters involve outright fraud that does not leave much room for intellectual debate.

As a Commissioner, I nevertheless had to devote a lot of time on consumer protection issues because that wing of the agency actually had more people and consumed more resources than the competition wing did. Consumer protection issues also attracted more Congressional interest than competition issues did at that time. Finally, I had to spend a lot more time getting up to speed on consumer protection because I really didn't know much about it when I arrived.

I did have responsibility for consumer protection matters in my later years at General Motors, but the issues largely involved the question of whether certain advertising claims were supported or whether certain important cave-ats had been omitted. Inquiries of this kind tend to be highly technical and case-specific and, besides, there are a lot of consumer protection questions that do not involve ad substantiation.

Tom Muris, who arrived as Chairman in 2001, had a more extensive background and greater interest in consumer protection issues than any Chairman who had served for 20 years. I have previously published a lot about his contributions in this, and other, areas,[33] which I do not need to repeat here. In summary, Tim and his bureau head Howard Beales made us aware that there was a lot more intellectual meat in even the most obvious violations than we had assumed.

For example, even if liability can be readily determined, the issue of appro-priate relief can be challenging. Do you want to litigate, if necessary, to get the maximum dollar recovery, which is often uncollectible but which will attract maximum attention and serve (1) to educate consumers and (2) to deter potential law breakers. The downside is that maximum relief may consume scarce resources in litigation and delay the elimination or correction of the offending ads. Somewhat different policy issues are presented if the liability issue is itself a close call. The targets in cases of this kind are more likely to be substantial and respected companies, who can afford the best lawyers. They also want to protect their reputations, and *any* publicity about a government dispute can cause greater financial harm for them than the actual penalty that might be imposed if the government wins.

This may mean that they are willing to promptly rectify any possible errors of commission or omission, provided it can be accomplished quietly without a public and potentially burdensome Commission order. If quiet resolution is impossible, however, they have the resources and incentive to do vigorous battle. A quiet resolution is tempting, but the Commission's overall credibility can be impaired if it publicly appears to focus only on the little guys. On the other hand, credibility may be even more adversely affected if it brings a case and loses. Moreover, win or lose, the challenged ads may continue to run longer than they would if the case had been disposed of quietly.

The Commission itself may be concerned if an attack on a particular ad campaign is misunderstood to mean that an expert agency of the U.S. government believes certain products or services are wholly worthless - something that could well happen. I remember that I once inquired of staff about the comparatively lenient treatment that had been recommended for a particular company, which seemed to have violated an existing Order prohibiting certain claims about its flagship product. The answer was "This is a very healthy product and we don't want the public to avoid it."

A policy decision of this kind actually raises a potential issue with more far-reaching consequences. If it is good policy to go easy on companies that are selling products we believe are "good" for people, does this mean we should take a particularly harsh view of ads for products that we think are "bad"? Should the Commission perhaps, go further and claim that even truthful ads about products we consider harmful are "unfair." This, of course, would look like the stance that the Commission had advocated some 25 years before under the tenure of Chairman Mike Pertschuk - a stance that gave rise to a furious backlash against the would-be "National Nanny."

The Commissioners unanimously agreed that we didn't want to go there, but Tim Muris took the lead in implementing a different approach to the same objective. He recognized that there was a big difference between restrictions imposed by government fiat and those imposed by industry self-regulation. At that time, in the early years of this century, the Commission had an active initiative in response to widespread concerns about the growing incidence of obesity. We had increased our close scrutiny of advertising for magical remedies that would allow the buyer to lose weight, while continuing the lifestyle that had helped cause the problem in the first place. Among other things, the Commission had given wide circulation to a glossary of so-called "Red Flag" claims about weight-loss claims that were demonstrably false.

Tim Muris thought that it would be a good idea to enlist the cooperation of the mainstream media in the campaign. He asked them to voluntarily reject any ads that contained "Red Flag" claims for worthless products, just as they reject ads that are obscene or otherwise objectionable.

One time I accompanied him on a trip to New York, with a large group of media representatives. The reception was mixed. Some were in open agreement. Others were resistant, because ads with their phony claims were nevertheless a significant source of revenue, even for respectable publications. A number of counsel raised an objection that had to be taken seriously. You are suggesting that we take action as a group, they said, but that raises serious antitrust issues. A collective refusal to do business with a particular kind of advertiser could be characterized as a "group boycott," and it is long-settled law that collective boycotts are always illegal, even if they appear to be motivated by worthy reasons. (The issues are similar to those mentioned in the preceding major Chapter on the discussion of "social" justifications for agreements among universities on student aid.)

I can fairly take credit for the development of a reasoned response to this objection. In summary, it proceeds as follows. Principles of consumer protection law and competition law have a common economic foundation. Competition law deals with distortions on the supply side, and consumer protection law deals with distortions on the demand side. They both can cause direct consumer harm and a misallocation of resources. These effects sometimes have to be balanced. For example, collective action to restrict the supply of worthless products does not harm consumers at all, and collective action to reduce the demand for these products can help them a lot.

In other words, this is just another case where rigid adherence to traditional legal doctrine is a bad idea. As I recall it, the first time that I publicly articulated this idea was at a seminar conducted by a private law firm in January, 2004, and I later published a short piece on the subject in the Antitrust Law Journal. [34]

At the seminar, I was approached by a longtime friend who was then the General Counsel of an Association of Soft Drink Producers. She said: "I assume your toleration of some group boycotts would not apply if we collectively agreed to avoid placement of our most-sugary drinks in school vending machines." My reply was: "I wouldn't assume that at all." About a year later, I read that Commission staff had quietly reviewed such an agreement, and raised no objections. It hadn't even required action at the Commissioner level.

I also credit Tim Muris for the constructive redirection of the Commission's "privacy" initiatives into areas that really matter. When I was a relative neophyte on the Commission in the election year of 2000, the issue of "privacy" seemed to be high on the political agenda. We Commissioners were engaged in an extensive discussion internally and with Congressional people, about possible remedies for the loss of privacy in the computer age.

I thought then, and still think, that much of this concern was misplaced. If you ask a cross-section of the public an open-ended question about their concerns, "privacy" is never up there as a major problem. If you ask about "privacy" specifically, the answer may depend on how you phrase the question. If you ask people whether they worry that people with access to computer traffic will create a secret profile of their preferences and opinions, you are evoking the shades of George Orwell's "1984" and will elicit expressions of alarm. If you ask whether they object if advertisers keep track of their purchases in order to make them aware of things that cater to their individual interests, you are likely to get a different response.

The fact is that people today, who increasingly live in an urban setting, have far more personal privacy than people who grew up in small towns, where everyone knew everyone else's private business. I didn't grow up in a small town, but rather a suburb of a medium-sized city, and we still didn't have much privacy. In that pre-antibiotic age, for example, the usual childhood diseases like mumps or measles - not to mention the more serious ones like diphtheria or scarlet fever - were regarded as a dangerous communicable risk. When someone in the house had one of these ailments, the Board of Health would nail a big poster on the front door, with a WARNING in red letters so people would stay clear.

In my family of five kids, that sign seemed to be up on the door a good part of the time. No such thing as "privacy of personal health information." Contrast that with the situation today where "privacy" concerns seem to trump communication of warnings about even more lethal ailments. In fact, a lot of city dwellers have so much anonymity and privacy today that articles are written about urban angst. People don't care about your personal life when they don't give a damn about you - so, you go online and blurt your secrets to the world, in the hope that someone will notice.

Anyhow, this was my view, but I usually was pretty discreet about voicing it as a public official. I slipped once, however, with consequences that are amusing in retrospect. In the event, described in the previous Chapter, when

I spoke after Peter Drucker, my subject was internet marketing. I focused on things like the problems of assuming reliability in transactions at a distance, but said very little about privacy. Predictably, I suppose, privacy was one of the first things raised in the question period.

I launched into an abbreviated version of what I have just written. Then, perhaps "intoxicated by the exuberance of my own verbosity" (a memorable phrase I first heard from my mother), I said that a lot of people who profess to worry about such things were needlessly "hysterical." The remark passed without comment but Stephanie, who was in the audience, told me later that her first thought was "Oh! Oh!" My reaction was "So what. I'm 3,000 miles away from Washington, and no one will notice." The next morning, the San Diego paper carried a story with a headline that said something like: "FTC Commissioner calls privacy advocates 'hysterical' " Another shrug of the shoulders. No one in Washington will take notice of an item in a San Diego newspaper.

I'd forgotten about the agency's clipping service that regularly circulates news articles anywhere that refer to the Commission or its people. My four experienced advisors saw it. When I returned to the city a few days later, they all asked to meet in my office. Very solemn. The message was simple: "Is it agreed that we will not in the future refer to one of the Commission's constituent groups as 'hysterical'?" I guess I never did. (But, I still think so.)

When he took office a year later Tim Muris sensibly redirected the privacy debate in two ways. First, he emphasized the need for the privacy of personal *financial* information where leaks can potentially result in direct monetary harm. We brought a number of cases in that area.

Second, he proposed action to prevent privacy invasions that directly annoyed almost everyone on a daily basis. I refer, of course, to the now-famous "Do Not Call" rule, which has drastically reduced the number of unsolicited marketing calls - that always seemed to be clustered at dinnertime.

In retrospect, it seems like an easy decision, but I remember that all of us who had to vote on it had some serious worries at the time. The consumer response might have been so huge and so fast that the system for compiling the list would crash. In addition, the Commission really did not have the resources to enforce the Rule if there was massive disobedience. If either or both of these things had happened, we would all look foolish. Neither did: AT&T did the magnificent job that they promised, and violations were surprisingly uncommon.

Among other things, we all aided in the effort by explaining the way the Rule would operate to advertisers and the specific activities that were exempt - notably, political or charitable appeals and sales calls when there has been a pre-existing relationship. I remember a trip to Fargo, North Dakota, of all places, to explain the Rule in a public town meeting - seated alongside Senator Byron Dorgan, the same guy who had held up my nomination over a quarrel involving something else. (Mutual tact prevailed, and the subject did not come up. We got along fine.)

The Rule proved so popular, so quickly, that there was an immediate response when some Federal District Court out West enjoined its enforcement on First Amendment grounds. Both branches of Congress passed an identical bill to specifically authorize the Commission's Rule, and the President signed it - all in about 24 hours! I believe that the only faster response in this Country's history was the Declaration of War after the attack on Pearl Harbor!

The Rule also provided the occasion for the third and the best standing ovation that I ever got. (I've already talked about the first, and will describe the second shortly.) A business group that recognizes outstanding performance by a branch of the federal government included the Do Not Call rule in the annual awards just a couple of years later. The award ceremony was held at a dinner in that great room at Union Station, which is available for such things.

Apparently, the ceremony typically features a senior member of the agency that is recognized, who formally accepts it and introduces the person or people who actually did the work. Tim Muris would have been the logical guy to accept, but he was not available and I was asked to do it for the Commission.

There were some really incredible accomplishments recognized that night. I remember particularly a woman in some scientific capacity who had actually produced a new form of matter, to be ranked with gases, liquids and solids! I also remember an FBI team that had detected and blocked a potential terrorist attack. All very impressive stuff, that fully merited the enthusiastic applause of the large audience.

Our award was announced close to the end. When I stepped up to the podium to accept, everyone stood up, and whooped and cheered for the longest time. I hadn't yet said a word! It was an experience I will never forget and obviously will never have again. Tim Muris and the people who did all the work, led by Eileen Harrington, deserve the credit. I don't.

The Bully Pulpit

One of the perks that I most enjoyed as a Commissioner was the ability to think out loud before an audience whenever I felt like it. The Chairman could not really do it because, despite the routine disclaimers, it is naturally assumed that someone in that position speaks for the agency. I had a lot more freedom, and took advantage of it.

I got many more invitations to speak than I could accept, so I could be selective. Events that would attract a large or more sophisticated audience were preferred because I really wasn't interested in preparing a primer. Probably a bit of intellectual snobbery. For a time, the ABA leadership was dominated by people who liked to ski and scheduled Winter events accordingly, which I always avoided to the extent I decently could because I don't like to visit cold places in the winter. I generally refused to give what I called "laundry list" speeches about what the Commission is doing right now. I preferred to speculate and hopefully, give people something to think about.

I could also practice my own principles for effective public speaking, which evolved over years of experience and observation. The most important thing for any speaker to remember is that you should try to establish a *personal* connection with the audience, not just read a prepared statement. Think of it as your half of a dialogue, even if the other half is silent.

Let me summarize a few things I have learned.

• Never, ever read a speech, unless you are a very good actor who can conceal the fact that you're doing it. You can write it out in advance, and privately read aloud what you have written, if that will help you to organize the points that you want to make, or help you to remember them and estimate how long it will take you to say what you want to say. Bear in mind, however, that the actual talk will always take longer than it will take to read a draft - even if you think you are reading the draft at a measured pace.

• Do not try to cram too much information into your talk. Do not think of a speech as an oral version of an article. The audience will only be able to remember three or four salient points, anyhow. I learned this when I was at General Motors. The "op-ed" pieces I wrote for the Chairman did not read at all like the occasional speeches I wrote for him. (It is amazing how many supposedly experienced advocates will read an overly long paper at breakneck speed, because they don't want to leave anything out, and it just goes by listeners in a blur.)

• Use your Power Points sparingly, if at all. Sometimes a thought can be presented more vividly by a graph or a chart, and it doesn't hurt to post the list of three or four salient points that you want the audience to remember. But, remember that you want the audience to look at *you*, not at a screen, and they will always stare at the screen if there is a lot to read. Moreover, you don't want to waste a lot of your valuable time tinkering with a machine at the start.

I actually have never used a Power Point in my life. When I was on the Commission, sometimes visitors would bring computers into my office, and expected me to look at Power Point pages as they talked. I usually told them to put the damned things away and just converse with me.

• You also should look at the audience yourself - left, right and center, alternatively. Don't just take in the crowd in a glazed way, but randomly make eye contact with individuals. It will help to keep you conversational, and, believe it or not, will automatically help you to slow down and talk at a pace that people can follow without straining. Your speech will naturally become "conversational."

(Ronald Reagan was called "The Great Communicator" because he would address a crowd of a thousand like he was sitting with a few people in their living room. He must have realized that's actually what he was doing because most people listen to the President's speeches on TV at home. Later on, accomplished speakers like Bill Clinton have done the same thing because people have gotten used to this style, even in an auditorium.)

• If you look at people, you will also get instant feedback. If they are smiling and nodding their heads, they are "getting it." If they are looking puzzled, with arms folded, you should go back and try to express an important point in a different way.

• If there is a large crowd, remember to speak clearly into the mike! This is worth repeating: REMEMBER TO SPEAK INTO THE MIKE! People on panels are particularly likely to forget it. These days, they may sit facing each other in easy chairs, to create the illusion of an informal exchange. This is fine, but too often they just talk to one another and are completely oblivious to the fact that there are a lot of people out there who also want to hear what they have to say.

• If you are chairing or moderating a panel, enforce the time limits - even against someone who thinks he is the Lord God Jehovah - so, the people who speak later don't get squeezed. If you are speaking yourself, remember that time will pass a lot faster than you think it will, and continuously monitor your progress against the clock.

It's not as hard as you might think. Any experienced litigator should be able to keep track of time limits and adjust. You have to do it in oral arguments when judges ask an unusual number of questions. I don't claim that I always followed my own rules perfectly, but I did the best I could and have tried to pass on these principles to people I have mentored.

Most of the speeches that I gave were never written down, but I would reduce one to writing later if it seemed to go over pretty well. Everything I have ever written for public consumption - including this memoir - started out as a longhand draft on lined paper. I didn't like to delegate this part because, for better or worse, I wanted everything with my name on it to be expressed in my individual "voice." I suppose there's some ego involved in this, but I also think it's a way to play fair with a reader. I'm amazed by the brazen chutzpah of some prominent "authors" who later disassociate themselves from a controversial statement in their own memoirs. If you disagree with anything published in my name, I'm the guy to blame.

The appendix to this memoir is a list of all the written speeches and articles that are still available on the Commission's website. They are a fuller articulation of most ideas expressed here. A couple of my favorites aren't there, because the only memorable parts were off-the-cuff remarks.

The first was early-on, when I made a few offhand remarks at a Bar lunch. I had very recently been amused by a couple of well-known lawyers who swaggered into my office - apparently trying to show a new Commissioner, or their own clients, how tough they were.

Please listen: Orson Swindle, Marine flier and POW, is a tough guy; antitrust lawyers are not. In an attempt to make this point with a silly story, I referred to the then current commercials for Miller's beer, which featured some high-iron men, or firemen, mopping their sweaty brows at the end of a hard and dangerous day, and breaking for "Miller Time." I asked the audience to imagine the appeal of a commercial that featured an antitrust lawyer in his office suit, mopping his brow alongside a pile of boxes, and announcing: "That's the toughest Second Request that I've ever handled; it's Miller Time." Dream on.

The other one that I remember was when the ad-lib was the occasion for my third standing ovation. I was asked by a well-known financial firm in New York to give a lunchtime speech on supermarket mergers, which we then happened to be reviewing in large numbers. The firm was producing an all-day seminar in an apparent attempt to interest some clients or would-be clients in deals of this kind.

When I gave a talk to a group with which I was not familiar, I tried to arrive early and sit in on a business session - if I were permitted to do so. I arrived at this seminar just in time to hear an enthusiastic speaker from the host firm say that the supermarket business was characterized by low profit ratios and that there was little room for future innovation. All true, based on my limited experience at the time. (So-called "big box" outlets like Walmart have since made a big difference.)

The speaker then went on to say that the market was looking for earnings growth, above all, and a good way to get it was to buy another supermarket chain. A lot of potential deals were available right now, but you people better hurry to be first in line. Perhaps I didn't understand the ways of Wall Street, but this part made no sense at all.

When the time came for me to speak, I began with something unplanned. I thanked my hosts for a good lunch, and offered my apologies because I was about to say something that might offend people who had treated me so well. I then repeated the gist of what I had just heard, and said something like:

> "I may be naive, but I do not see how a chronically low margin business can create shareholder value by buying, probably at a premium, another company with the same problems. It all

sounds to me like the perhaps apocryphal story about the residents of an isolated town who survived the depression by taking in each other's laundry."

Half of the audience - undoubtedly the guests - immediately rose and applauded. The other half - my hosts - sat in sullen silence.

There are a couple of amusing and perhaps instructive sequels. A few days later, Lisa Kopchik, one of my advisors who routinely read a trade journal about the supermarket business, came into my office with a big grin on her face. The latest issue of the journal carried a glowing article about the well-attended seminar, and made a number of derogatory comments about my little talk. I was described as a "pointy-headed-bureaucrat from Washington" who had tried to dampen the enthusiasm of the crowd.

I agreed it was hilarious. There is, however, a more serious sequel. The firm that had sponsored the event, and touted its superior ability to read the market, was one of the first to go belly up early in 2008.

The "Collegial" Experience

People have very different temperaments. Some people have a strong personal agenda, confidence in their sense of what is right, and are not afraid to stand alone in the crowd. They can be outstanding, or disastrous, leaders - depending on the quality of their judgment. Other people tend to be more detached and tentative. They tend to see both sides of tough issues, and question their own conclusions if they find that they are alone. They perform best in a collegial setting, where others share the responsibility for decisions.

It should be obvious to anyone who has read this far which of these I am. And, that helps to explain why I so enjoyed my years on the Commission.

The Federal Trade Commission is a collegial institution, that is not directly answerable to any single authority. The Chairman is like a CEO in some respects: He is the one who makes personnel appointments, from inside and outside. He is also the one who typically initiates various affirmative programs. In both of these areas, he could theoretically be overruled by a majority vote of his fellow Commissioners, but they typically will defer to his wishes on these matters. In those areas, we functioned rather like "outside" corporate directors.

However, on the substantive decisions about matters litigated before the Commission, or on the decision to actively seek relief in litigation elsewhere, the Chairman has only one of five votes. Since there has been very little "party" discipline in recent years, any Chairman has to rely on individual powers of persuasion.

There are advantages and disadvantages to a system like this. The greatest disadvantage is the obvious fact that the collective decisions typically take a longer time. The process may not work well in emergency situations when quick action is required. The obvious advantage is that decisions are more likely to reflect a consensus view - particularly if the decision makers are "independent" as the Commission is designed to be. This is particularly important in a system of popular sovereignty that depends on a stable legal system.

It's an interesting, if perhaps irrelevant, fact that most of the newly created competition authorities around the world are multi-member commissions like the FTC, but are part of the executive branch like the DOJ. Make of it what you will.

In my tenure at the Commission, I served with three Chairmen: Bob Pitofsky, Tim Muris and Debbie Majoras, and five other Commissioners: Mozelle Thompson, Sheila Anthony, Orson Swindle, Pamela Jones Harbour, and the current Chairman, Jon Leibowitz. Each one of them helped me, in one way or another. Some of these things have already been described; I couldn't begin to list them all, unless I doubled the length of this narrative. What I can say is that those appointed before me were all generous with their time and counsel, when I was first finding my way, and all of them then and later tolerated my opinions and forgave my faults to a greater extent than I expected or deserved.

I am also deeply indebted to Deborah Blunt, the Staff Assistant who ran my office, and to Chris White in the General Counsel's office who advised me on ethical concerns. They both kept me out of trouble. Before I leave this subject, I want to talk about the real "collegiality" I experienced at another level. Every Commissioner is allowed to select four Attorney Advisors, from within or outside the agency. The way you use them is a matter of individual choice.

During my tenure, all of us used advisors to communicate views informally among our peers. The so-called "sunshine" rules limit the ability to have private discussions of Commission matters with more than two Commissioners in the room. Our advisors are, however, allowed to communicate our views in larger groups, and these exchanges made a substantial contribution to our overall efficiency. Beyond that, advisor responsibilities varied in the different Commissioner suites.

I personally relied on my advisors to do exactly what is suggested by the position's title, that is to "advise" me. Each one of them was a seasoned lawyer, median age around 40. Almost all of them had a lot more experience with the agency than I did, and often knew what was going on before I did.

They were never selected because of their personal political or philosophical views; in fact, it could be an advantage if their initial reactions to pending matters differed from mine. We had free-form discussions of these matters every Tuesday morning at the large conference table in my office. I deliberately chose to sit at the side, rather than the end, to emphasize that everyone was free to speak candidly.

I did, however, sometimes take the occasion to acquaint them with some of my particular interests that went beyond the matters that were up for decision. The reason was because I relied on them to undertake the initial screen of the voluminous pile of written material that descended on the office every day. Much of it involved non-controversial subjects, like the authorization to bring an action against outright fraud, where prompt unanimous approval was expected. I relied on my advisors to find the material that they knew I would want to see and, in order to do that, they had to know what my general interests were. If they hadn't been able to rely on their skill, I never would have time to think about anything else.

As mentioned before, I personally wrote every word of material that was circulated over my name, inside or outside the agency. However, I relied on my advisors to do some basic research if needed, to provide citations to relevant authorities, and to comment on the substance when they disagreed or thought of additional arguments.

Advice sometimes flowed the other way, as well. It was their choice. I would express some views on longterm career choices and even some personal matters, if they wished. I know a lot about the lives of some in the office, and virtually nothing about some others. I will, however, always consider all of them as valued friends.

After I left the Commission, those who were still in town used to take me out to lunch on my birthday every year. The most recent one (number 80 in 2011) may be the last because I don't live in Washington any more, and seldom visit. If any read this, I want to tell you again how much I have appreciated your contributions, and how fond the memories are.

You each deserve an individual essay, as all my fellow Commissioners do, but I can only list your names, roughly in the order that you came on board: Holly Vedova, Lisa Kopchik, Tom Klotz, John Smollen, Mark Eichorn, Dara Diamond, Katherine Schnack, Eric Wenger, Mike Wroblewski and Beth Delaney.

It was not easy to take leave of all this, but the icing on the cake came two years later when then-Chairman Debbie Majoras gave me the Commission's highest award for service - named after Miles Kirkpatrick, the man who is rightly credited with restoration of the Commission's solid reputation in the early 1970s. (I knew Miles Kirkpatrick when I was a young lawyer.)

The ceremony for this award was impressive, as it always is, because only one is given each year. Stephanie, our son, David, two sisters and their husbands, a niece and her husband, and many, many old friends and colleagues were there. Some I hadn't seen for years. Two Supreme Court Justices (John Roberts and Ruth Ginsburg) and one Circuit Court Judge (David Tatel) - each of whom has already been separately mentioned - were there. This old guy was overwhelmed. Still am, when I think about it.

My acceptance talk was never written out, and obviously has never been printed anywhere. There's a muddy video of it somewhere in the pile of stuff I brought out from D.C., but I can't find it right now. I do remember that it was primarily an expression of appreciation for the opportunities that I was lucky enough to have while I was at the Commission, and concluded with the statement that my service was "not only an honor, but a joy." Those are the right words.

I know; I know: my delighted reaction seems inconsistent with some things I have said before about lists of the best and awards. I'll take refuge in Emerson's observation that "consistency is the hobgoblin of little minds." Just because I think the whole award process can be arbitrary doesn't mean I shouldn't enjoy it when my own name gets picked out of a hat. The same goes for the other "lifetime" awards I received from the American Antitrust Institute in 2005 and the Global Competition Review in 2011. It's nice to think that a few people, at least, think I've contributed something, even if that word "lifetime" has a somewhat chilling undertone.

September 11, 2001

I mention these events at the end of the Chapter, even though they occurred relatively early on in my Commission term, because they had a profound and lasting effect on my views of the world, as they have for so many other people. In an eerie way, they awakened old memories, too, because the strong sense that something had profoundly changed in the world reminded me of my impressions when the Korean War started in 1950 - something I described many pages ago.

The day started like any other; I got into the office about 9:00. Shortly after that, one of my advisors rushed in and said: "Turn on your TV. A bulletin I just saw on the internet reports that a plane has crashed into one of the World Trade Towers."

We turned on the news and saw one tower, with a heavy cloud of dark smoke billowing out the top. No one seemed to know how the apparent "accident" had occurred on such a clear day. I remember that I told the growing group in my office that a bomber had flown directly into a high floor of the Empire State Building during WWII, and the building had survived. But that was in a storm at night, and even bombers were not all that large by present-day standards.

As the talking heads in the box and in the office speculated back and forth, the image of another plane appeared on the screen. It appeared to travel in slow, slow motion - perhaps because of the angle of the shot, or perhaps because hearts stood still - and exploded into the other tower.

Anyone who reads this is likely to remember the events that followed that day. The crash into the Pentagon (we could see the smoke from our building); the crash of an airliner in Western Pennsylvania; the collapse of the towers; an estimated 20,000 deaths (which, fortunately, was exaggerated); and mounting reports of heroism and horror.

My own experiences were a little different than most. We had in the FTC building that day about ten of the country's leading industrial organization economists, who had been invited to lead a discussion of "what we don't know, but wish we did." Some had come a long distance, and no one could go anywhere because all flights had been grounded; the metro had been shut down; and the streets were jammed with cars standing still. So we went ahead with the conference anyway. The presentations and panel discussions were excellent - at least, whatever I can remember of them. There were occasional interruptions, when someone would enter the room to report that a tower had collapsed, and we would just gulp and move on. I don't know why the transcript was never published; perhaps the participants were too dispirited to undertake the usual review and minor smoothing of syntax.

By late afternoon, we were finished. No public transportation was available, but I was close enough to walk home. The streets were almost deserted; the only visual sign of life was the collection of military vehicles, and the only sound was the occasional roar of the fighter planes circling the city. It was like those images in the old horror movies of an empty city following some worldwide disaster.

Our house was directly under the flight path from Andrews Air Force Base to the White House lawn, and Stephanie and I watched in the backyard as a parade of helicopters brought various high level leaders back from their bunkers, somewhere.

In the following days, we had a series of mistaken bomb reports and repeated drills in the Commission's building. We would dutifully file out the door and gather at our assigned rendezvous in a nearby park - only to return after milling around for an hour or so. One day, I was deeply occupied with something, assumed it was just another drill, and decided just to ignore the warning buzzer. Unfortunately, I got caught at it by a young man in a uniform with a sniffer dog on a leash. I guess it was a genuine bomb report. He was very polite, but very firm: "I'm sorry, sir, but you'll have to leave." I asked if he had any idea when we would be able to return. The man in the uniform pointed to his dog: "He's in charge, sir. He'll let us know."

One more post 9/11 event that I want to describe - not because it really has anything to do with my education or experiences as a lawyer, but because it relates some of my reactions as a citizen and says some things that I still believe today. Think of it as a segue into the final Chapter.

Before the attack, I had agreed to give an after-dinner talk in mid-September for the business school at Pepperdine University, a highly respected graduate program. It coincided with another talk I had planned to give on the following day at a program sponsored by the Commission's Los Angeles office. I also had some interest in the place because Stephanie had attended the undergraduate school at Pepperdine before we were married, and I used to drive up from the base at Miramar and visit her there on weekends.

Both speeches were obviously postponed after the 9/11 attack, but I agreed to do both if they could be rescheduled in similar close proximity. They were rescheduled on successive days in November, and I planned the trip again.

I had some ideas about the Commission's role in the new world, and did not expect either talk to be particularly challenging. About a week before I left, however, I received a copy of Pepperdine's printed program for its event. My talk was not described as the usual message that you might expect from an FTC official to a business school audience. It was the capstone of what was an award ceremony that would include recognition of a graduate who had died a hero's death on September 11.

Tom Burnett, an athletic young man with a bright future and a lovely family, was one of the people who had overpowered the terrorists on the flight which had crashed in Pennsylvania, and thereby had probably saved either the Capitol building or the White House. How in the world could I make a contribution to this event, much less be the speaker with the most allotted time? Unlike speakers before me, I did not know Tom Burnett personally - all I knew about him was what I had read in the newspapers. My unease deepened when I noticed that his widow, Deena Burnett, would also be on the program. It was probably the hardest assignment I ever had, and I didn't have much time to prepare.

I needn't have worried so much. Everyone there was friendly and appreciated my willingness to travel across the country to participate in what was such an important event for the school. Deena Burnett, who sat with me at a speakers' table, was so gracious and serene that she put everyone at ease. I was able to speak from the heart in a way that we antitrust lawyers seldom get to do, and try somehow to relate the things with which I was familiar to the inspirational tone of the event.

This is another talk that was never written down and, of course, never printed. The Commission's Los Angeles office had taken a table at the event, however, and Jeff Klurfeld, the Region's Director, took a video. When I got a copy of the tape from Jeff, Debbie Blunt made a transcript for me, and I attach this transcript as Appendix B.

I feel these things as deeply now as I did then, and if I had to provide a summary of what I think about the important roles of my profession, the agency in which I worked then, and most of the clients I have represented, this would be it. I tried somehow to connect these things with my gratitude for the sacrifice of those people who have given so much to all who are privileged to live in this wonderful country.

The speech was well received, but I cannot tell whether I really was able to tie these things together. My hosts were very polite people. If you look at Appendix B, you can judge for yourself.

LAST THINGS

Return to Private Life

My term as a Federal Trade Commissioner expired late in September, 2005. It is permissible and customary, however, for a sitting commissioner to serve until a successor is confirmed, and my successor Tom Rosch was not confirmed until mid-December. It would be more convenient for each of us to transfer the title, as it were, at the end of the year, and that's what we agreed to do. I have no idea whether it was legal or not but important matters are rarely decided at the Commission in late December, anyhow, so I'm also sure it made no difference.

Even though I was 74 at the time, I really wasn't quite ready to give up the occupation I loved, and I returned to my old firm - now known as HoganLovells after combining with a leading firm of similar size in the UK. The deal was that I would not be called a partner, since I had no intention of functioning like one. I did not want to assume full responsibility for client matters, ever again, but would be glad to help out in any matter if I were asked. Think of the difference between a regular member of the starting lineup and a utility infielder.

I was pleased to work as a backup resource or advisor, subject to the overall direction of younger partners, many of whom once worked under mine. I'm thinking of people like Phil Larson, Janet McDavid, Mary Anne Mason, Joe Krauss, Tripp Monts, Lynda Marshall, Bob Leibenluft, Steve Steinborn, and Sharis Pozen (now Acting head of the DOJ's Antitrust Division). I've had some interesting things to do, and could tell some stories about them, but they're not my stories to tell now; the various partners-in-charge can tell them if they wish, and I would hope that they do. It has been a pleasure.

Actually, the experience has been a useful preparation for life outside the office. I'm not there yet, but I expect that I will become increasingly dependent on younger people for the day-to-day business of living if I survive into deep old age. I already seem to spend an inordinate amount of time in the offices of various medical specialists. And, I damned well have to be humble about taking advice.

I have to recognize, however, that my contributions as an active lawyer are just about over. What has it all meant? Have I ever done anything that really makes a difference? Some 30 years ago, I spoke at a program on a topic that I cannot remember. It had to involve some current controversy, however, because the other speaker was Michael Pertschuk, a former Chairman of the Federal Trade Commission with whom I had disagreed on almost everything. I have to assume that we went at it again, hammer and tong, but in a jovial way.

I must have been overwhelmed with a sense of futility because, during a lull in the proceedings, I passed him a note that said: "Mike, I wonder if someday all these arguments will seem as silly as the 17th Century religious wars seem to us now?" Mike Pertschuk read the note, chuckled a bit, and wrote back: "I agree with you."

I suppose that nothing that any of us do will make any difference in the very, very long run. (It appears that the earth will be swallowed by the sun in some six billion years.) So, that's not really a very satisfactory answer. Most of us don't get to choose the issues of our era, so we have to do the best we can unless we choose to drop out of society altogether.

I have tried to do the best I can, within the limits of my inheritance or my self-imposed frailties. I hope that the damage done by my inevitable failures has not been too serious. I do want to close with some comments on things that remain.

Life Begins at Eighty

In the deep depression year of 1935, they made a lighthearted movie called "Life Begins at Forty." Well, I did experience a lot of invigorating changes around the time that I turned 40. I was adjusting to an entirely new manner of life without chemical assistance, and about to embark on the high adventure of a big new job at General Motors. But, I have experienced even more invigorating changes in this, the year I turned 80.

I want to talk a little bit about the experience of being 80, for those much younger people who might read this memoir. I know what it feels like to be your age, but you don't know what it feels like to be mine. Most people are too reserved to talk about something like that, but I'm not. So, I'll tell you.

It does not mean the end of adventures, but they may be adventures of a different kind. Just three years ago, for example, Stephanie and I had an experience unlike any we have ever had before. Although we each have had opinions about the candidates in national elections, neither had ever become involved in the electoral process itself. That changed in 2008, when John McCain ran for President.

I had met John McCain a number of times at small functions to which I had been invited by Orson Swindle, the Senator's close friend and fellow POW. (Orson and I, of course, served on the Commission together, and have remained in touch over the years.) Stephanie's acquaintance goes back much further.

John McCain's father had been an Annapolis classmate of Stephanie's father, Howard Abbott, who was lost with all hands in June, 1941, when the submarine O-9 failed to surface after a test dive off Portsmouth, N.H. Stephanie's mother collapsed under the strain of the terrible days that followed, and Stephanie and her younger brother were taken in briefly by the Navy family in quarters next door - the McCains.

She remembers very little about it today, except for the feelings of confusion about why she suddenly was living next door and annoyance at "a very noisy little boy." (She was then almost seven, and the future Senator was just short of five, so the annoyance was not surprising.) Senator McCain's amazing mother, Roberta McCain recalls it all very well, however, as just about "the saddest thing I remember."

So, we were both enthusiastic about the primary and national campaigns, did volunteer work, and maxed out at various fundraisers. Orson arranged for Stephanie's appointment as a McCain delegate from D.C., and for our special treatment as "family friends" at the Convention in Minneapolis. It was an experience that neither of us will ever forget - even though the ultimate outcome of the election was disappointing.

In fact, unexpected experiences like that one seem to be better than they ever were. A recent article in our local newspaper discussed the results of a rather surprising nationwide poll. There was a positive correlation between the age of the respondent and expressions of general contentment. In short, older people seemed happier than younger people.

The reporter was astute enough to speculate that the causation may run the other way. It may be that people with a positive view of life just live longer. I could also speculate that we may be more content because whatever happens next, we've had the opportunity to live a full life, and can't feel cheated. It's also possible that older people may have been trained in an era when it was considered unseemly to complain. (I know I was - but, then, I really had very little to complain about.) All I can say about it right now is that I have enjoyed life more and more with each passing decade, and this past year has been the best of all, before the sad events described below – but, even these witness that contentment can prevail to the end of our days.

I suspect the pleasure of relocation to my favorite place has something to do with it. The freedom associated with the offload of so many possessions also has something to do with it. With all due respect to the good clients I have served and may sporadically continue to serve, I've had even more fun in my present occupation of telling individual stories. (It's an occupational hazard in old age, however, and we always have to be mindful of the glazed-over appearance of younger eyes.)

I think there is also something else that sustains morale. Some people deliberately seek out physical risks. They are attracted to the most dangerous branches of the military or they may engage in extreme sports like base jumping or attempts to scale the highest peaks in the world. Somehow, close encounters with mortal threats makes them feel more "alive;" knowledge of the fragility of their existence makes them appreciate it so much more.

Octogenarians do not have to deliberately seek out reminders of mortality; it comes with the territory. I appreciate the company of my peers more now than I have since I was a member of that exclusive club called "Teenager." My peers today are sharing the same experience of heightened awareness. It is not depressing at all. For the most part, our contemporaries are cheerful, and sometimes hilarious. We have the comradery of survivors. And, yes, we do sometimes talk about our increasing issues of memory and mobility, the mysterious pains that come and go, and the various operations we have had or are about to have. But I don't find it depressing. I'd like to think that we do these things in the spirit of Shakespeare's imagined veteran of the battle at Agincourt, who will "strip his sleeve and show his scars." from the wounds sustained "on Crispen's day."

Death in the Family

Shortly after the preceding paragraphs were drafted, we got word that my oldest brother Dan had a terminal cancer, and was living with his younger daughter Pamela, her husband, and a full time caregiver across the country in Connecticut. No one could predict the timeline but he declined quickly and died on October 3, 2011 at the age of 82.

Although the three brothers were close in age, (we survivors are 81 and 80), Dan always had been the leader of the pack. He was not only a tall man in his prime (some 6'3), but also reached his full height by his early teens, so he was much the biggest and strongest then. That's important when you're a boy.

He also had more drive and discipline than the rest of us. He graduated first in his Georgetown College class at the age of 19, completed a two-year MBA program at Dartmouth, and secured a direct commission as an Ensign in the Navy Supply Corps at the onset of the Korean War.

Shortly after that, he married Elizabeth ("Liz") Mullen, herself a brilliant and sophisticated girl of 20, who had – because of her mother's chronic illness – served in teens as the official hostess for her father, a prominent Supreme Court Justice in New York City.

After the birth of their four children, Dan and Liz decided that they were not interested in the pursuit of fame and fortune in the Big Apple, and bought a horse farm in Simsbury, Conn., surrounding a house that dated from 1740. Neither one of them cared to ride horses, but their children loved them and all became exert riders. As expected, this common interest unified the family and they formed a close bond that survives to this day.

Dan took over the management of a small auto leasing company in Hartford, which my father and a couple of his business associates had bought as a sideline venture, in order to accommodate a once-close friend's widow who wanted to cash out. Dan ultimately bought off the children of the other investors and built the company into a consistently profitable family enterprise that is today run by two of his children, now in their middle age. The significant thing is that he never wanted to create an empire, although I am sure he had the talent, because he wanted to keep family control of the company.

I mention these things, not only as a tribute to someone who deserves a far more extensive memorial – and may someday get it – but also because his example, in youth and in later life, has ultimately made a significant contribution to my own views of the world. He and Liz always understood what was really important.

In his last weeks, Dan faced the inevitable end with calm and good cheer. He had good reasons to feel serene. He and his recently departed wife Liz had an unusually close marriage that lasted for over 55 years. They lived the life they chose to live, and succeeded at it; and they raised a closely-knit family, whose company they enjoyed above all others. In the traditional expression: "He could look back on a life well lived."

The last time we spoke on the phone, about two weeks before he died, he sounded much the same as he always did, and said he felt "fine", though obviously tired. I had already told him a number of times how much his example had meant to me, so we talked mostly about Yankee baseball because it was an interest we had shared for over 70 years, albeit a somewhat tender subject these days. (I only learned later on how much the physical effort to talk on the phone drained him, but he always wanted to do it.)

There was a touching sequel. When we learned of Dan's death, Stephanie was able to make the somewhat complicated travel arrangements on short notice and we made the long trek to Connecticut the next day. The day after that, there was an old-fashioned Irish wake, which was attended by the remaining siblings, and most of the numerous nieces and nephews whom we too seldom get to see. The atmosphere in these events, which are relics of the old world, is somber but determinably optimistic. It's a celebration of life, too, and I hope that my survivors will realize that when they gather for me.

We were amazed when Peter Mullen showed up. Peter was Dan's closest friend at Georgetown, his scholastic rival, and became his brother-in-law when Dan married Liz. He and Dan had made very different life choices, but were always close. Peter became a highly successful corporate lawyer in New or City, and for a number of years was the managing partner of the fiercely competitive and lucrative Skadden Arps firm. ("Peter was the only guy in the place who never feuded with anyone," was the way a Skadden lawyer once described for me the secret of his success.)

The reason we were surprised when Peter appeared was that we knew he had some months before undergone an appalling and debilitating operation for some illness that I never quite understood. He was, without doubt the most physically ravaged person I had ever seen who was still (barely) mobile. But, I was glad to have the opportunity to talk to him, because Peter and his wife "Billie" were close neighbors when Stephanie and I lived in New York's Peter Cooper village late in the 1950s. They were a few years older, and introduced us to the ways of life in that somewhat close-knit community.

Peter and I exchanged some amusing memories of those experiences, and he spoke about his present disability and admittedly poor chances for improvement. But, he seemed in good spirits, and we talked until he grew too tired and began to lose his track. He died 10 days later.

It seems somehow appropriate that these lifelong friends, with intertwined families, would die almost simultaneously. RIP.

Their mutual bravery, as they stared down death, should reassure younger people who may be anxious about the passage of time. We who now live in thin air may feel some sweet nostalgia about the physical agility and stamina that we enjoyed in our youth, but it is coupled with a deeper appreciation of life's quiet pleasures and acceptance of things that we are unable to change. And, there is no fear.

"Death, be not proud though some have called thee mighty and dreadful, for thou are not so."

(John Donne c. 1620s)

Some Speculations

As the end of life draws near, it is also natural that people will reflect more on metaphysical things. It's not a consuming obsession for me, and really not particularly scary, but the ever-present reminders of mortality not only heighten the appreciation of life but also suggest the inevitable question: "Is this all that there is?"

I read everything that is accessible to someone unfamiliar with higher mathematics about the origins of the universe and the evolution of human life.

I don't pretend to be an expert on things scientific, and I do not have the awe-inspiring intellect of an Einstein who was able to intuit revolutionary concepts, which were later confirmed by empirical observations. What my legal education and experience did give me, however, is the ability to distinguish between what is "proof" that something had to have happened in a particular way and a demonstration that it *might* have happened that way or that it sometimes actually did.

For example, the principal competing theories today about the origins of the universe are the alternative speculations that a "Big Bang" created just the universe we perceive or that multiple explosions created myriad "multiverses". The latter, although still a minority view, seems to be growing in popularity because of the awkward fact that so many fundamental physical variables in our observable universe seem to be precisely tuned to permit the evolution of habitable planets and of human life. This fine-tuned condition inevitably suggests the possibility, if not the need, for some intelligent design, and many scientists, by the nature of their calling, feel obliged to resist this explanation. If there are myriad universes - perhaps an infinite number - even the most unlikely combination of variables could have occurred by random chance.

The shortcoming of both theories, however, is that they each depend on the existence of certain determined physical principles, and particles or fields of force, that just happen to have been there forever - mostly in passive quiescence. Neither really solves the mystery of creation because certain initial conditions still have to be taken as a given. Almost a century ago, the then-famous astronomer John Haldane said: " … my suspicion is that the universe is not only queerer than we suppose, but queerer that we *can* suppose." Discoveries since his time suggest that it is "queerer" still, with no end in sight. I don't know why intellectual respectability requires me to believe that the ultimate source of the queerness is mindless.

There is a story, which is colorful enough to be taken as true even if it isn't, that in ancient times the leading cosmological theory was that the earth was carried on the shoulders of a giant, who in turn was seated on an elephant, which was in turn standing on the back of a giant turtle. A skeptical critic at the time was supposed to have asked: "But what was the turtle standing on?" The answer was: "Another turtle, of course; it's turtles all the way down." The geniuses who think about these things have made amazing discoveries in the search for ultimate reality; and to probe deeper and deeper into the worlds of the very large and the very small. Some of these discoveries have turned out to have very practical applications. But, so far as I can see, we're still stuck in the turtle stack.

The same logical flaws appear in popular discussions of the links between physics, chemistry and biology. In addition to the initial mysteries of creation, theorists have attempted to find an explanation of how an insensate group of particles or energy or something more exotic could have organized themselves into chemical elements, living organisms, and ultimately beings who are intelligent and curious enough to inquire about these things. Again, however, mathematical calculations, experiments that show some self-organization can happen in certain circumstances, or even observations that show it has happened somewhere sometime in the past, also depend on unexplained underlying assumptions and, of course, do not "prove" that it *must* have happened without intelligent intervention everywhere.

This conclusion is particularly important in light of the current lively debate between the advocates of "evolution" and "intelligent design." If "design" advocates are lampooned as people who believe the universe, our world and all its inhabitants were created in "six days," per the biblical account, the position is obviously ridiculous. If, however, the dispute is more accurately portrayed as a debate between the theory that the *only* engine of evolution is "natural selection," or "survival of the fittest" versus the belief that evolution can also be directed in a purposeful way, then there is something legitimate to argue about. (For example, if homosexuality really is inborn, where's the reproductive advantage?)

Expressed another way, a lot of popular science writers seem confused about the fundamental difference between an accurate "description" which will give rise to testable predictions, and an "explanation" of how and why certain things happen. The holy grail of a single equation that will encompass all known fundamental forces would not "solve" the mysteries of the universe around us. An equation can provide a precise description of what will happen under certain conditions, but it does not explain anything. (Besides scientists have just discovered the existence of a new force that seems to accelerate the expansion of the observable universe, which no one knows much about yet.)

It seems to me that the belief in purely natural explanations for our world or the belief in an intelligent creator is simply a matter of philosophical preference. I prefer to believe in a purposeful intelligence beyond our understanding, because the idea is more comforting and the alternatives are no less mysterious.

I am not at all reluctant to talk in greater detail about my personal spiritual beliefs with family and friends, but this is not the place to talk too long. What I can say is that I have experienced a strong sense of comfort in times of extreme pain and potential anxiety, when I asked for it. I am confident that it will be there the next time I need it, even if though there is no way for me to be sure of the source.

I am aware of the fact that some experiments have shown that these sensations are associated with activity in a particular location of the brain. But, this doesn't mean they always originate there. A picture or a message on my computer screen is produced by activity in the machine, but the machine is not the ultimate source.

It is also natural, I suppose, that I sometimes speculate (not often) about what, if anything, lies beyond. Again, this is a question that logic will not solve. Only a mystic will feel sure and - for better or worse - I am no mystic. I have no problem, however, with the notion that some essence of the "thing" that is me could survive without any connection to a physical body. As a crude analogy, think of a Beethoven symphony. It clearly is "something" but where is it? Is it located in a series of notations on pieces of paper, in a tape recording of a performance, or in the memory of someone who listened to it? Suppose all the known pieces of paper and recordings had rotted away, and all those who had heard the symphony were dead. Does the symphony then cease to exist? Suppose further that aeons down the road, archeologists uncover a score, figure out how to read it, and play the notes. Does this mean that the "something," a Beethoven symphony, has suddenly winked back into existence after having been extinct for so long?

All this begins to read like those speculations about whether mathematical proofs are created, or merely discovered like a buried treasure. Or, the discussions of theoretical physicists who speculate about whether a physical thing really can be said to exist, or an event to happen, without a sentient observer. That's a big mystery, too, but scientists don't think it's beneath their dignity to talk about it.

This discussion may seem to stray far away from the underlying themes of this memoir. But, I don't think it really is. It is just a perhaps outre illustration of the way that I have been taught to think about things - that perhaps limited perspective of a lawyer who is better at clarifying questions than answering them.

Since I don't know of any way to be sure about the reality of an existence after death, I am free to imagine what I want. If it turns out that I am wrong, there will be nothing left of me to be disappointed. If you want a clue about what appeals to me look at the well-known sonnet, *The Soldier,* by Robert Brooke. Like so many people in military service during a war - in his case World War I - and almost all old people anytime, he reflects on what might survive after his death. In line 10, he imagines a transformation into "A pulse in the eternal mind, no less." Make of it what you want, but I happen to think that's the most profound (and optimistic) line in the English language.

A Final Word

Since I cannot do a thing to affect what will or will not happen after my increasingly-rickety frame gives up, I should close with some things that I am still determined to do.

I am determined to spend more time with my children and grandchildren, as well as my brothers and sisters. Along with my wife Stephanie, whom I profoundly hope will be beside me all my days, these closest relatives are still the best friends that I have and the joy of my life. I also still treasure the friendship of many people with whom I studied in school or worked in my various jobs, and only a few have been mentioned by name in this memoir. Most of us actually spend more time with our office "families" than our own, and we get to know each other very well - albeit in different ways. The same for old classmates, at a particular time.

Any reader would run out of patience long before I completed a discussion of purely personal friends, so I won't even try. I'll just mention two sets, one old and one new, to illustrate different dimensions of friendship.

DeVier Pierson, already mentioned, has probably been my closest personal friend for many years. Although he will insist he is a much younger man (by a month) and we spent our early days in very different places, we have in many ways led parallel lives. I don't know anyone who understands me better, and vice versa. He and his wife Shirley are also the most hospitable people in the world. Even though we live a continent apart for most of the time now, they fortunately do have a vacation house in Newport Beach right up the coast.

I am grateful as well that I have come to know Michael and Gail Jordan, new friends for me here in Coronado. They both have Navy history, as well. Mike was a photo interpreter on active duty, stayed in the Reserves, and retired as a Captain. Gail, a high-school classmate of Stephanie here, actually is part of a family with five generations of career military service. She and Mike have gone out of their way to introduce us to people here and get us involved in a number of interesting volunteer activities. She has also been patient enough to type this memoir for me.

I would like to maintain a connection with HoganLovells in some capacity, as long as the firm wants me to. I am grateful that I have had the opportunity to practice there, off and on, since January, 1983, and many partners are still close personal friends. I am still willing to offer advice and act as an advocate, to the best of my ability, if I'm asked to do so. However, I have lost the zest for battles I am not required to join.

It's refreshing to be removed from the ceaseless partisan bickering in the Washington air. I believe that the enemies of our country and our civilization underestimate our resolve when they hear the clamor that is stimulated by an adversarial media. In wartime, particularly, I believe it is wrong to encourage disparagement of our country's leader - whether I voted for him or not. I deplored the vitriolic criticism aimed at President Bush, and I won't do the same today.

I feel at home with the uncomplicated patriotism of the people who live here. Most of them have had direct or close indirect experience of military life, and know where the warts are. But, they have never grown cynical or lost faith, and they have been disciplined to express their political views, if any, in a temperate way. I know of no group in our society with people more unpretentious, generous and brave.

To my knowledge, I have no outstanding quarrels with anyone. If someone who sees this thinks that I do, please let me know and I'll try to set things right.

The questionnaire that I had to fill out for the Senate Commerce Committee before my confirmation as an FTC Commissioner asked what I thought were the most important activities of any national government. I said that the two essential things were to protect a country's frontiers, in order to provide peace and security for its citizens, and also to have a legal system that allowed for the peaceful resolution of disputes. I believe that military people and lawyers - despite the fact that they sometimes have to do battle - each are ultimately preservers of the peace. I am pleased to have had the opportunity to make a small contribution in both roles.

It's time to wind this story down. For all who read it, including one time allies or adversaries and loved ones or friends - particularly those of a certain age who, like me, may soon undertake that last journey to a destination we can only imagine - the spirit of my final message is best expressed in the words I heard some sixty years ago on the day I became an officer in the Navy:

> "May all your cruises be on calm seas,
> And may all your missions be peaceful ones."

THOMAS B. LEARY

ACKNOWLEDGEMENTS

A project like this requires the support of many people. I want to extend particular thanks to Gail Jordan, who typed my longhand manuscript and offered numerous suggestions from the perspective of a non-specialist reader. Our daughter, Alison Leary Estep, who works in the public relations field, provided valuable advice about the publishing world and explored various options for me. And, finally, Alison's colleague BeckyJo Bourgeois designed the cover, navigated the thicket of various formats, and made the final arrangements with the publishers. They more than made up for my ignorance about these things.

(TOP LEFT) Mary Smith Leary, Tom Leary's paternal grandmother, 1885; **(TOP RIGHT)** Daniel Leary, Tom Leary's father, 1950; **(ABOVE)** Reunion of FTC Advisors, December 2007; left to right, Tom Klotz, Michael Wroblewski, Beth Delaney, Mark Eichorn, Tom Leary, Katherine Schnack, John Smollen, Holly Vedova, Deborah Blunt (office manager), and Lisa Kopchik.

(ABOVE LEFT) FTC Kirkpatrick Award Ceremony. Tom Leary with three FTC Chairmen, with whom he served, 2007; left to right, Tim Muris, Debbie Majoras, Tom Leary, and Robert Pitofsky; (ABOVE) Margaret Barrett Leary, Tom Leary's mother, 1920; (LEFT) On the Great Wall with Stephanie at Simitai, China, June 2004; (BELOW) One of the last pictures of the five Leary siblings together, Spring 2010; left to right, Barrett (80), Margot Badenhausen (71), Dan (81), Mary Caroline Clark (75), Tom (78)

(TOP) The Leary siblings; left to right, Barrett, Dan, Margot, Mary Caroline, and Tom Leary, Christmas 1939, West Orange, NJ; **(ABOVE LEFT)** Tom Leary's wife Stephanie, 1965; **(ABOVE RIGHT)** Immediate family on cruise together, 2009; left to right, back, Alison Leary Estep, Tom Leary, Stephanie Abbott; middle, Robert Estep, Thomas Abbott Leary, David Abbott Leary, Kelly Leary; front, Barrett Estep, Lauren Estep, Erin Leary

FOOTNOTES

[Note: For simplicity, the citations to my previous speeches and articles on the Federal Trade Commission Website are cross-referenced by number to Appendix A. The citation to this list is https//ftc.gov/speeches/leary/shtm, and is not repeated over and over again.]

1. See Leary, True Stories, Appendix A, No. 17.

2. Goldfarb v. Virginia State Bar, 421 U.S. 733 (1975).

3. Erie v. Tomkins, 304 U.S. 64 (1938).

4. Gerald Gunther, Learned Hand: the Man and the Judge (Knopf 1994).

5. U.S. v. Pan American World Airways, 193 F. Supp. 18 (S.D.N.Y. 1961), rev'd other grounds 371 U.S. 296 (1963).

6. Foremost Dairies, 60 F.T.C. 944 (1962), modified, 67 F.T.C. 282 (1965).

7. See 115 U.S.C. Sec. 1407.

8. U.S. v. Grinnell Corp. 384 U.S. 563 (1966).

9. Fortner Enters. v. U.S. Steel, 394 U.S. 495 (1969); U.S. Steel v. Fortner Enters., 429 U.S. 610 (1977).

10. Continental T.V. Inc. v. GTE Sylvania, Inc. 433 U.S. 36 (1977).

11. Sylvania, supra. n. 10, at 51 n. 18.

12. Leegin Creative Leather Products v. PSKS, Inc. 551 U.S.877 (2007).

13. See Leary, State Auto Dealer Regulations, Appendix A, No. 28.

14. United States. v. Arnold Schwinn & Co., 388 U.S. 365 (1967), a case later overruled by <u>Sylvania</u>, supra n.10.

15. Thomas Leary, What Is the Real Issue, published in ABA Section of Antitrust Law, INDUSTRIAL CONCENTRATION AND THE MARKET SYSTEM, at 278 (1979).

16. See 18 U.S.C. 1961-68 (1970).

17. Codified, as amended, in 15 U.S.C. Sec. 18a.

18. See, e.g., Leary, McDavid & Larson, How to <u>Avoid</u> Negotiations on Second Requests, ANTITRUST (Summer 1999), at 41.

19. The illustrative cases mentioned are Cargill, Inc. v. Montford of Colorado, 479 U.S. 104 (1986); California v. America Corp, 490 U.S. 93 (1989); California v. American Stores, 495 U.S. 271 (1990); Brook Group v. Brown & Williamson, 509 U.S. 209 (1993); State Oil v. Khan, 522 U.S. 3 (1997), and Leegin v. PSKS, 551 U.S. 877 (2007). We supported the winning side in Cargill, Brook, Khan, and Leegin.

20. See 18 U.S.C. Secs. 3551-3586.

21. Quotation is from True Stories, Appendix A, No. 17.

22. See Dream the Big Dreams, Appendix A, No. 1.

23. FTC v. H.J. Heinz Co. 116 F. Supp.2d 190 (D.D.C. 2000), <u>rev'd</u>, 246 F 3d 708 (D.C. Cir. 2001).

24. See An Inside Look, Appendix A, No. 23.

25. Schering-Plough Corp. v. FTC, 402 F.3d 1056 (11th Cir. 2005) <u>cert.</u>, <u>denied</u>, 126 Sup. Ct. 2929 (2006).

26. See Pfizer, Inc. 81 F.T.C. 23 (1972).

27. 15 U.S.C. Sec. 45.

28. Quote is from Special Challenges, Appendix A, No. 13.

29. U.S. DEPT OF JUSTICE & FED. TRADE COMMISSION, STATEMENT OF ANTITRUST POLICY IN HEALTHCARE (1996) <u>reprinted in</u> 4 Trade Reg. Rrp. (CCH) 13, 153 (Sept. 5, 1996).

30. See Health Care Interview, Appendix A, No. 3; Antitrust Implications of Clinical\Integration, Appendix A, No. 18.

31. See Comment on Merger Enforcement, Appendix A, No. 25.

32. Economic Roots of Antitrust, Appendix A, No. 8.

33. See The Muris Legacy, Appendix A, No. 7.

34. See, Self Regulation, Appendix A, No. 10; Competition Law, Appendix A, No. 11.

THOMAS B. LEARY

APPENDIX A

Speeches and Articles by Thomas B. Leary Commissioner

Available on the FTC website at http://www.ftc.gov/speeches/leary.shtm.

(1) Dream the Big Dreams
    This is the written version of personal remarks delivered at the
    Commissioner's Farewell Reception on December 22, 2005

(2) Federal Civil Remedies for Antitrust Offenses: Statement of
    Commissioner Thomas B. Leary Before the Antitrust Modernization
    Commission
    This is the Statement that Commissioner Leary delivered before the
    Commission on December 1, 2005

(3) Health Care: An Interview with Commissioner Thomas B. Leary
    This is an interview with Commissioner Leary conducted by the ABA
    Antitrust Section Health Care Committee Newsletter, published in the
    ABA's Antitrust Health Care Chronicle, October 2005, Vol. 19, No. 3.

(4) The Bipartisan Legacy
    This is the written version of a speech delivered at the American
    Antitrust Institute's Sixth Annual Conference at the National Press
    Club in Washington, D.C. on June 21, 2005. The remarks are to be
    published in a future edition of the Tulane University Law Journal.

(5) The Legitimate Uses of Social Security Numbers, and Their Misuse for
    Identity Theft Purposes
    Testimony of Commissioner Leary Before the Committee on
    Commerce, Science, and Transportation of the United States Senate,
    June 16, 2005

(6)   Category Management: An Interview with FTC Commissioner
      Thomas B. Leary
      This is an interview with Commissioner Leary conducted by the ABA
      Section of Antitrust Law, Sherman Act Section 2 Committee, pub-
      lished in the Sherman Act Section 2 Committee's newsletter, Vol. III
      No. 2 (Spring 2005)

(7)   "The Muris Legacy"
      This is a later written version of a speech delivered at a program of the
      American Bar Association, Section of Antitrust Law, held in connection
      with the Annual Meeting of the Association on August 7, 2004, just
      eight days before the effective date of Chairman Muris' resignation.

(8)   "The Economic Roots of Antitrust," An Outline
      This outline was prepared for a presentation at the International
      Seminar on Antitrust Law and Economic Development, held at the
      Chinese Academy of Social Sciences Institute of Law in Beijing, China,
      on July 1, 2004.

(9)   "A Second look At Category Management"
      This paper is based on oral remarks delivered on May 17, 2004,
      at the 23rd Annual Food Marketing Institute Legal Conference in
      Tucson, Arizona, and also on June 23, 2003 at the American Antitrust
      Institute's Roundtable Discussion on Antitrust and Category Captains,
      in Washington, D.C.

(10) "Self Regulation and The Interface Between Consumer Protection and
      Antitrust"
      This is a slightly modified version of informal remarks delivered at
      a lunchtime seminar hosted by the Dewey Ballantine law firm in
      Washington, D.C. January 28, 2004 (PDF 21k)

(11) Competition Law and Consumer Protection Law: Two Wings of the
      Same House.
      This is the written version of a speech delivered at the FTC 90th
      Anniversary
      Symposium on September 22, 2004, in Washington, D.C. It is pub-
      lished in 72 Antitrust L.J. 1147 (2005). (PDF 28K)

(12) "Antitrust in a Technology Economy: What's New and What's Not." This is a written version of the speech delivered on June 6, 2003, at the Stanford Conference on Antitrust in the Technology Economy, jointly sponsored by the ABA Section of Antitrust Law and Stanford Law School. (PDF 28K)

(13) Special Challenges for Antitrust in Health Care
This article is a written version of a speech given at a forum on Antitrust and Health Care jointly sponsored by the Health Lawyers Association and the ABA Sections of Antitrust Law and Health Law (May 15, 2003), and is published in Antitrust, Spring 2004, Volume 18, No. 2, at 23. (PDF 367K)

(14) The FTC and Class Actions
Based on oral remarks before the Class Action Litigation Summit, Washington, D.C., on June 26, 2003.

(15) The Dialogue Between Students of Business and Students of Antitrust
Given at the American Antitrust Institute's program on "Stretching the Envelope" on April 22, 2003. It is printed in 47 New York Law School Law Review 1 (2003). Similar remarks were presented at the Notre Dame Research Workshop and Conference on Marketing, Competitive Conduct and Antitrust Policy on May 3, 2002. (PDF 49K)

(16) A Structured Outline for the Analysis of Horizontal Agreements
This revision of a paper first presented a year ago was prepared for distribution at the Conference Board 2004 Antitrust Conference (Mar. 3-4, 2004). (PDF 27K)

(17) Lessons from Real Life: True Stories that illustrate the Art and Science of Cost-Effective Counseling
This article is a later written version of remarks delivered on October 25, 2002, at the ABA Section of Antitrust Law Antitrust Masters Course in Sea Island, Georgia, and is published in the March, 2003 edition of The Antitrust Source, www.antitrustsource.com (PDF 83K)

(18) The Antitrust Implications of "Clinical Integration: " An analysis of FTC Staff's Advisory Opinion to Medsouth
This article is based on a speech delivered at the Saint Louis University Health Law Symposium on April 12, 2002, and is published in issue 47:2 of the Saint Louis University Law Journal at page 217. (PDF 47K)

(19) Allies in A Common Cause
This paper is based on the transcript of informal remarks delivered at a Conference on Dietary Supplements of the Food and Drug Law Institute, Washington, D.C., January 18, 2003. (PDF 21K)

(20) The Spell of the Gherkin
before the Castro C. Geer Chapter of the Federal Trade Commission Alumni Association Annual Business Meeting, Washington, DC. December 18, 2002.

(21) Efficiencies and Antitrust: A Story of Ongoing Evolution
Prepared remarks before ABA Section of Antitrust Law, 2002 Fall Forum, Washington, DC., November 8, 2002.

(22) The Federal Trade Commission and the Defense of Free Markets
before David T. Chase Free Enterprise Institute, Eastern Connecticut State University, Willimantic, Connecticut, October 7, 2002
(PDF 30K)

(23) An Inside Look at the Heinz Case
This comment is adapted from a speech before the Association of the Bar of the City of New York, NY, December 4, 2001, and has been published in Antitrust, Spring 2002, Vol. 16, No.2, at 32.

(24) The Essential Stability of Merger Policy in the United States
Prepared remarks before Guidelines for Merger Remedies: Prospects and Principles, Joint U.S./E.U. Conference, sponsored by the University of California at Berkeley School of Law, Berkeley Center for Law & Technology, and Ecole Nationale Superieure des Mines de Paris, Paris, France; published in 70 Antitrust L.J. 105 (2002)

(25) A Comment on Merger Enforcement in the United States and in the European Union
Prepared remarks before the Transatlantic Business Dialogue Principals Meeting, Washington, D.C., October 11, 2001.

(26) Antitrust Issues in the Settlement of Pharmaceutical Patent Disputes, Part II
This essay is based on a speech before the American Bar Association Healthcare Program, in Washington, DC., May 17, 2001, and is published in the December 2, 2001 edition of the Journal of Health Law, Vol. 34, at 657.

(27) The Need for Objective and Predictable Standards in the Law of Predation
before the Steptoe and Johnson and Analysis Group/Economics 2001 Antitrust Conference, Washington, D.C., May 10, 2001.

(28) State Auto Dealer Regulation: One Man's Preliminary View
before the International Franchise Association 34th Annual Legal Symposium., Washington, DC, May 8, 2001, and also published in the ABA's Franchise Law Journal, Vol. 21, No. 2, Fall 2001, at 65.

(29) The Patent-Antitrust Interface
based on a speech before the American Bar Association's Section of Antitrust Law Program, "Intellectual Property and Antitrust: Navigating the Minefield," Philadelphia, PA, May 3, 2001.

(30) Antitrust Economics: Three Cheers and Two Challenges
This paper is based on talks before a conference sponsored by the economic consulting firm of Charles River Associates, Washington, DC, November 15, 2000, and on July 7, 2001, at the meetings of the Western Economic Association, and more recently updated.

(31) Antitrust issues in Settlement of Pharmaceutical Patent Disputes
This essay is based on a speech before the Sixth Annual Health Care Antitrust Forum, Northwestern University School of Law, Chicago, IL, November 3, 2000, and is published in Vol 14 of the Antitrust Health Care Chron., Winter 2000/2001 at 4.

(32) Distribution Law Developments At The Federal Trade Commission before the Distribution and Dealer Termination, 21st Anniversary Seminar, Law Journal Seminars, New York, NY, June 28, 2000.

(33) The significance of Variety in Antitrust Analysis
This essay is based on a speech before the Steptoe and Johnson 2000 Antitrust Conference, Washington, DC, May 18, 2000, and is published at 68 Antitrust Law Journal 1007 (2001)

(34) The Two Faces of Electronic Commerce
April 28, 2000

(35) Unfairness and the Internet
This essay is based on a speech before the Wayne State University Law Review, "Unfair Practices and the Internet" Symposium, Detroit, MI, April 13, 2000, and is published in Volume 46:4 of the Wayne State Law Review, Winter 2000, at 1711.

(36) Freedom as the Core Value of Antitrust in the New Millenium
before the ABA Antitrust Section 48th Annual Spring Meeting Chair's Showcase Program, Antitrust at the Millenium: Looking Back and Moving forward, Washington, DC, April 6, 2000.

(37) Antitrust Law As A Balancing Act
before the Tenth Annual Seattle Computer Law Conference, Seattle, WA, December 17, 1999.

APPENDIX B

Honoring Our Heroes

Thomas B. Leary

I was originally going to talk about the Federal Trade Commission – and I will say a few things about the Federal Trade Commission – but that is not going to be my main topic tonight. I did not realize until I got the final program, about a week ago, that Thomas Burnett was a graduate of Pepperdine and that he, along with some other graduates, was being honored tonight. With your indulgence, I would like to change the theme of my speech to talk about: What we can do to honor our heroes.

One of the things that we can do to honor our heroes, obviously, is to remember them on occasions like this. Telling stories about them – some day probably building monuments. The most interesting thing to me is the way our taste in monuments seems to change. On the old monuments, the heroes were treated as being in the pantheon of the gods. Today, we put their names there, and we encourage people to look at the names and think of them as individuals – as classmates, as neighbors, as spouses. I think we honor our heroes best by remembering their humanity, and that is part of what we are doing tonight.

The second way we honor our heroes is by reflecting on the values that they sacrificed for. Now, we say our fundamental value is freedom but what do we mean by that? In World War II, they had the posters of the four freedoms, the Norman Rockwell posters, and you may have seen them even if you don't have first-hand memories of World War II: Freedom of Speech, Freedom of Religion, Freedom from Fear, Freedom from Want. Those were noble and inspiring themes for that time. We have since learned that freedoms are nuanced, they are complicated, they sometimes conflict. Sometimes people exercising freedom of speech can instill fear in other people. Sometimes we get confused between freedom of religion and freedom from religion. And freedom from want remains intractable. The average disposable income for individual Americans has grown almost four times since World War II. It's amazing - real dollars increased almost four times! Yet, we still have pockets of want. And one of the reasons we have pockets of want is because in order to eliminate them completely, we would have to impose a level of social control that would be unacceptable in this country – because it would interfere with people's freedoms.

There are other freedoms that we are primarily concerned with at the Federal Trade Commission. I think that you as representatives of the business audience ought to be primarily aware of them. We read that the things the terrorists hate most about this country are what they perceive to be the excesses of our modern consumerist society. They think it is rampant materialism and vulgarity. I guess at times we all share some of those sentiments. I know I have my list of pet peeves about modern society and I am sure you have your own. I do not care for grungy unisex clothing. I really do not like much of what is on network television. And I think a lot of popular music is unspeakable. Are these the freedoms we celebrate, the freedoms to produce these things? I say, yes, we do. We celebrate them because these aspects of society, for better or for worse, reflect some very, very noble ideas that are much older than our own nation.

One of the great ideas of the Western world, which emerged centuries ago, was the notion that people could choose their own occupations based on their inclinations and their aptitudes, rather than by accident of birth or political favoritism. Now, this evolved over the centuries, and we were very slow to apply this principle to all of our citizens. But we accept it today. We accept that what we do is not dependent upon on who our parents were or sovereign grace. And we also recognize that people are free to sell whatever products or services they wish. There are exceptions because there are certain things that are too dangerous or insulting to human dignity. But, by and large, we don't worry about whether products are worthy or unworthy. There is a corresponding and reciprocal freedom on the buyer's side. We call it consumer sovereignty. We can buy what we want regardless of whether someone else thinks it is good for us. That is the essence of the society that the terrorists hate.

At the Federal Trade Commission, we respect seller choice and buyer choice. We don't give permission to people to do things. We ate the FTC resolve abuses in the system. On the antitrust side, for example, we will step in when some private party tries to prevent some other private party from competing. But that's honoring the principle of freedom to compete. And on the consumer protection side, we step in when there is false or misleading advertising. Apart from that, we are umpires. We do not drive the wheels of commerce. We just try to prevent people from putting sand in the gears. That is what our job is.

Now, by definition, a free society where people are free to sell or buy whatever they want is not going to please everyone. But I still think it is an important element of our society, and I think it is worth making sacrifices for.

Go beyond that. This is where so many of you come in. Freedom of choice and consumer sovereignty, as well as seller freedom, do not mean much when most people are living at a subsistence level. They only become meaningful as a society becomes productive and as wealth grows. Freedom is essential to the creation of wealth and wealth is essential to the enjoyment of freedom. There is a circular relationship there. And we in government do not create wealth. Only you in the private sector can do that. Only you. And this is where the contributions of the other awardees and so many of you in this audience come into play. We need your daring. We need your ingenuity for a productive society that is worth fighting for. That is the third way we honor our heroes, by continuing to be productive.

Now some people in the business community that I have talked to seem to be paralyzed. They seem to be reluctant to make big decisions. They are nervous. They think we need to wait until the dust settles down. We need to wait until we get a better picture of what the threats may be. I do not think that is going to happen, next month or next year. I think you people who create wealth are going to have to live with a new level of uncertainty. It is going to have to be embedded in your business planning. You are going to have to learn to survive in that environment. You can do it. If you think about it, you have dealt with uncertainty all of your lives. Even in a time of peace and prosperity, most new businesses fail. We know that. We look at mergers in the Federal Trade Commission. Most merger transactions don't deliver the value that people expect. Uncertainty is part of your lives. And you know how to deal with it in an organized way. That is what you learn in school and that is what you learn by experience. This is a different kind of uncertainty, which you will learn to deal with like you deal with all the other uncertainties in your life.

I will conclude with the last and what I think is the most important obligation that we owe to our heroes. When I was a little boy, my mother told me that I had an obligation to be cheerful. It was not easy for her. She was a very nervous person but she fought everyday to be cheerful. Because she believed it was a premier virtue. It was a premier virtue, of course, because it is not only more considerate of our fellow human beings, but because it is an expression of faith in a benevolent creator and the ultimate triumph of the good.

We owe it to people like Tom Burnett and other heroes to be cheerful. You know it is possible to be serious and dedicated, and cheerful at the same time. Think of the people in the old days who marched into battle singing songs with bands playing and banners flying. Think of the cheerful irreverence of the GI's in World War II. Think of the people who are laughing at their fears today.

I saw an article in the paper this morning down in San Diego which really tickled me. It was an article on celebrity wimps. You know, these people who are macho movie actors and various other people in macho occupations who are afraid to fly in airplanes. This article was talking about an Australian national rugby team that was afraid to fly to some overseas tournament. They were shamed by the fact that flight plans had been made by some Catholic girls' hockey team and a kids' music act called the Wiggles. Can you imagine? So the Wiggles shamed them into it and they decided they would fly. I don't know about you but I think that is hilarious. It is hilarious and it is inspiring, too.

I think it is important that we are meeting here on an occasion of cheerful good fellowship like this dinner. Bin Laden says we are terrified in this country, terrified to do anything. I see you in this room and you do not look very scared to me. He is living in a cave! Who is scared of whom?

Let's be thankful. Let's be thankful we can still do these things. Let's be thankful for a man like Tom Burnett. Let's be thankful for other people like him who are going to be asked to take terrible risks as we go forward here. Most of them are very young. But they are sturdy, they are brave, and they will do it. So we will honor them. We will honor them by remembering. We will honor them by celebrating our sometimes untidy freedoms. We will honor them by continuing to be productive and creative, and always, always, we will do it with faith and good cheer.

Thank you for making me a part of this event.

---

*Commissioner, Federal Trade Commission. This text is a transcript, with minor edits, of a video-recorded talk given on November 13, 2001, at the Graziano School of Business and Management Alumni Awards Dinner, Pepperdine University, Los Angeles, CA. On this occasion, a posthumous award was presented to the widow of Thomas J. Burnett, one of the heroes of United Airlines Flight 93, which crashed in Pennsylvania on September 11, 2001. There is no written version of the talk.

THOMAS B. LEARY

APPENDIX C

Outtakes

The following are additional stories related to some matters discussed in the main body of the book.

Journalistic Experiences

When I was deeply involved with the daily newspaper at Princeton, the head of our graduate Board of Trustees was a remarkable man named Julius Ochs Adler, then a General Manager and Vice President of the N.Y. Times. Shortly after he graduated in 1914, he won a Distinguished Service Cross and a Silver Star in World War I, and attained the rank of Major General after extended service in the reserves and a term of active duty in World War II.

He was a dynamic individualist, who gave a lunch for the Senior student editors in the Times building each and every year, and personally gave us a tour where we could see the huge and noisy presses which turned out the paper each day.

The *Times* was then acknowledged as the premier paper in the country, respected not only for the breadth of its coverage but also for the balanced moderation of its editorial positions and the strict objectivity of its news stories. When the *Times* endorsed a political candidate, it meant something.

As student editors, we were taught by graduate mentors like General Adler that a well written news story should never contain a hint of the reporter's subjective opinions. Has that ever changed!

Let me mention a relatively recent example. For years I have read *The American Lawyer,* a news magazine that, in my opinion, often covers various legal developments in more knowledgeable depth than any other publication. I also believe it is relatively objective.

That is why I was unpleasantly surprised several years ago when it ran a long cover story about Senator Orren Hatch, Republican from Utah, who is generally "conservative" but not reliably so. Facially, the article appeared to be balanced: the Senator is portrayed in a fanciful cover picture with both a devil's horns and a saint's halo. When I read the story, however, it was obviously not a balanced portrayal at all. So, I was moved to write a letter to the magazine's Chairman, then Steve Brill. These are some of my comments:

> "…I am sure your article believed the article was fair: after all, Hatch is portrayed as a likable fellow who is not particularly conservative in all issues. But the rhetoric is hardly balanced."

> "Hatch is described as 'strident' and 'blind' when he agrees with conservatives but 'thoughtful' and 'moderate' when he agrees with liberals. It apparently never occurs to the author that anyone could have a principled objection to a 'civil rights bill' or the Equal Rights Amendment; Hatch's opposition to both is 'grisly'. When Hatch speaks for a liberal cause, however, he is 'moving' and shows 'courage'."

> "These examples are not isolated. A Senator like Helms at the extreme right of the Republican party is a 'scorched-earth idealogue'; a Senator like Metzenbaum at the extreme left of the Democratic party is an 'old liberal warrior'."

> "A double standard is applied to political rhetoric, Hatch's rhetoric is deplored; the rhetoric of his opponents is presented without comment as a legitimate point of view. (An 'evil GOP creep'.) The most offensive calumny by far is Eleanor Smeal's claim that Hatch is a 'fascist', but your author quotes it to show that Hatch may be an extremist, not Smeal. Imagine the uproar if the slander had gone the other way."

> "The bias is probably not intentional. Your author may be surrounded by people with a similar world view, and none of them

can imagine that there are intelligent people of good will out there who have different opinions. They are wrong."

A few days later, Steve Brill called me up, with the article's author on an extension line. He asked me whether I wanted the article printed. I said I didn't care about that; I wasn't trying to show anyone up. I just wanted them to think about what I had said.

To my considerable surprise they both agreed that I had a point. They really were unaware that their biases showed because they were surrounded by people who agreed with their own underlying assumptions.

Liberals are not the only people with biased assumptions, of course. A lot of our personal friends share common assumptions that tilt in the other direction. However, many Republicans distrust the mainstream media because surveys show that it is overwhelmingly staffed by people who are Democrats. And, often it shows.

Navy Days and Later Echoes

Reflection on my experiences in the Navy – compressed into a relatively brief period of time, but still vivid in memory – diverts my mind into a number of pathways, of limited relevance.

The powerful impact of my close-up view of President Eisenhower, for example, calls to mind a number of encounters, with other Presidents. Some were more amusing than inspiring. My grandchildren may be interested, even if no one else is.

I never saw President Roosevelt, up close or at a distance, but I remember well some of his speeches – particularly, his stirring Declaration of War on the day after the Pearl Harbor attack, which was broadcast over the loud-speaker system at school. I was only 10, and caught up in the patriotic fervor of the time. This lasted throughout the War, and my room was so filled with model warplanes, ships, tanks and guns that my mother claimed it was impassable.

Once, I literally bumped into President Truman. It must have been in the late 1940s, and I was with my parents in Washington, D.C. on a visit to one or both of my older brothers at Georgetown. We were having dinner in the Shoreham Hotel, and the President was giving a speech in the Hotel's Ballroom that same night. I was alone in the men's room when one of those big guys in a black suit came in and stood by the door. He prevented anyone else from entering, but just nodded and waited courteously for me to complete my mission. When I walked out through the door, I literally collided with President Truman, who was obviously waiting his turn. Nothing memorable was said, but I was then struck by the fact that he looked much more impressive than he did in his pictures, and I have been since struck by the fact that the President was so loosely protected in that more innocent era.

I never saw President Kennedy when he was in office, but I did see him up close in the late 1950s, when he was still a Senator from Massachusetts. When I was at Harvard Law School, I was still active in the Navy reserve and spent one weekend a month at the Naval Air Station in South Weymouth. One day, we were told that the Senator would come by to inspect our unit early that evening.

After we had completed our daily activities, we spiffed up a bit and adjourned to the Officers' Club to wait for the call to go down to the hangar and line up in ranks. Well, Senator Kennedy was then, as always, chronically late, so we naturally passed the time drinking beer. The wait went on and on, and so did the beer consumption.

When he finally arrived, with Jackie, we were initially in a very relaxed frame of mind. The Senator looked impossibly young, and his wife was gorgeous. I don't know whether we looked very military or not, but at that point I don't think we very much cared. The Senator passed right in front of me, looked me square in the eye, and I tried to look serious and resolute.

I guess we did alright, because there were no adverse comments, then or later, but as the ceremony progressed, the inevitable physical effects of beer became increasingly evident. I know I was not alone because of the twitches and grimaces of my buddies close by. I began to wonder whether I should just collapse in ranks if things got too explosive.

When the seemingly endless event concluded and the Senator and his wife exited the hangar, we didn't wait for any orders to dismiss but made a collective dash for relief – men's room, ladies' room, bushes outside; it didn't matter. Thus concluded my only encounter with Jack Kennedy. And, I promise there will be no further mention of micturation.

I never saw President Johnson, close up or at a distance, but Stephanie did. It's her story, but I don't think she'll mind if I tell it here.

In the Summer of 1957, when we were traveling around the Northeast on the Harvard Law Review censorship project, Stephanie and I spent a few days in Washington. I wanted to do some work in the archives there, and she wanted to see the sights on her first visit to the Capitol. I gave her some ideas, and particularly mentioned that I had always enjoyed the sight of the Senate in session. I remembered that all you had to do was show up, and perhaps wait for a short time in line. So, that's what she did. Neither of us knew that security had been tightened in the Capitol since the Puerto Rican Nationalists had fired some shots in the House Chamber about ten years before. It was necessary to get a pass from the office of your Congressman. When Stephanie got to the front of the line, she was stopped by a guard because she had no pass.

She was overcome by frustration, because she knew nothing about the rule and furthermore had no idea who her Congressman was because she was a California girl, temporarily living in Massachusetts and married to a guy from New Jersey. So, she says she simply started to cry.

At that point, a very tall man – trailed by a posse of young followers – stopped and asked her what was the matter. (A very tall, beautiful young blond woman will have that effect.) Between sobs, she told her sad story. At that point, the tall gentleman pulled out a card, signed it and gave it to her.

"We'll just make you an honorary Texan", he said. She showed the card, and sailed through.

When I joined her in our hotel room later in the day, she told me all about the event. When I asked her who the gallant gentleman was, she said she had no idea - but, she still had the card.

It was signed "Lyndon Johnson", then the Majority Leader in the Senate, and probably the most powerful man in the country after President Eisenhower.

Stephanie is a staunch Republican, then and now. But she never will utter a word of criticism about that tall Texan, Lyndon Johnson.

After Johnson, came Presidents Nixon, Ford and Carter. I never saw Nixon and Carter when they were President – only before in the case of Nixon (at the Eisenhower Inaugural Ball) and after in the case of Carter (in an elevator someplace). I saw President Ford at a rather dull fund raiser in Detroit, where General Motors had taken a table. I saw President Reagan several times, close up or at a distance, but there are no particular stories attached to the events. The same for Presidents Clinton and President Bush, the younger. I have never seen President Obama, and doubt that I ever will.

There is, however, a nice story about the elder President Bush. In the interim period between his 1988 election and his 1989 inauguration, there was a big dinner in a Washington hotel that honored the outgoing President Reagan and the incoming President Bush. I would never go to such a thing on my own – too expensive – but some of my former colleagues at General Motors asked me to fill an empty seat at the Company's table.

The Master of Ceremonies for the event was Jack Kemp. He did a magnificent job. (I was disappointed later by his rather lackluster performance as a Vice Presidential candidate in 1996.) Remember he once played professional football as a quarterback. As he made the usual introductions of celebrities in the audience, he would reach under a podium, pull out a football and sail it across the immense ballroom to the celebrity just mentioned. Miraculously, he was not only precisely on target, but every celebrity managed to catch it – despite their varied states of physical agility – thus, avoiding a lot of broken crockery.

The first half of the dinner was a moving farewell for President Reagan. Jack Kemp introduced him as "The Last Lion" still standing in a century of out-size personalities. (I believe, with the benefit of hindsight, that the description still fits.) Reagan then made a short speech and graceful exit; the second half focused on President-Elect George Bush.

The highlight of this half was the conclusion. After Bush made his brief remarks, and the enthusiastic standing audience had been seated, he started to lope slowly up the central aisle of the room. Kemp threw threw another perfect pass; Bush effortlessly caught it over his shoulder and ran through the back door into the corridor. What an exit!

These stories are of no particular historical or educational significance, but I like to call them up.

Stories Related to My Wall Street Experience

In the subsection about some non-antitrust cases I worked on at White & Case, I mentioned a tax case for U.S. Steel, during which I had become immersed in the steel making process at all levels. My closest companion on those long trips was a company tax lawyer named Charles ("Chuck") Corry, a guy about my own age.

Chuck Corry had a relaxed and amiable disposition. He did not appear to be particularly ambitious; in fact, he once told me that his career ambition was to become Manager of Taxes for the Corporation. Unlike most lawyers, who tend to talk their heads off, Chuck very rarely volunteered a comment about anything controversial; in fact, he could be downright laconic. As it turned out, that was a quality that later served him well.

I lost touch with Chuck Corry after I left White & Case in 1971, but I learned about his career progress over the years from other business contacts in the steel industry. He assumed general financial responsibilities beyond the tax area, and became a major architect of the company's product diversification outside the steel business. His low profile and modest demeanor served him well; he avoided controversy and factional rivalries; and he made no enemies. He was rewarded for his discretion when he became Chairman and CEO in 1989, and served with distinction for six years.

Chuck's success demonstrated that, contrary to popular wisdom, nice guys do indeed sometimes finish first. I admired him further when I read just a few years ago that he had publicly objected to the leveraged buyout (LBO) of a company in which he held a minority stock interest. It was particularly refreshing to read that he, a former CEO, had said too many LBOs benefitted the top officers disproportionately.

I don't know much about corporate law, but I seem to remember from Law School that the benefits of special knowledge that company executives acquire rightly belongs to the shareholders. Yet, it is commonplace for top executives, who can perceive value greater than the market recognizes, to capture that value for themselves in an LBO. Of course, it is true that these buyers have to offer fair value to the other shareholders, but large financial institutions are flexible and adroit enough to provide the requisite certifications of fairness for a wide range of valuations. The legality of this still puzzles me.

My favorite story about Chuck Corry, however, was told to me later, with vast amusement, by one of his close friends. Corry was in the habit of traveling with a pistol in its case, for some reason. This had not attracted any particular notice because he normally flew on a company plane. One day, he apparently had forgotten all about it because he was arrested for carrying a weapon in his luggage when he attempted to board a commercial flight out of Washington's airport.

The arrest of such a prominent CEO was a one-day wonder in the D.C. press, but there was no further mention of it and I didn't find out what happened until sometime later. Apparently, local prosecutors were satisfied it was an innocent mistake, and accepted a misdemeanor plea. There probably was a fine levied which was presumably not a problem, but the prosecutors were concerned about the appearance of unduly favorable treatment in the case. By agreement, Chuck Corry had to spend a night in jail.

The companions for a one-night stay in a D.C. jail are not the kind of people with whom a CEO would normally feel comfortable. Chuck Corry's natural discretion, however, was equal to the occasion. I'm told the initial conversation with his cellmates went roughly as follows:

> Thug 1: "What's you in for, man?"
>
> Corry: "Weapons."
>
> Thug 2: (Wide-eyed) "Did you ever . . . I mean sometime . . . uh, off someone?"
>
> Corry: "Not in this town."
>
> All Thugs: (Silent awe.)

There's a lesson in here, somewhere, but I' don't think I'll ever have the occasion to apply it.

The second story is a footnote about legal writing. In the main narrative I mentioned some of the things that David Hartfield had taught me about legal writing, and the simple notion that lawyers should try to talk like "a normal human being". On reflection, I think I should have amended that to say "a normal, reasonably articulate human being". Most judges will not be familiar with the currently popular jargon of youth. For example, I believe that people my peers once knew as "hepcats" or "hep" are now known as "hip". I think "hip" people today are what we would have called "cool", but the current equivalent of "cool" seems to be "hot". And "bad" is now a term of endearment.

Perhaps the extreme example of hipness, or coolness or hotness, is a conversation I overheard in one of my favorite eating establishments when I am traveling alone, namely a diner that serves bacon and pancakes all day. When you are eating alone, you cannot help but hear the conversation of those close to you – in this case two young and attractive women. They said "you know" and "like" a lot, and I've forgotten most of the other unintelligible remarks. But the following memorable exchange was loud and clear, and has confounded me ever since.

> Female 1: (With evident resignation) "You know, you never know, you know."
>
> Female 2: (With sympathy) "I know."

After some years of reflection, I believe what they were saying is something related to a basic theme of this memoir, but I cannot be sure. However, I would not endorse it as a good example of clear, lawyerlike communication.

A Final Story

This might be a good place to end, but I want to include one more story that still makes me feel good. I mentioned in the Washington Chapter that I have always welcomed the opportunity to mentor younger people. As I look back on a long life, the realization that I may have contributed to their success in some small way is a lasting source of satisfaction.

I sometimes have been asked to talk about the legal profession to groups of law students and undergraduates who are thinking about it. After a session with one such group, at a Midwestern University, I was approached by a formidable young woman in a campus police uniform. She asked if she could talk to me privately after the others had filed out of the lecture room.

When we were alone, she said she had graduated from the same University with good grades and had always wanted to be a lawyer. But, an early unsuccessful marriage had left her alone with a daughter to support, and she had shelved her dream. Recently, however, she had applied for, and been accepted at a night program offered by the University's Law School. Her biggest concern, she said, was that she would have to work her way through; it would take five years; and she would be 45 by the time she had finished. Did I have any advice about what she should do?

I said that the experience of Law School may be very different from what she expects, but she will know early on whether it is something she wants to stick with. However, age should not really be an issue. "You will be 45 in five years, whatever you do, and you might as well be a lawyer if that's what you want." The comment sounds simple, bordering on banal, but she brightened up and said she really hadn't thought of it that way.

Some years later, I got a note in the mail from someone with an unfamiliar name at an unfamiliar address. The writer reminded me of the long-forgotten conversation just described, and said it had tipped the scales for her. She had graduated from the Law School, and was now pleased to be working in the office of a local prosecutor.

One more pleasant memory to add to my lifetime collection. My accidental choices seem to have turned out pretty well.

Printed in Great Britain
by Amazon

70542352R00192